CONTENTS

Judith Chalmers was born in Manchester and made her broadcasting debut at the age of 13 in BBC's Children's Hour. In 1959, after 11 years in the North working for both radio and television, she moved to BBC Television in London and was appointed Senior Presentation Announcer. Judith also worked as a commentator and reporter for programmes such as Come Dancing, Royal Ascot, Henley and BBC Television News. She also spent four years presenting Woman's Hour.

In 1972, she joined Thames Television and the following year presented the first edition of 'Wish you Were Here . . . ?'. The programme has been a tremendous success and is regularly in the Top Ten ratings.

Judith's other television appearances for ITV have included hosting Miss World for five years and she commentates at Royal State occasions, The Royal Film performances and The Derby.

The Home Service, on Channel 4, is a new series of magazine programmes she presents based on her own idea which deals with all aspects of owning a home.

Judith is Travel Editor of Woman's Realm and has written for several other magazines. She is Chairman of The Appeals Committee of the Women's National Cancer Control Campaign and is an Honorary Lady Taverner. In 1984, she was elected to the National Consumer Council and the following year was appointed the only lady member of the Peacock Committee set up to investigate the financing of the BBC. She is a Freeman of the City of London.

Judith Chalmers married Neil Durden-Smith in 1964 and they have two children, Emma and Mark.

FOREWORD

There are two questions I am always asked. One is where do I go on holiday? The answers are in this book. The other is how have holidays changed since 'Wish You Were Here...?' began? The answer *is* this book.

Like wine and avocados, holidays used to be only for the few. Today they are written into our calendars as indelibly as Thursdays. Holidays plural, note: we are into the age of two and three holidays a year now, you know. That is one of the changes.

Perhaps the biggest change of all is the way holidays have become part of our expectations. Holidays now are indispensable. We expect to have holidays as we expect to have cars and kitchen units; more than that, holidays are an entitlement. They are written into contracts of employment and they are taken by nearly 30 million of us a year. There is even a charity, the Holiday Care Service, set up to find holidays for those whose health or circumstances would otherwise prevent them from having one.

And people's expectations *of* their holidays are greater now. They want to travel farther and to see more. Fifteen years ago America was a dreamland, now it features in more brochures than Italy. The same is starting to happen with Australia and whoever could have imagined in the early Seventies that a book like this would include Samoa?

Today's holidaymakers want to be up and doing. As well as a suntan they want an experience, be that of new cultures, new food, new landscapes, new sports or new pastimes. They also want the best. And therein lies a minefield. What is best? One man's Malta, so to speak, is another man's Portugal.

We might agree on the simple things — that the best bread is still to be found in France and the best showers are in Finland; that the best service (general) is to be had in the States, the best service (luxury) in India; that the best taxis are in Germany and the best trains in Switzerland. There will be dissenters even here. But try arguing about which country has the best food or wine or scenery (let alone the best beaches or mountains) or make a case for The Best Holiday, and you would do better to plead that the earth is flat.

If there is one thing I have learned in 15 years of 'Wish You Were Here...?', it is that there is no such thing as the ideal holiday. So 'best' in these pages is 'best' of its kind — best in quality, best in value, best for you if you like that sort of thing. That is why Majorca is here along with Sydney and Benidorm appears with Bath.

It is more difficult in compiling a book like this to decide what to leave out than what to put in. In the chapter on cities, for instance, the exclusion of Venice, Florence, Paris and Rome requires an arbitrariness verging on the godlike. But then so too would the omission of Hong Kong, New York or Amsterdam, all of which I have included. There are only 50 holidays within these covers, 50 *of* the best.

In my quest for the best I have been happy to rely upon the advice and experience of other travellers and 'professional holiday-takers' to enable me to include places with which they are familiar and I am not. The selection is mine but it could not have been made without the assistance of my fellow travel writers, Robin Dewhurst, Susan Grossman, John Graham Hart, Rob Neillands, Tony Peisley, David Wickers and Carol Wright. I am grateful to them for their expertise.

This is a book for armchair holidaymakers. Dip into it to enjoy a place on the page or use it to plan the holidays, short or long, that will take you to the places themselves. Let it spirit you to Suffolk today and the Seychelles tomorrow and, since it is a book which lets you write your own tickets, why not drop in at Bermuda on the way. Let it bring you the excitement of New York, the wonder of India, the adventure of Africa and the beauty of Britain. Let it make your next holiday be your best.

ISLANDS

All islands really should be approached by boat. That way you feel sure they are islands — after all there is no point in an island if it is easily reached. That is why it is such a waste when you *have* to arrive by air. As for the Channel Tunnel — we might as well be one end of an underpass, like a roundabout or Switzerland.

If the truth be told, my best holidays could all be on islands. Islands have a mentality which is exactly right for relaxing. You feel cut off, out of touch, hard to find even by telephone, truly away from it all. Inhibitions fall away faster on islands.

Islands are less demanding than the mainland. For a start they are smaller. They should be small enough to explore in a week, so any time after that can be spent going back to favourite places.

And islands tend to have strong characters, and it is this which makes their holidays unforgettable. That certainly is true of Corsica, the most spectacular island in the Mediterranean, and of Jamaica, the most spectacular island in the Caribbean. Rhodes combines the sophistication of big resorts with the simplicity of much smaller Greek islands; Majorca is the least-known island in the world that is visited by four million holidaymakers a year; Bermuda is enjoyed as much by the people who live there as by those who arrive by air; Scilly can be approached by boat.

MAJORCA

Turn your back to the sea, shake the sand from your feet and head inland. Within a few minutes you've left behind the concrete and chrome tower blocks, the bars belting out the latest pop hits, the tea just like Mum makes; ahead lies Majorca as Pedro has kept it for centuries.

The countryside fairly hums with heat. Lanes wind through scented almond and apricot groves. The silvery green leaves of twisted olive trees catch the eye as they shimmer in an unexpected puff of breeze. A moped shatters the silence as it zaps towards the coast like a demented mosquito, probably bearing a waiter to serve lunch in one of the package holiday hotels by the sea. A grizzled, tanned peasant, with all the time in the world, jogs gently homewards in his donkey cart for food and a siesta.

You could be almost anywhere in the southern half of the Mediterranean's most popular holiday island. But in this instance, it is the road from Cala Millor to Artá, crowning a hilltop and still within sight of the sea.

In time and temperament, Artá is light years away from the man-made fun factories on the coast. A small, austere town, its narrow streets are almost permanently shuttered against the heat of the day. In cramped dark bars, they talk of farming and fishing rather than suntans and sangria. And the cost of your wine will be a fraction of what you would pay on the coast.

Climb up to the fortified church of San Salvador, aloof above the furrowed roofscape bleached by centuries of sunshine. Hidden in a shadowy corner of a cool courtyard, a tiny shop sells religious souvenirs, postcards and handmade baskets, often woven on the spot from dried and shredded palm leaves by the dextrous, flicking fingers of Juana Ana Massanet or a friend. It's a home craft for which Artá has long been famous; now slowly dying as a quicker peseta is to be made in the bars and on the beaches of the tourist resorts. And, if you're hot and thirsty, Juana will sell you a beer or *cuba libre* from the fridge in the corner. One civilised side of Majorca is that you are never far from a drink.

Artá is a timeless corner of Majorca. The odd thing is that relatively few holidaymakers ever reach it. It's the same story for other small towns like Campos and Lluchmayor. Even odder is the brown stone farming village of Petra. Everyone goes to Valldemosa, where the scandal-prone French writer George Sand and her Polish lover, the composer Chopin, spent an unhappy winter in 1838. Today they place a fresh rose on Chopin's piano every day of the year. Yet who knows about Petra? It was the birthplace in 1713 of Junipero Serra, the enterprising Franciscan missionary whose settlements eventually blossomed into Los Angeles, San Francisco and San Diego. Comparatively few visitors see his house, furnished in period style, or the museum, which is actually owned by the city of San Francisco. His statue stands in a palm-fringed square near a street grandiosely called Calle California.

Few visitors make it to San Marriog, either, although it is in its way a shrine to tourism. This stately villa was the home of Archduke Ludwig Salvator, the man who first introduced Majorca to Europeans. He arrived in 1867 and spent 40 years writing a six-volume study about the island. Today, his house is filled with momentoes and the exquisite sub-tropical gardens lead to a clifftop white temple made from Carrara marble. Concerts are held here in summer.

It is hard to believe in places like these that Majorca plays host to around four million tourists every year, nearly half of them from Britain. But then this is the Mediterranean's best known, least known island.

Parts of the south and east coasts are girdled by a relentless rim of high-rise resorts. They are not pretty but they are fun. Magaluf, Palma Nova, Arenal, C'an Pastilla, Calla Millor, Paguera and so on are the places that lead people to say that Majorca is 'spoiled'. Not a word I like, as it usually means that a lot of people are simply having a good time.

Even so, the real charm of Majorca lies away from these fun palaces. Even in the more populous parts you'll find oases of peace — like delectable Cala Figuera and Playa Canyamel, a sandy bay encased by rocks, pines and high wooded hills. Here, the Hostal Cuevas is a small white hotel perfectly positioned above the beach; just 12 bedrooms, a seaview terrace for pre-dinner drinks and a traditional-style dining room with lobster often on the menu.

Hostals are personally-run small hotels, offering a better standard of food and service than the average package hotel but with fewer facilities: no lifts, for instance, or marble foyers or reservation staff who speak six languages. They may actually only speak Spanish.

By far the most exciting coast is the spectacular north-western stretch from Puerto Andraitx to Formentor. Grey, stone villages cling precariously to mountain sides, suspended between sea and sky. From Estellenchs, caught in a cleft of wooded hills, you can walk all day and barely see another soul.

The Moors first sliced the mountain side into terraces and gave Banalbufar its name. Today, the same fertile flight of terraces drops 400 feet from the sober huddle of village buildings to a small stone and rock beach. The sun is obscured in the morning but turns the hideaway stony cove into a soporific suntrap later in the day. In the evening they take drinks on the terrace of the Hostal Mar y Vent in the village high above; open the shutters of your white-washed bedroom furnished in Mallorquine style and you have a breathtaking view of the terraces spilling down to a brochure-style blue sea. Here, English is spoken, and there's a swimming pool and tennis court.

Visually, Banalbufar is a stern, uncompromising Spanish village. In contrast, Deya is Majorca at its most obviously picturesque — a cottagey jumble of stone streets and winsome gardens with olive, almonds and carobs dipping to a stony cove, a hot half hour's walk away. Under the little bar's bamboo sunshade, sipping cold beer and munching fried squid and salad, you again wonder if this is really Majorca.

Writer and poet Robert Graves came to Deya in 1926, liked it and stayed. Today it has a conscious arty charm and a gentle hint of late Sixties' lifestyle. You can stay simply in the village or, aloof from the jingle of goat and sheep bells in its own secluded grounds, at the grand and elegant Es Moli. A mini-bus takes you to its own private beach.

All these places are within half an hour or so of Palma. If you don't want to drive, take the old-fashioned train to Soller and savour the glorious untarnished scenery — a genuine armchair view, for that's just what you get with a first class ticket. Soller is unchanged Majorca, a workaday town among fragrant orange, lemon and olive groves, its busy little streets and shady squares bustling about their own business. It's one of the few places left where villagers still take the *paseo*, the traditional evening stroll.

A creaking tram trundles an unhurried three miles to Puerto Soller. This was a top resort long before the package holiday boom, which has now left it quietly behind. Cradled in a vast amphitheatre of hills, the setting is superb. Stop here for a long, leisurely lunch, eating fresh fish and sipping cold white wine in one of the little harbour-side restaurants frequented by fishermen ... just what holidays are all about.

As you may gather, I have a particularly soft spot for Majorca. It was our very first location for 'Wish You Were Here ... ?' back in 1973. I stayed in Puerto Pollensa. It's still as peaceful and attractive now as it was 16 years ago with a style that is missing from larger resorts. The harbour is the focal point and, outside the peak season, there's always space on the narrow sand beaches shaded by those gloriously scented pines that, to me, are instant Mediterranean.

The hotel I stayed in then is still a favourite: Illa d'Or, ten minutes from the centre, just far enough from the hustle and bustle of day trippers who pour in for lunch. It's an older hotel, furnished with antiques; no pool but you can swim in the sea and sunbathe in peace on the terraces.

Lofty mountains rise behind and one road squiggles like toothpaste from a tube to Formentor, a slender promontory smothered in evergreens, cut by rocks and fringed by a superb slither of uncrowded sand. The views are outstanding and so is the exclusive and prestigious colonial-style Hotel Formentor, regarded by many as the best in the Balearics. It's as far from the bucket-and-spade image as you can possibly get, and was one of Sir Winston Churchill's favourite spots.

Palma, like the rest of Majorca, is underrated. The vast Gothic cathedral, a perfect backdrop to the harbour with its elegant yachts, is as impressive as anything on the French Riviera. The shopping is outstanding too, with more choice, better quality and lower prices than you'll find in most resorts. There's a good variety of night-life — again at half the cost of the French Riviera. You must make time, at least on one evening, to go to Abacos, one of the most unusual night-time places I've come across. As you go through the heavy wooden entrance-door, Vivaldi or Beethoven gently soothe you from discreetly-hidden speakers. There are mounds of colourful fresh fruit, lavish flower arrangements and rabbits or birds in spacious cages that surround you in the cool garden. An 'Abacos Special' is what you should order. It's served in an enormous glass with sugar round the rim and can take ages to drink, which is just as well because there's so much to enjoy, including the people, in this fascinating old house.

Majorca is as synonymous with package holidays as Benidorm. Yet the old Spain remains well and alive for those who seek it. In country villages, you can find the local speciality, *pan amb oli*, slabs of rough bread spread with olive oil, topped with fresh tomato and wafer-thin slices of dried mountain ham. In the narrow tangle of Palma's back streets the little *tapas* bars still flourish. Places like El Pillon or Casa Gallega, crowded with Mallorquines who just can't resist snacks of delicious titbits and a glass of wine before heading home for lunch.

If someone created a blueprint for a tourist island to suit all tastes, they would surely invent a Majorca.

CORSICA

'*M'excusez, monsieur, mais c'est la route pour Bastia?*' The old man looked up from his grizzled dog, paused and then spat fiercely and accurately over the low stone wall. 'Speak English,' he growled.

There's a lot of fierce spitting goes on in Corsica and has been for the last couple of thousand years. Mostly it's to do with whoever happens to be running the place at the time. At the moment it's the French, but to the Corsican, one ruler is very much like another. Greeks, Etruscans, Carthaginians, Romans, Vandals, Byzantines, Saracens, Genoese, French — they've all held the island at one time or another and he's not cared much for any of them.

Apart of the fierceness of his spitting, the Corsican is noted for the fierceness of his pride and independence. This is the only corner of France where I've found anyone who would rather you spoke English than French. Unfortunately, this old man's English appeared to have been exhausted by the first two words he uttered so in the end his natural courtesy forced him to chew out a few words of direction and God-speed in the tongue of the latest oppressor.

The truth, of course, is that France oppresses Corsica about as much as Westminster does the Isle of Wight and although proud and independent, the vast majority of Corsicans have little interest in pressing for 'freedom'. The last time an official poll was taken, only three per cent of the population favoured a break with France.

However, there is no doubt that the continual invasions and occupations of the island have helped form the unyielding character of the Corsican. As each fleet arrived so he fled to the mountains and seemed to draw his strength from the weathered granite itself. And just what strength that granite could impart, the whole of nineteenth century Europe was to feel when one small Corsican set out to rule the world — and so nearly succeeded.

Napoleon Bonaparte is, of course, Corsica's most famous son but although he took an active and rebellious interest in Corsican affairs, he and his family found little support here. Indeed, he and his clan were virtually thrown out of the island in 1793 and when he took supreme power in France ten years later, he more or less ignored Corsica except for repressing any sign of rebellion. So hated was he that in 1811, the Corsicans threw in their lot with the British and when he abdicated they tore down his statue and hurled it into the sea.

With all this turbulent history you might expect to find Corsica today a brooding place but instead you find one of the loveliest islands in the world. The variety is bewildering. The west coast is a succession of dramatic coves some sharply notched, others softly carved out of layered limestone. The heart

of the island is a towering mountain range — vast granite blocks shuffled by the hands of giants. Over the peaks to the east, green lowland plains roll down to the sea, silver in the distance.

But as famous as its shores or mountains is the Corsican maquis, an evergreen and impenetrable mass of low-growing trees, shrubs, climbing plants and fragrant herbs which covers more than half the island. The scent of the maquis drifts across mountain and plunging valley and far out to sea. Napoleon once said that even with one's eyes closed there would be no mistaking Corsica. If you want to see the maquis at its best, go in spring or early summer when the whole interior of the island is a carpet of flowers.

But where to start exploring this exceptional isle? Well, why not with the capital, Ajaccio. Napoleon was born there, and today he's certainly more popular than he was during his lifetime. His statue is everywhere. One moment on horseback, another standing defiant. Here in a classical robe. Now in his famous cutaway coat. There in a natty Roman toga.

Before you take the wheel of your mandatory hire car, catch the train from Ajaccio and ride high into the mountains to Corte. Slowly you wind up through the hills and over the viaducts upward and upward until there it is, the ancient capital high on a massive crag. Its citadel dominates the heart of the island.

South from Ajaccio, though, is my favourite corner of the island. I remember the first time we took the road down round the Bay of Ajaccio toward Petreto-Bicchisano and stopped for lunch at the Hotel de France. Despite its grand name, the Hotel is a small, family-run road-side inn whose speciality seems to be luring in unwary travellers and then wrecking their schedule for the rest of the day.

Corsican food is a delight. French country cooking at its best — game in season, sheep and goat cheeses, chestnut-flavoured sweetmeats and puddings, blackbird paté — if you can bring yourself to eat blackbirds — and wonderful *charcuterie* from the island's small, native pigs. The seafood, too, is superb —

particularly the *bouillabaisse* and the red mullet. Corsican wines range from fruity whites to powerful reds and there are a number of interesting local liqueurs like *myrta* and *cedratine* to try.

If you manage not to be waylaid, the road south will take you to Propriano, once a small fishing village but now the liveliest resort in this part of the island. Dozens of cafés, restaurants and bars crowd its harbour area and the nightlife goes on well into the small hours. If you've any energy left, though, try the scuba diving — it's some of the best in the Med.

Within easy reach of Propriano is Sartene, centre of one of the island's most important wine-growing areas. Vines are everywhere, their twisted stumps marching over the hillsides like armies of arthritic gnomes. Perched high on a hill, Sartene seems not really to have joined us in our time but instead decided to linger in its past. One of the oddest Easter rituals takes place here when a masked and stumbling penitent drags a heavy cross through the narrow granite streets to the taunts of the crowd.

South again and you come to Bonifacio, the most dramatic of all Corsican towns. Its site is extraordinary. It almost seems to grow from the 200-foot crumbling limestone cliffs upon which it stands, staring defiantly over the straights towards Sardinia where you can go for a day-trip. Once a pirate stronghold, the ramparts of the old town would shrug off a battleship and, within its walls, each house is a fortress.

Turn the corner of the southernmost tip of the island and you begin to discover some of Corsica's best beaches. The Plage de Palombaggia just south of Porto Vecchio is arguably the prettiest. Backed by a ridge of pines and dunes, it's divided by red rocks into little sheltered coves you need share with no one. We had one of our best summer holidays here some ten years ago in a small rented house at the end of a bay. The beach was our back garden, the children dug for clams which made the most delicious soup, and came running back to the house one morning excitedly calling out that some people walking along the beach were actually speaking English!

Although the south certainly has a lot to offer, so, too, does the north-west. Calvi is another historic citadel town with great charm and a lovely Old Town. It was whilst besieging Calvi in 1794 that Nelson lost his right eye when he was hit by a stone — all that the defenders had left to hold off the might of the British fleet. Calvi is also a popular seaside resort, and to the east of the town there's a long, safe and sandy beach with every possible watersport.

The best time to visit Corsica is spring, early summer or early autumn. Try to avoid the July/August peak period if you can, particularly mid-August when the French descend from the mainland and the island raises its prices in welcome. If you are limited by school holidays, then perhaps the last week of August is likely to be the least crowded.

When Napoleon finally decided to flee Corsica, he sent his mother a message: 'This country is not for us.' That was his first mistake....

SCILLY

Call them just plain Scilly: never, ever, the Scilly Isles or Scillies. This exquisite archipelago of a hundred or so granite outcrops lies just 28 miles off Britain's western tip of mainland. They feel many miles more foreign.

Only five of the islands are inhabited by a population of some 2000 with the largest, St Mary's, being home to more than three-quarters of them. Fringed by

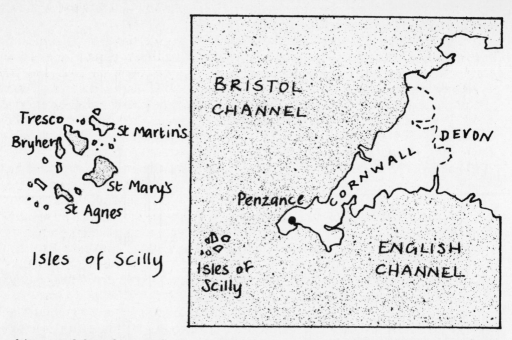

white sand beaches and surrounded by transparent emerald waters, these beautiful hybrids of land and seascape, flavoured by a daily lifestyle that seems more conducive to the pages of a book of nursery rhymes than twentieth century realities, have hardly been discovered by mainland neighbours, let alone visitors from abroad.

You can travel here from Penzance, on the Cornish mainland, either by helicopter, a 22-minute hop, or on board the Scillonian ferry, a two-and-a-half hour, often lumpy ride — on account of the ship's flattish bottom which is a necessary item of anatomy for negotiating the shallow harbour waters at St Mary's. Either way, the best introduction to the islands is aboard Vic's 1949 tour bus. Both bus and Vic, who is 83 years old and a drag artiste in his spare time, are immaculately preserved. Nowadays Vic tends to leave the driving to his nephew Ron who has admitted to topping 60 but prefers not to 'flash my age around if you don't mind'.

There are few vehicles on St Mary's, which is just as well, seeing as there are only 11 miles of road, including the streets of Hugh Town, the 'capital' of the islands. 'Look,' said Ron, 'there's our car-park two-thirds full with just two cars. This is a world of raging activity. Look over there, that's Mr Smith off to get his morning paper. And that's number four, where Wynne lives. She usually gives us a wave. Can't see her though. Must be doing her washing.' Ron's commentary is priceless. 'We don't have any snakes, deer, squirrels, badgers or foxes,' he continued, 'but we do have dogs, rats, rabbits and chamber maids. We used to breed Scilly Asses but now the only silly asses we ever see come from the mainland. But I never tell them that, especially if they've just lost their breakfast on the *Scillonian* off Land's End and wished they'd never left Penzance.'

The Scilly welcome, coupled with the peace, pure air, warmth and overall beauty of the islands, has long attracted a discerning clientele, though never in sufficient numbers to detract from the glorious assets. The most famous regular summertime visitor is former Labour Prime Minister Harold Wilson, who has a modest bungalow on St Mary's. In vivid contrast to Lord Wilson's political colours, look at the flowers in his front garden — it is filled with 600 heads of Tory blue agapantha blooms.

Travelling between the inhabited islands of Tresco, Bryher, St Agnes, St Martin's and St Mary's is remarkably easy. So is visiting the outlying rocks to watch the colonies of gulls, cormorants, oyster catchers, curlews and the occasional grey heron, plus seals and, on lucky days, playful dolphins. Every morning, during the long summer months, the dozen or so ferrymen gather on Hugh Town quay (a place known locally as Rat Island, a reference to its earlier residents). There they decide on a range of options and schedules — depending on the state of the tide and general weather pattern — and then disperse to call on all the St Mary's hotels to tell visitors in mid-cornflakes just where they can go that day.

The flotilla of boats leaves at ten in the morning, and again in the afternoon, carrying between a dozen and 70 people. Most are bound for the 20 or more brilliant beaches which miraculously manage to remain uncrowded even in the height of summer. 'It's just like the West Indies,' adds Ron. 'for weeks on end all you get to see are men in loincloths and ladies' legs. Some ladies wear nothing but shoelaces. Disgusting it is. But if it's raining you'll find 2000 people crammed into seven cafés, 28 shops, three pubs and three ladies' lavatories.'

'Scilly' comes from the Latin *sulli* meaning sunny. Because of the influences of the Gulf Stream the islands enjoy the warmest of British winters. It is that which accounts for the flourishing flower and bulb industry and the profusion of plants that thrives in the famous Abbey Gardens on Tresco, established by Augustus Smith in 1834. Shielded by windbreaks of Monterey pines and hedges of laurel, pittisporum, escallonia and eunymus, the gardens are home to more than 4000 plant varieties, including native species from South Africa, Australasia, the Mediterranean countries and the Canaries, many of which cannot be seen anywhere else in Britain.

After exploring Tresco, breathing its purest airs and watching the sun and clouds cast brilliant shafts of light across its gentle scenery, John Hicks, skipper of the 'Swordfish', steered us across a tossing sea way out to Scilly Rock itself. 'Is it always this rough?' one of the passengers asked. 'Rough?' queried John. 'This isn't rough. This is what we call a nice movement. The only thing that's rough is me.' All the boatmen charge the same £1.30 for their basic round-trip voyages. 'Those boatmen,' Ron explains, 'will do anything for £1.30. They spend all the summer chasing the visiting ladies and the chamber maids. You should see 'em at the end of the season. On their knees they are.'

Be sure to stop for a pint at the New Inn on Tresco and take a look at the wall chart showing how the savage seas of Scilly have, over the years, been the graveyard of some 2000 ships. The description of each wreck reads like a history of sea trading: vessels with salt from Spain, silks from Italy, rice from Rangoon, elephant tusks from Africa, cotton from Galveston, hides from Argentina and tea from Fuchow. Also on Tresco is a small museum, called Valhalla, where the figureheads of many galleons have finally come to rest, each with a sad tale to tell. If you want first-hand proof of the ferocity of the seas, head for the Devil's Kitchen (just beneath the lighthouse of Hell Bay) whenever there's a hint of a blow from the south-west and you'll be glad to feel the ground.

As well as his performances as a drag artiste in community cabarets, Vic also played a starring role in the maritime history of the islands. Nicknamed 'the human foghorn', Vic used to stand sentinel on Peninnis during bad weather and blow a bugle to guide the skipper of the old *Scillonian* through all the dangers masked by fog. He performed the task for some 25 years until the *Scillonian* struck a rock on a day when the fog was too dense even for Vic's penetrating blasts. Radar was installed shortly afterwards.

The maritime zenith of the Isles of Scilly coincided with the last days of sail. Hundreds of magnificent vessels called here to wait for a fair wind to carry their cargoes up the English Channel or north along the western coast. They also came to recruit pilots for the last stage of their voyages. Or, to be more precise, the Scilly pilots recruited themselves, for no sooner had a ship been sighted than competing pilots and their crews would row out to meet her in their traditional six-oared gigs. The first pilot to lay a finger on the ship's wheel got the job. Trans-Atlantic liners, which used regularly to salute the landfall of Bishop Rock lighthouse, the tallest in Britain, are a rare sight on the horizon, let alone a flotilla of vessels anchored in St Mary's Bay. But tradition dies hard. Every Friday, throughout the summer months, the islanders hold gig races, maybe competing against visiting teams from the mainland.

But Fridays are different. They make Scilly seem quite frenetic. The rest of the time little happens — if there happened to be a word in the English language that could translate the idea of *mañana* it could be aptly applied to these isles. There are no Sunday papers in Scilly. Or, to be precise, there are Sunday papers but they don't arrive till Monday morning. But it doesn't seem to matter. They could wait till the end of the week for all that anyone really cares.

JAMAICA

A strange affliction overcomes people after a holiday in Jamaica. However hard they try, they find they can't walk fast or run for a bus, let alone worry about being late for work.

It doesn't last, but there is definitely something about Jamaica that seems to put a person's internal alarm clock on the snooze setting. It is like an LP record playing at 32⅓ rpm, a slight but definite slowing down of the pace of life.

Jamaica is simply the Caribbean of everybody's dreams. When we are putting those eight crosses on the coupon or digging the car out of another 'surprise' winter snowstorm and we dream of being wafted to the balmy Caribbean, the island we imagine looks just like Jamaica.

It is perhaps not quite the most beautiful of all the islands — Grenada probably just has the edge, and Martinique and Guadeloupe claim a touch more sophistication (they are *French* Caribbean, after all!) — but Jamaica comes closest to having it all: the sweeping white sand beaches, the blue mountains and the colours and scents of tropical flowers. There is also every kind of holiday accommodation, as well as sophisticated facilities for land and water-sports. Most important of all, there is the Jamaican character which knows that having a good time is not only desirable, it's an obligation.

This character is something the visitor is immediately aware of. There are, after all, not too many airports around the world which greet their arrivals with a glass or two of rum. Only Montego Bay (Mo' Bay to those in the know) goes out of its way to provide just such a warming welcome.

Where Jamaica really begins to come into its own is at the hotel. It has more genuinely top-class hotels than any of the Caribbean islands and they include places to match any of the world's premier hotels. Seven have banded together

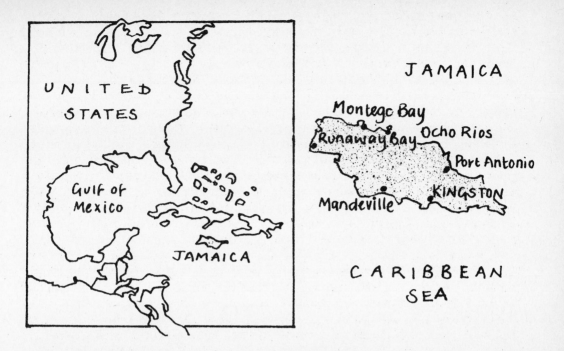

UNITED STATES

Gulf of Mexico

JAMAICA

JAMAICA

Montego Bay

Runaway Bay Ocho Rios

Port Antonio

Mandeville KINGSTON

CARIBBEAN SEA

to call themselves 'The Elegant Resorts of Jamaica'. For once, the copy-writers have got it right because no one could argue that Plantation Inn, Jamaica Inn, Sans Souci and the rest are anything other than elegant. They all either sit on or overlook their own private beaches and are set in lush, colourful grounds. The rooms are in cottages, bungalows, villas or apartments.

But while many of the island's hotels have million dollar settings, it is their style that sets them apart. Only high tea served with white gloves would entice the windsurfers away from their sailboards and this is a daily event at most of the 'Elegant' hotels.

There are plenty of other memorable experiences served up on Jamaica. Sip a Pina Colada at Rick's Café at Negril as the sun goes down over the miles of white sand beaches on the westernmost tip of the island, and it is easy to understand why the place became such a mecca for the hippies of the Sixties. It is still relatively undeveloped even though it found fame recently when the area's largest hotel changed its name from Negril Beach Village to Hedonism II and so ushered in the vogue for the 'all-inclusive' hotel where one price covers everything — drinks, watersports and even cigarettes.

The reason for the change was much more prosaic than the names of other inclusive hotels that followed throughout the Caribbean — Ecstasism, Eden II among them. Jamaica's political and economic problems of the 1970s had pushed inflation up and even the most well-heeled of visitors was feeling the pinch when buying drinks and meals on the island. The concept of a hotel where everything is included in the basic holiday price was an immediate winner and the fact that no money needed to be carried around was a security bonus.

We British have been slower to take to these new style hotels than the Americans but they are undoubtedly excellent value. Some, like Eden II (once the Hilton), Sandals, and Couples are just for cosy twosomes with no groups, and in particular no children, allowed. Others, including Hedonism II, Sandals

Royal Caribbean, Jamaica Jamaica, Casa Montego, Jack Tar and the recently-opened Negril Inn and Boscobel Beach (once the Playboy) are for everyone. Even Sans Souci has recently gone all inclusive.

But there is always going to be a place for hotels like Shaw Park Beach, a particular favourite with British visitors for its quiet charm and unpretentious service, not to mention a fairly eccentric British manager. Even without all-inclusive prices, it is one of the best value places to stay. There are some fun places to eat nearby at the Pineapple Place shopping plaza, which is also a good spot to start looking at the distinctive black coral jewellery, one of Jamaica's best buys.

Even in the smartest of stores, there can often be some leeway on the price but save your best haggling lines for the street markets. The one near the main coast road in Mo' Bay looks a bit dull with all the stalls numbered and seeming to stock the same craft items but if you show a flair for haggling patter, the place comes to life as the other stallholders come to watch, offer advice and see if you can put one over on one of their number.

The beach salesmen who come and offer you all manner of deals while you take the sun should be treated with some caution. If encouraged they can be so persistent as to be a pest and often, if what they are selling doesn't make you fat, it is certainly fragrant and illegal!

If Jamaica has a fault, it is that the hotels have taken it upon themselves to provide so many creature comforts that visitors rarely feel the need to venture outside. The high price of hiring cars and the dismal standard of most of the roads is further discouragement. It is quite possible to get all the exercise you need without leaving the hotel grounds because those 'grounds' usually include an array of tennis courts (floodlit for cooler evening play), all the wherewithal for water-skiing, scuba-diving, windsurfing and even para-gliding, and often a golf course, too. In Jamaica, you won't by now be too surprised to learn that the nineteenth hole is always found halfway round the course. After the ninth and it's time for a Red Stripe beer. And where else can you say that the water hazard that claimed your ball was the Caribbean; that you had a lucky rebound off a palm tree and a free drop after a goat stole your ball?

But, if you do make the effort to get out and about, it is well worth it. There are several working plantations which have organised tours to show off their past and present. The island's colourful pirate past is recalled in the former capital, Port Royal; Mandeville is a Caribbean rarity — a mountain resort, and near Mo'Bay are two great houses with fame earned in quite different ways: Greenwood was built by a cousin of Elizabeth Barrett Browning and Rose Hall was once ruled over by Annie Palmer, a white witch.

One extraordinary trip has evolved out of one woman's strange rapport with the island's birds. Lisa Salmon, the 'Bird Lady of Rocklands', quite literally has exotic birds eating out of her hands. You will, too, if you are the lucky one chosen to feed the Doctor Bird, the island's national bird, or the red-billed streamertail Hummingbird. There are organised tours, but you can also go independently to her Anchovy Sanctuary near Mo' Bay if the tourist office rings ahead for you and you can be there after 3.30pm.

If there is one quintessential Jamaican experience, it is rafting, an 'excursion' which involves visitors in doing absolutely nothing — in style. Simply allow yourselves to be punted down river (either the Rio Grande or Martha Brae) on a raft made for two — just. There is nothing to do except watch the world drift gently by, stopping for a picnic lunch washed down with a Red Stripe or three.

Try it and you'll wonder why no one ever thought of it before. There's no shooting white water rapids and no singing gondoliers, just an awful lot of peace and tranquility. That is not something with which a Mo' Bay evening is over-endowed. The island's tourist capital positively pulsates at night, with discos called things like Inferno and the Hellfire Club.

You can eat out under the stars at a number of restaurants and hotels. Dining is not cheap but it can be good value and everyone should try some of the Jamaican delicacies like jerk pork, curried goat, rice and peas, ackee and saltfish, roast yams, and banana fritters. Provided you have immediate access to a cold drink, try a pattie. Sold at every street corner, these pastries are full of highly-spiced meat which have an effect of vindaloo proportions on your taste buds.

Jamaica is one of the largest of the Caribbean islands, being 146 miles long and 51 miles at its widest point. The capital, Kingston, is in the south-east, but visitors on holiday spend most, if not all, of their time on the north coast where all the beach resorts are to be found — from Port Antonio at the eastern end through Runaway Bay, Ocho Rios, and Montego Bay to Negril in the west. Errol Flynn, Sir Noel Coward and Ian Fleming have all called Jamaica home in their time. Perhaps most significantly, Christopher Columbus, who, let's face it, was no mean mariner, became stranded on the island for a year when a couple of his ships foundered putting into what is now New Seville.

Foundered? Stranded? A likely story, Mr C.

RHODES

Only the Greek gods with their outrageous sense of theatre could possibly have designed the setting for the Rhodian village of Lindos.

As you round that last bend on the southern coast road, there it is shining beneath you — a sparkling bay overlooked by a hilly promontory up which struggles about as pretty a whiter-than-white village as its creators could possibly get away with. However, not quite satisfied with the effect, they then set off the whole ensemble with Crusader battlements surrounding a 2500-year-old acropolis.

From that viewpoint high on the road above, you know you've found it. The perfect place. The ultimate bolt hole. And ten years ago you would probably have been right. Then, very few knew of it and even fewer holidayed here. Today, as you drive down the last half mile, you soon discover it's a very different story.

Lindos now is no get-away-from-it-all haven but one of the liveliest resorts on the island. By day it's roasting-room only on its two white sand beaches and by night its restaurants, bars and discos heave till the small hours. And yet such is the resilience of this unique little village that even when the visitors outnumber the locals by three to one, its charm still manages to win through. In early or late summer, it's the delight it always has been. Only in July and August do the gods really desert it.

All its cobbled streets are narrow enough to admit only a donkey and so there are no cars in Lindos. Neither are there any hotels. It doesn't, in fact, even have rooms in its tavernas — all its visitors stay in pretty walled villas or simple private rooms. The nearest hotel is the Lindos Steps but that's a bay away to the north.

Lindos is tourism's final frontier in Rhodes. Draw a line across the island from Lindos to the hilltop castle of Monolithos in the west and you've a pretty good guide to what's developed and what's utterly untouched.

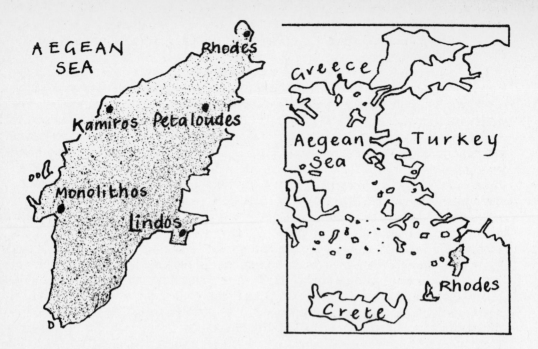

North of this line are the island's main resorts and the capital, one of the most fascinating towns in the Mediterranean. South there is virtually nowhere to stay but some breathtaking views, wonderful isolated beaches and a hundred-and-one perfect places for a picnic. It's this variety that makes Rhodes so special. At one end of the scale you have miles of superb deserted coastline and at the other excellent modern family hotels. You have 5000 years of fascinating history and at the same time resorts where, if you are over 30, they don't know whether to serve you or embalm you. Add to all this the sometimes surprising fact that the British are still the Rhodians' favourite foreigners and you have the recipe for a perfect island.

Personally, I like Rhodes best early in the season, at the end of May or in early June before the crowds arrive and while the Rhodians still have time to stop and share an ouzo. The flowers, too, are best early and the whole countryside has a fresh, newly-minted glow. The island's name came from the ancient Greek for 'rose' and today they are still everywhere, along with the ubiquitous bougainvillaea — a purple tide pouring over everything that's too slow to get out of its way.

But what perhaps I love most about Rhodes is the way the past wraps itself around you until you almost feel part of it. From here in the twelfth century BC a fleet sailed to join Agamemnon on his way to Troy. Rhodian ships served, too, with the Persian hero-king Xerxes and later with Alexander the Great.

When Alexander died, Rhodes refused to join with one of his successors, Demetrius the Besieger, in an attack on Ptolemy in Egypt, and the seeds were sown for the creation of one of the great Wonders of the World — the Colossus of Rhodes.

On receiving the Rhodians' refusal, Demetrius, living up to his name, laid siege to the island. After a frustrating year he called it a day and sailed away leaving a vast bronze siege engine which the Rhodians then sold. With the proceeds they built a statue of Helios, their protector sun god. It was the biggest statue the world had known. The Colossus, as it became known, was only 30 feet shorter than the Statue of Liberty. Alas, it survived only 70 years before an earthquake brought it crashing to the earth somewhere around 225 BC. No trace is left.

The next besieger of Rhodes was none other than Julius Caesar's murderer, lean and hungry Cassius. He had more luck, breached the walls and sacked the place, carrying off virtually everything that wasn't nailed down and most that was.

But today no period in the island's history is more visible than when it was the headquarters of the last of the Crusaders. Driven out of the Holy Land, the Knights of the Order of St John retreated to Rhodes and held off the combined forces of Islam for more than two hundred years before finally having to surrender to Suleiman the Great in 1523.

Rhodes Old Town is a monument to their determination and one of the best examples of a Crusader city anywhere in the world. The knights lived in 'inns' depending on their language. The inns of France, Germany, Italy, Spain, Auvergne, Provence and England all stand as solidly as ever along with one of the most interesting buildings in the Knights' Quarter, the knights' infirmary which now houses the Archaeological Museum of Rhodes.

Among its treasures is a rightfully famous little statue of Aphrodite. She is only 18 inches high and is kneeling, holding out her hair to dry after a swim. She's been waiting for that hair to dry for more than 2000 years.

Next to the museum is a small cobblestone street, the historic Avenue of the Knights which 500 years ago was the main street of the inner city and which houses most of the inns. As you amble up the gentle hill past the vaulted gateways with their faded coats of arms, you feel as if you are stepping slowly back through the centuries, as if any moment one of the vast oak doors will swing aside and a mailed knight will stand before you.

At the top of the Avenue is Kleovoulou Square and the Palace of the Grand Master, a 300-room castle restored beautifully, if a little eccentrically, by the Italians when they held the island. The mosaics, some brought over by the Italians from Kos, are among the most famous in the world.

Rhodes Old Town is also, of course, an excellent place to shop, particularly for handmade items like shoes and jewellery. While Rhodes isn't entirely tax free, many items are considerably cheaper than in England and it's well worth comparing a few prices. The designer boutiques of the New Town often offer some of the best bargains and when you need a rest from shopping, it's lovely to sit outside the city walls at one of the number of outdoor cafés, where you can sip a cool drink and watch the vast array of boats along the waterfront weaving in and out of their berths or bobbing at their moorings.

Another bargain in Rhodes is a motorcycle or Suzuki jeep — not that they are cheaper than anywhere else, you just seem to get more discovery for your drachma. The main resorts — Rhodes Town, Falaraki and Lindos — are all on the east coast, many of the prettiest and most interesting places to visit are inland or on the west coast.

If you take the road south from Rhodes and then turn inland, you climb up to the ancient hilltop village of Filerimos, founded perhaps 2500 years ago. Little remains of its early origins today except for a pretty monastery and church, but the breathtaking views of the coastline make it well worth the diversion.

Another left off the main road will take you inland once again toward Petaloudes and the extraordinary Valley of the Butterflies. Here every year in the pine woods, literally hundreds of thousands of butterflies gather between June and September. Clap your hands and the air fills with dancing colour.

And so on to Kamiros with its Doric ruins, all that is left of a once great city. Time it right and you could arrive at the little port of Kamiros Skala just in time for lunch at one of the harbourside tavernas. Fresh fish from an open air grill, a glass or two of retsina, caiques creaking at their moorings and the sun pouring out of the sky — why even consider going on?

Well, because only a few miles further on is the Crusader castle of Monolithos which is without doubt one of the most beautifully situated castles anywhere. Perched high on the top of a vast rock overlooking the blue below, the fortress is now in ruins but the view will stay with you forever.

Monolithos is the limit of most people's travels but if you're really feeling in the mood to get away from it all, keep heading south. You won't see another tourist all day. If you want to stay the night in the south, the only place is the Skiadhi Monastery. There are no monks there but the elderly couple who now run the place will almost certainly give you a bed.

In the morning, as you leave, you may hear a soft call behind you. 'Chairete, English — be happy.' On an island like this, who could not be?

BERMUDA

Despite what many people think, Bermuda is *not* a Caribbean island. It is a pink pimple on the map of the Atlantic, 1000 miles north of the Caribbean, and small enough to make you wonder whether the pilot will even find it, let alone land on it.

Easy for a pilot to miss, maybe, but all too easy for a sailor to hit. Among the hundreds of ships claimed by the band of reefs that surround Bermuda was the *Sea Venture*, flagship of Admiral Sir George Somers. In 1609, *en route* from England to Jamestown, Virginia, a storm altered the course of his ship which was subsequently wrecked. The spot, the tip of an ancient underwater volcano, was then known on the charts as the 'islands of the devils'; Sir George's mishap was to determine its political destiny.

Although it was a Spaniard, Juan de Bermudez, who had first discovered the island a century before Somers, he failed to claim it. Hence Bermuda became what is now Britain's oldest surviving colony. In 1984, amidst a variety of pomps and circumstances, it celebrated its 375th anniversary. Princess Margaret came to unveil a new statue of Sir George, who went on to become the island's first Governor. His heart, in fact, lies buried on Bermuda although his body was dispatched to England pickled in rum (a state not unlike that of many tourists returning from their holiday).

Bermuda is a gentle, wholesome, dependable, very civilised tourist destination. You'll feel quite at home in its parishes with names like Warwick and Devonshire, traffic driving on the left, cricket matches, little red ER postboxes, cucumber sandwiches and toasted muffins for tea and bobbies in British uniforms, minus the trousers. Those famous Bermuda shorts are *de rigeur* for a number of respectable callings, including the clergy, banking, the law and even for politicians. That is doubly surprising when you learn that the island dress code denounces, for example, the public sporting of hair curlers and the exposure of bare chests on the streets. Bare breasts are banned throughout the island.

As its geography implies, Bermuda is really a mid-Atlantic hybrid. More than

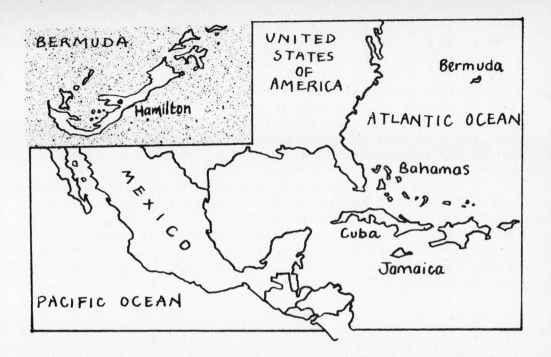

three-quarters of Bermuda's visitors come from the United States and the Bermudan dollar is intimately linked to the American. It has been popular with Americans ever since Mark Twain came and told his fellow countrymen: 'You can go to heaven if you want. I'll stay right here.' More practically, Americans come because it is near — one-and-three-quarter-hours' flying time from New York — sunny all year round and, as one New Yorker succinctly confided, 'so deliciously British'.

For its size, Bermuda has one of the highest concentrations of up-market accommodation anywhere in the world, ranging in scale — and price — from the Southampton Princess, with its 600 rooms, seven restaurants, 11 tennis courts and two pools, to family-run self-catering complexes like Astwood Cove with 18 self-contained, air-conditioned apartments clustered around a pool. The hotels are distinctly American in the nicest sense, right down to such caring little touches as enough ice in your drinks to sink the Titanic and always a choice of dressing for your salads. Everything works, including the staff who wander round with cheerful smiles saying 'Hi, and how are you folks today?'. They are also inclined to wish you 'a Bermudiful day' — though never for a second time if you groan loudly enough the first.

Bermuda, despite another popular misconception, is not in fact an island but an archipelago of some 150 miscellaneous outcrops and islets that, from the air, are shaped in the form of an anorexic prawn. The seven inhabited islands cover a mere 22 square miles, smaller even than Guernsey, and all are linked by bridge or causeway. But what Bermuda may lack in size it more than compensates for in beauty, particularly along its shoreline. Sheltered by a belt of coral reefs, Bermuda's beaches must surely rank among the world's most fabulous.

Although the majority of the 80-odd beaches (some white, some coral-pink but all spotless) are privately owned, the chances are that your hotel will own one anyway, or have exclusive use of one nearby. Since nowhere in Bermuda stands more than a mile from the sea, all the hotels on the island can justifiably claim to lie within the proverbial stone's throw, albeit a Daley Thomson one.

Although New York City is only 700 miles to the north west, Bermuda's turquoise waters are warmed by the Gulf Stream, hence the profusion of such *flora exotica* as banana trees and bougainvillaea. With average year-round temperatures of 70°F and seven hours of sunshine a day, the island fills an ideal, though fairly expensive, niche in a world short on perfect places to go for a spring or autumn holiday. At these times, temperatures hover in the 70s, nudging the upper 80s during the summer months. There's a fair amount of rain, twice that of Manchester for example, but most of it falls at night or in short, sharp shocks which are soon ushered away by bluer skies. Bermudans, with their ever-ready line in euphemisms call these outbursts 'liquid sunshine'.

For many visitors there has been little in the way of significant change since Mark Twain described Bermuda as 'the right country for a jaded man to loaf in'. For those who want to play it the hard way, Bermuda also offers an impressive menu of sports, including 100 tennis courts, sailing, snorkeling and windsurfing, some of the world's finest light tackle and deep sea fishing, more golf courses per square mile than any other country on the globe and, of course, cricket.

The overall laid-back mood — which must have a good deal to do with the lack of income tax, unemployment or racial tension (between the island's two-thirds black, one-third white population) — is even reflected in the island's 20 mph speed limit. There's also a maximum car length of 16½ feet — although the Governor, the US Consul and the mortician are specifically exempted from this restriction.

Tourists are neither allowed to bring their own nor even hire a car. There are not enough road miles to go round and even the locals are limited to one car per family. There are plenty of taxis however, many driven at no extra cost, by fully qualified guides, but most visitors, as I did, choose to explore the island's 150 miles of road by rented moped. Several companies will deliver a mount right to the hotel, hand over a crash helmet and show you how you can avoid that most painful of Bermudan experiences colloquially known as 'road rash'.

The scenery is hardly spectacular, but rather like a well-tended garden, with exotic blooms bordering well-manicured lawns and pastel-hued houses, each one topped by a lime-washed roof to catch and cleanse the rain. Don't come to Bermuda in the hopes of making forays to unexploited nether regions — with even a modest bungalow costing around £250,000, real estate is far too highly prized for the developers to allow too many green fields to escape their clutches, let alone tracts of wilderness.

Neither does Bermuda offer a great deal by way of conventional sightseeing. Hamilton, the capital, has its restaurants, bars and chic stores (including Trimmingham's, the island's version of Harrods, where you can stock up on fine china and cashmere sweaters), while the pretty old capital of St George, laced with streets like Old Maid's Lane, Slippery Hill, Aunt Peggy's Alley and Needle and Thread Lane, is famous for its Town Crier. He is the only resident with non-regulation length hair and who punishes gossiping women on the ducking stool every day for the amusement of unemancipated tourists. There's also an excellent Maritime Museum in the old naval dockyard, a bobby on traffic duty who performs his telegraphics from a large birdcage and, for the best bird's-eye view of the island, Gibbs Hill, one of the oldest lighthouses in the world. Not, needless to say, older than the *Sea Venture*. Otherwise the good Admiral Somers would have been able to give Bermuda a wide berth, which would have been a great shame for Britain.

CITIES

There could hardly be more convincing evidence that today's holidaymaker is a sophisticate than the fact that Liverpool is now selling itself just as hard as a tourist town as Southport up the coast.

Cities are natural holiday resorts. Often they have rather more zing and spice in the way of attractions than the man-made holiday spots that have got where they are because of their beach.

Yet it was only a few years ago that a holiday wasn't a holiday unless it was beside the sea. Or a lake. Or up a mountain or down a river and then only if the river was the Nile. Cities were out. They were where you went to work. An annual escape from the old commercial and industrial centres, like Liverpool, was the very definition of the twentieth century holiday.

There were exceptions. Bath was one, Amsterdam another, but they were roosts for culture vultures. For most people the idea of going *to* a city for pleasure was, if not unthinkable, certainly something they had never thought of. Today, though, the idea of taking a two or three day break in a city in Britain or abroad, is one of the fastest growing styles of holiday.

Cities actually have it all: history, art, shops, restaurants, hotels from doss-houses to Dorchesters and the gamut of entertainment from sin to symphonies. Cities like Sydney and Hong Kong have beaches too.

And this is my choice of seven of the best holiday cities in the world: Edinburgh, the most urbane; Sydney, the most civilised; Bath, the most elegant; Amsterdam, the most romantic; New York, the most thrilling; Liverpool, the most surprising; Hong Kong, the most fun.

EDINBURGH

At heaven's door St Peter welcomes a man wearing a kilt and asks him where on earth he comes from. 'Edinburgh,' says the man proudly. 'Ah!' says St Peter, opening up the pearly gates. 'You can certainly come in, but you'll not like it here at all.'

Scotland's capital is an earthly gem, a world-ranking city of great beauty. But Edinburgh is really a tale of two cities. Just before the London train comes to rest at Waverley Station it slices right between these two Edinburghs, passing down a green ravine that really deserves a raging torrent rather than a few pairs of spindly rails. Out of the right hand windows you glimpse the Old Town, strung high and mightily along the crest of an ancient volcanic ridge, the city's natural spine. At one end stands Edinburgh's most famous sight, the Castle, rooted in its plug of basalt. One swift glance at its prime location will tell you why, despite its turbulent history, it was never successfully stormed. Except, that is, by tourists.

The Castle is the globally recognised symbol of the city and star of everything from picture postcards to tins of shortbread biscuits. The hill on which it sits has probably played a defensive role since the Iron Age although the first real fortress was erected on the site in the seventh century and has had a rather promiscuous history ever since, tossed between its English and Scottish occupants. Today it plays a whole host of roles, including army barracks, chapel, home of the Scottish royal crown, stage set for the annual Military Tattoo and, from its battlements, a prime spot for excellent views of the city.

Old Town Edinburgh grew up in medieval times, huddled beneath the Castle's protection from Enemy England just down the road. The trouble was that it kept on growing and growing. Drawn to its main street, a teeming population lived in high-rise squalor. Imagine the scene at nine each evening when the cry of 'gardezloo' and drums would announce the moment when everyone packed into the ten-storey tenements could tip their entire household refuse out of the windows on to the street below. 'Auld Reekie' indeed, as Edinburgh was fittingly called.

That street, today known as the famous Royal Mile, is now without the stench. It is 'royal' because it links the Castle with Holyrood House, the official Scottish palace of the Queen — though most intimately associated with Mary Queen of Scots. But if you want to blend with the natives, call it High Street, Cannongate, Lawnmarket, Esplanade or Castle Hill, depending on where you're standing; Royal Mile is really just a guide book description.

Apart from exploring the Castle, possibly Britain's most popular historic monument outside of London, there's the well-preserved fifteenth-century house of fiery preacher John Knox and the seventeenth-century Gladstone's Land, a six-storey tenement now refurbished as a typical home of the time, with the original shopbooths displaying goods of the period. Almost opposite the house is the Museum of Childhood, one of the country's most fascinating museums. Among the most imposing buildings is Scotland's seventeenth-century Parliament and St Giles' Cathedral, Edinburgh's — and arguably Scotland's — most important 'kirk'.

Mind you don't tread on the heart of Midlothian, the heart-shaped pavement motif that marks the site of the Old Tolbooth prison. The tradition of spitting on the heart, as a mark of contempt towards the authorities, is still practised by some of Edinburgh's older citizens. But do take time to tread around the old courts and the narrow passageways known as the Closes, with their steep stairs and dark corners where Burke and Hare still loom in the imagination, waiting to donate the bodies of intrusive tourists to the Infirmary to further the cause of medical research. But don't condemn the Scots for that — Burke and Hare were Irish.

The real problem about visiting the Old Town is not what to see but what to leave out. Don't miss Bobby or the locals will never forgive you. South of the Royal Mile at the top of Candlemakers Row stands Greyfriars Church with its famous statue of Bobby the Skye terrier who kept almost continual watch over his master's grave for 14 years until he, too, died and was buried in the same graveyard.

When Old Edinburgh reached bursting point plus, the city fathers threw a bridge over to the neighbouring parallel ridge of land and the second city was born. The New Town is 'new' only in relation to the Old. It is a classic, brilliant testimony to Georgian architecture, a world of stark, rather austere, no-nonsense stone buildings often coated with a sombre grime but always embellished by iron railings and fancy balconies, panelled and fantailed windows, foot-scrapers and torch-snuffers and even the original roadside blocks from which Edinburgh Society could mount their sedan chairs without putting their backs out.

The New Town is everything that the Old Town wasn't. It is light and spacious, planned on a well-gardened grid with aptly named George Street at its core and Princes Street as its southerly boundary. Two squares punctuate either end of the grid. One, St Andrew, is best overlooked, but there is a remarkable exception even here, in the shape of the public banking hall of the Royal Bank of Scotland which has all the exuberance of an Arabian palace. Charlotte, the square at the other end of George Street, is a masterpiece (mistresspiece?), particularly the north side designed by Robert Adam to look like a palace rather than a string of individual buildings. At Number Seven is the Georgian House, the National Trust's New Town equivalent of Gladstone's Land, furnished, decorated and preserved exactly as it would have looked in its Georgian heyday. Next door, at Number Six, is Bute House, the official residence of the Secretary of State for Scotland.

There are also impressive circuses in the New Town, not for performing animals but magnificent terraced circles of buildings like Royal Circus and Moray Place whose front doors are discreetly adorned by highly polished brass bells, knobs, knockers and name plaques of advocates, physicians, chiropodists and the professional like. So highly polished, in fact, that you can see if your hat's on straight from as far away as the kerbside.

Unlike Glasgow, and countless other metropolises south of the border, Edinburgh was largely overlooked by the Industrial Revolutionary fervour of the late eighteenth and early nineteenth-centuries, and so avoided the accompanying ugly sprawl. Its economic misfortune was an aesthetic stroke of luck. And, thanks to one of Europe's most influential conservation policies, Edinburgh New Town remains largely unsullied by modern times. But there are exceptions: both St Andrew Square and Princes Street were hacked around by developers until the lessons were learnt. Nowadays you virtually require special dispensation from the Lord Provost before they'll let you put up a window box.

Come up from London on the night sleeper and you'll find the New Town still yawning in the wee hours of dawn. Poor old Sir Walter Scott, sitting alone in his Gothic rocket of a monument, looks down upon a ghostly Princes Street, its store doors still tightly closed to all but the cleaners. If you're staying overnight, a hotel I've enjoyed is the good old traditional North British, a former railway hotel, which stands staunchly at the end of Princes Street. The last time I stayed, my room looked out over the dramatic skyline of Edinburgh, a staggering view by day or night. And as for those lovely cast-iron baths, they're almost like your own miniature swimming-pool. By lunchtime, Edinburgh's main shopping thoroughfare is so crowded that walking can seriously damage your health. Just as the one o'clock gun booms out from the Castle precincts and all Edinburghers decide to check their watches, head-on pedestrian collisions are not uncommon.

Edinburgh is a shopper's town with Jenners on Princes Street the Harrods of the North, the *crème de la crème* of retailing as Miss Jean Brodie would no doubt have called it. But, megastores aside, the Scottish capital is also the place to find shops like shops used to be, from the old-fashioned grocers where nothing is ever too much trouble for the assistants in the stiffly starched white collars, to scores of antique emporiums, some little more than junk caverns, but all worth a browse for anyone with an eye for a bargain. Edinburgh's also the place to get yourself a new bagpipe — the craftsmen at the sixteenth-century workshop of J & R Glen on Lawnmarket at the top of the Royal Mile can kit out an entire pipe band.

There's also a third Edinburgh, in between the Old and the New: Princes Street Gardens, laid upon the bed of an ancient loch. The National Gallery of Scotland is here — although most of the townsfolk who take to the grass during the summer are as likely to be drawn there by the chance of a tan as much as a thirst for culture (since their city shares the same latitude as Moscow, who can blame them?). It is also the venue for concerts, children's shows, buskers, country dancing and all manner of happenings, especially during the Edin-burgh Festival which takes place every year in August and September.

Unusually for a capital, Edinburgh is a city with masses of doorstep greenery and glorious countryside views. The pewter-shaded waters of the Firth of Forth, the Pentland Hill — Robert Louis Stevenson's 'hills of hope and home' — and Arthur's Seat, an ancient volcano, the mere mention of which is apt to send a geologist into tremors of passion, are all a haggis throw from the city centre. For a glorious perspective on the lot, head for just one of the city's seven hills, Calton Hill, with its Nelson's Column and mock, unfinished Parthenon — the National Monument. If you happen to be on Calton Hill at one o'clock you can watch the time ball plummet as the cannon is fired in the distance. And no matter how convincing the locals sound, the cannon doesn't shoot the ball down. That's a lot of old porridge.

SYDNEY

Sydney, for me, starts on top of a cliff. A hundred feet below, the Tasman Sea disintegrates in a shiny mist of spray.

We are on the South Head. Bondi Beach is behind us, four miles to the south; Botany Bay, where Captain Cook landed, is farther south still. To the north, toward Manly, across almost a mile of ocean is another cliff, the North Head. These two rock points form a ceremonial gateway to the grandest waters in the world, Sydney Harbour. The city centre is still four miles away, but this is where Sydney begins and should you go there you must not miss an inch of it.

Sydney *is* its harbour. London and Paris have their rivers, San Francisco its bay: Sydney's harbour transforms a pleasant, prosperous city into a place like nowhere else on earth.

Once upon a time it would have looked like a great deserted lake with rough rock shores, wildly indented with a thousand creeks and coves tucked into the forks of a thousand headlands and spits. Those fingers of land and inlets are all still there — Watson's Bay, Milson's Point, Double Bay — but now they are built over with shimmering yacht marinas and big white houses withdrawn among trees and lawns that slide down to the waterside.

But if the shores of the harbour are select — and you can't get much more select than the two million dollar price tags which they tie to property on the waterfront these days — the waters of the harbour are a free for all, permanently agitated with activity.

They are the marine equivalent of a bustling city piazza — Trafalgar Square or the Place de la Concorde with tides. Harassed ferries fuss about their schedules, laid-back yachts sashay down the wind, harbour cruises go poking round the sights. Self-important motor launches, self-conscious cruise liners, tentative freighters, shadowy warships and the non-stop hydrofoil to Manly criss-cross, circle and bisect the harbour.

There are events unique to the harbour too. On Sundays in summer the Sydneysiders turn out to watch the 18-footer races. These are hybrid, lightweight catamarans, professionally crewed, which skid across the water half the time tipped up almost on their sides. They are followed by television from helicopters and by punters who cram on to the decks of wallowing ferries commandeered for the day as floating grandstands. In January there is even a race for the ferries themselves.

The ferries run to the suburbs scattered round the harbour shores. They are *the* way to get around for sightseers, shoppers and commuters alike. Dumpy little boats with sagging gunwhales, wooden saloons and stubby funnels, they are to Sydney what the double deck bus is to London. You catch them in the city centre from Circular Quay (which incidentally isn't circular at all: it's dead straight).

The Captain Cook harbour cruises also leave from here. And what a route they follow. Hardly have you taken your seat on deck than they have made a smart turn to starboard and you are passing the gleaming cowls of the Opera House. With the Harbour Bridge behind you, it is at this point you stop pinching yourself and accept that you really are in Sydney.

Those high white bonnets of the Opera House, which Sir John Betjeman said looked like nuns in a rugger scrum, have become an emblem of Australia itself. At one time they were a symbol for every row there has ever been between an architect and his municipal employers. In this case the ructions only ended when the architect, a Dane called Joern Utzon, walked out. The building, financed by lotteries, was completed by committee in 1973, which is probably the reason why the Opera House inside does not have the same impact as it does outside. Utzon never saw it finished.

Anyway, there it is, right at the end of Bennelong Point, a brilliant white bud blossoming on the best site in Sydney right under the mightly steel arch of the Harbour Bridge. For a country whose stereotypes had previously been both macho and philistine, known the world over for its digger hats, beer and boomerangs, it must have come as something of a shock to find it was suddenly recognised for an Opera House.

The building is more than that in many ways. Physically it is more accurately described as a performing arts centre. There are guided tours most days.

Tickets for performances are like gold dust. The tip is either to book very early or get on a tour which includes a show. The Opera House, though, is more than just a building: it stands for a city with a strong cultural pulse, not only on Bennelong Point, but in all the other theatres, galleries, museums, jazz clubs and concert halls throughout Sydney.

Go to the 'Con', the Conservatorium of Music in Macquarie Street for the classics, to the Art Gallery of New South Wales in the Domain for an exhilarating collection of Australian art and to the Basement in Reiby Place behind Circular Quay for jazz. One of the particular pleasures of the city is the amount of live music, much of it outdoors in the streets or on the concourses like those at the Opera House and in Martin Plaza in the city centre. People pack the Plaza at lunchtime for programmes of music and dance. When I was there I saw a bagpipe band from Scotland, kilts and all.

Before the Opera House, Sydney was known by every school geography book for the Harbour Bridge — the 'coathanger' as the locals call it. Opened in 1932, its single 550-yard span, unmatched in its day, links the city centre with the North Shore. It carries an eight lane highway and two railway tracks but it has always had one foot planted firmly in the past. At the southern end is the place where modern Australia began.

Or rather, where modern Australia was unloaded. Two hundred years ago, on 26 January 1788, the first convicts were landed at Sydney. Along with four cows, six horses and 44 sheep, they were herded ashore to a hard promontory at the western end of the harbour. The Rocks they called it and the Rocks it remains today.

It did not take long for it to degenerate into a sleazy and dangerous slum, rum-sodden and brothel-ridden, where the men from the whalers pitched into the taverns and the bawdy houses and frequently into each other as well. It was a territory for gangs — known as 'pushes' — until an outbreak of bubonic plague left the area broken and dilapidated.

In the Rocks, as in so many other former slum areas in cities around the world, squalor worked as a preservative. So when the conservationists moved in during the early Seventies they found streets full of the sort of buildings that everywhere else had been bulldozed away to make room for office blocks. Had it not been for the area's decay, the houses in the Rocks, some of the oldest buildings in Sydney, would have undoubtedly been ground into the foundations of a yet another plantation of concrete towers.

Instead, the Rocks is now one of the nicest parts of the city. Dollops of money, paint and imagination have transformed the dereliction into a place with the feel of a Victorian village. There is even a village green, complete with a stone church and hundred-year-old houses with verandahs.

Old warehouses, like the Argyle Centre, have been turned into craft shops; there are pubs, like the Lord Nelson and the Hero of Waterloo, which have buffed up their bars and dusted off their marble, little lanes and quiet courtyards and boutiques selling designer T-shirts and 'everything' for the left-handed. There are gas lamps and cottages and trees with sunshine in their leaves and Campbell's Storehouse on the waterfront which used to house cargoes of rum, whale oil, cedar and seal skins and now contains shops, restaurants and the Australian Wine Centre where they hold free tastings.

Cadman's Cottage is in the Rocks. It is the oldest house in Sydney but that only means it was built in 1816. Not far away is the Old Sydney Inn, another restored building and a good place to stay. Pier One, where the liners berthed and the immigrants first set foot in Australia, is on the edge of the Rocks. Now it is a colourful mix of shops and cafés, markets, musicians and crafts.

A thousand feet above the city stands Sydney Tower, a spindly steel stalk with a big gilded tub on top of it. From the observation deck, or from either of the two revolving restaurants, you look out across the harbour, flecked with sails, towards the famous Taronga Park Zoo, right on the water's edge at Mosman. Immediately below is the wooded parkland of The Domain and the Royal Botanic Gardens, where Farm Cove is cupped like a rowlock between the Opera House and Mrs Macquarie's Point. You look out to the beaches, and there are at least 20 within 25 miles of the middle of the town.

Everyone has heard of Bondi. Like most people, I expected it to be remote and romantic. In fact it is spread out in front of a nondescript suburb with a frontage of seaside hotels and ice cream parlours. But the sands are marvellous, curving acres of them, invaded by surfers and protected by shark nets and glistening lifeguards just to prove this is Oz. You can swim most of the year. In high summer — that is from December to February — the temperature average is around 25°C (just under 80°F); in the depths of winter — June to August — it is nearer 16°C (about 60°F).

Sydney Tower is rooted in Centrepoint, one of the new shopping precincts in what is a surprisingly compact centre for so sprawling a city. You can see it easily on foot in the course of a holiday but the best way to cover the sights is to hop on one of the Sydney Explorer buses. They make a circuit of the top 20 tourist spots and you should never have to wait longer than 25 minutes to catch one from anywhere on their route.

The buildings in the centre all seem to have gone up either in the 1930s or yesterday, with almost nothing in between. There is some older architecture, for instance Strand Arcade, a three-tiered Victorian shopping arcade, all rich cedar wood and glowing stained glass.

Then there are the inner suburbs like King's Cross, Sydney's Soho, and Paddington, Sydney's Hampstead. Bijou terraces of Victorian houses are wrapped in wisteria and bougainvillaea and a delicate wrought iron tracery known as Paddington lace.

But, for all the Victoriana and the traffic that drives on the left, this *is* Australia. The gardens brim with poinsettia and hibiscus, the trees are Moreton Bay figs and the birds that flit from their branches are lorikeets. And at Watson's Bay you can arrive by boat and sit outside Doyle's Restaurant above a small beach with dinghies nodding on their moorings; you can order king prawns and barramundi, mud crab and oysters, sip a chilled Chardonnay from the grog shop up the hill and gaze up that long and lovely harbour towards Sydney in the distance. Sydney, for me, ends right there. After that there is nothing left but check in the memories for home.

BATH

You can judge the tenor of a town by the temper of its taxi drivers. So how reassuring to find a horse-drawn carriage parked by the curb, waiting for business. 'Tour in an original Victoria, circa 1870,' invited a discreet pavement sign. Ideally, in Georgian Bath, it should have been a single-seater sedan chair, manhandled on poles by two be-wigged and buckled bearers, but the high-wheeled, horse-clopping carriage caught perfectly the leisurely ambience of this most handsome of cities.

Mixing my fashions, I was tempted to take the Victoria straight to the Pump Room. In genteel Georgian times, socialites, impeccably dressed, would gossip, listen to the string quartet and delicately sip the spa waters. Today, dressed in what you like, you can take tea or coffee beneath the sparkling cut-glass chandeliers, gossip, listen to a trio and delicately sip the same spa waters. Though gulp might be better. As Dickens' Sam Weller put it, it tastes like 'warm flat irons'.

In fact, it was quicker to walk. And more fun. Round the corner floated the delicate cadences of woodwind music. Outside the Abbey, a dignified figure in a Regency wig, long patterned coat, breeches and buckled shoes was playing a recorder. Round another corner came the soulful sounds of jazz, played by a duo in jeans on sax and guitar. The sun shone and everyone seemed happy and relaxed. Diving down one alleyway bedecked with flowers I discovered the Fudge Kitchen, selling nothing but fudge made on the spot, and a shop selling virtually nothing but shirts mostly made in France. Another alley bristled with second-hand bookshops, art galleries and a wine bar offering vintages 'full and plummy' and vintages 'with a hint of raspberries'. And from within, a hint of Chopin.

Bath is a living museum, a graceful Georgian city fashioned in pale limestone. Built in a bowl of sheltering hills, embraced in a loop of the River Avon, its handsome crescents, terraces and squares rise in stone tiers. Today, it is a conservation showpiece. Yet, as a museum curator wryly remarked, in the 1950s and 1960s, more Georgian buildings were destroyed by locals than by Hitler. Now, he asserted, you have to ask permission to change a light bulb. Conservation and cleaning are constantly in hand. The city's birthright is being zealously protected for all our benefit.

Bath has prospered over the centuries because of its hot springs. Every day, some quarter of a million gallons gush out of the earth at a constant 46.5°C. They were first discovered, according to one legend, by the swine-herd prince, Bladud, father of Shakespeare's King Lear, around 500 BC. Bladud was banished from court as a leper. His pigs, also suffering from skin disease, foraged for acorns in muddy pools and emerged cured. Bladud sensibly followed their example and was also healed.

Disbelievers should walk to The Circus, where this story is commemorated in the giant stone acorns topping the regal sweep of majestic houses.

The Romans, at least, believed in the medicinal properties of the hot springs, building a spa and baths and dedicating a temple to the Roman goddess, Minerva, and the Celtic god, Sul. For around 400 years, Aquae Sulis, as it was known, became one of the most fashionable watering places in Rome's northern empire, its prosperity finally ending with the fall of the Roman empire and the rise of the sea level which caused the River Avon to flood the baths.

Today, the remains of the Roman Baths are unusually complete and among the finest Roman ruins in Britain. A clear, hot water stream pours from the Roman reservoir beneath the King's Bath, seen today just as in Roman times. The Great Bath is ringed with statues, a grandiose Victorian embellishment. Amidst the grandeur lies a human touch. The Romans made lead curses and some are displayed. One is written backwards. A man had his wife stolen and named ten men and women with the inscription: 'May they be made as liquid as water.'

The Bath you see today is largely a Georgian creation, fashioned by three men. At the turn of the eighteenth century, Bath was a medieval walled city, the now restored Abbey its focal point. It had been described as 'unsavoury, lewd and immoral' at various times. Then Ralph Allen came to Bath in 1710, became postmaster and made his fortune running a profitable and efficient national mail service. He bought stone quarries at Combe Down to build a new city from the pale limestone, sharing his dream with John Wood, a temperamental but brilliant architect from Yorkshire. He, and later his son, transformed the city into one of the most handsome in Britain.

The third man was Richard 'Beau' Nash, a 31-year-old penniless Welshman, who arrived in Bath in 1705, made £1000 in his first season at the gaming tables and was appointed Bath's first 'Master of Ceremonies'. A clever administrator and entrepreneur, he had a passion for order and propriety. He cleaned up the town, paved roads and installed street lights to make it safe at night; and ridiculed doctors who poured cold water on the healing powers of the hot springs. He cracked down on touts, including the notorious sedan chairmen; two of their pavilions, where they waited to be hired for about one shilling, or 5p, an hour can be seen, well restored, in Queen's Parade Place.

Beau Nash devised 11 rules of social behaviour; break them, and you would be ostracised by society. When Princess Amelia, George II's daughter, wanted to break the 11 pm dancing curfew at the Assembly Rooms, she warned Nash: 'Remember, I am a princess.' 'Yes, Madam,' he reputedly replied, 'but I reign here and my laws must be kept.'

Nash died penniless, thanks to his gambling debts and law suits, but he still surveys the legacy of an era he created. His bust gazes, across the immaculately restored Pump Room, on a scene he would no doubt recognise: the chatter of visitors sipping coffee or tea and munching Bath buns to a musical accompaniment, spa water on tap at 25p a glass. He would not have approved of everyone's dress sense, though.

The best way to catch Bath's unique flavour is to take a free walking tour from the Pump Room, run by knowledgeable, voluntary guides. They operate daily in summer, less frequently in winter, and last about two hours. Museums are not included but the walk takes in all the main points of historical and architectural interest, including that magnificent set-piece, the Royal Crescent, Britain's first crescent and still its most dramatic.

But then Bath is full of set-pieces. Pulteney Bridge, with shops built across it, is the town's answer to Florence's more famous Ponte Vecchio. Astride the Avon you'll find a truffle shop, a flower shop, a coin shop — that sells old farthings for 45p — a stamp shop, one window crammed with brass and another with homely knitwear. 'Be someone in silk,' urges the silk shop, while its near neighbour, Duck Son and Pinker, sells pianos and organs.

Up on the lofty heights of the Royal Crescent, Number One is immaculately restored and furnished in period style, a genuine glimpse of Georgian formality. Beau Nash would approve, though after seeing the fashions through the ages at the Costume Museum he would undoubtedly invoke one of his strict 11 commandments. Camden Works in Julian Road is the Victorian factory and office of J.B. Bowler, brass founder, engineer and mineral water manufacturer. When the business closed in 1969, no bill, letterhead, receipt or order was thrown away. The whole place has the cluttered atmosphere of a working factory, parts of which still clatter noisily away.

Bath is a short break city for all seasons. It has more museums than you could possibly cram into a brief visit. One leaflet lists 18, all different. It is also well nourished with restaurants, over 100 at the last count. The celebrated Hole in the Wall serves such delicacies as bisque of smoked trout and sorrel with malt whisky. Then there is the Sally Lunn, a flat round cake first made in the early eighteenth century by a bakehouse worker. You can now eat her speciality at the Sally Lunn House in 20 toasted ways, sweet and savoury, from plain with butter to one topped with venison and game casserole. Nearly opposite, another café serves the Bath Bun. Elsewhere, the generic English muffin adorns menus. Clearly, the calorie count in Bath can be high. But then, you can always walk it off.

AMSTERDAM

The Dutch have a saying: 'God created heaven and earth, but man made Holland'. Nowhere is that more true than Amsterdam — in Amsterdam man even made the land on which the city stands. Nowhere is it more difficult to believe.

Amsterdam looks like the work of The Creator, not of contractors. You would think it was an act of nature. Its colours are the colours of earth and foliage; it is scaled to the size of trees. Who can imagine that those rings of green canals, between which the city is squeezed, were dug and are not rivers; that the elms were deliberately planted; that auburn brick was ever placed on auburn brick and not bared by erosion?

Yet it is probably the most artificial city in the world. The ground beneath it was imported. The original settlement in the thirteenth century was built *on* a river: the dam on the Amstel. Four centuries later and the Royal Palace in Dam Square had to be founded upon 13,659 timber piles. There are another 8,687 beneath the Central Station. Amsterdam, you might say, piled into significance.

Much of the city is built on land reclaimed from marshes or the sea. Schiphol, the international airport, has unrolled its runways on the site of a sixteenth-century naval battle. Schiphol means 'ship's hole'. Actually Schiphol means some of the best duty-free shops in the world, but that's another matter.

Amsterdam is never quite what it seems at first sight. Here is the Calvinist capital of stolid Holland with one of the most lurid and ostentatious red light districts in Europe and a malignant trade in drugs, hard and soft, which is fuelling a rise in other crime. Amsterdam's long history of tolerance, which saw refuge given to the persecuted through the ages — Jews from Portugal, Huguenots from France and the Pilgrims from England — has now come to accept the sight of drug dealing on the streets and pallid young addicts dumped comatose on the pavements around the Central Station.

That is the distressed side of Amsterdam, distressing too for someone who has to admit the failings of an old friend. But this is still the city where one of the cheapest rides around town is aboard the orange trams which squeal and clatter and querulously clang their bells at any pedestrian who dares to cross their tracks.

It is where piping street organs still play in the squares; where, on one canal florists have set up their stalls on barges to make a permanent floating flower market and, on another, a canal boat has been made a home for cats; where the Amor porno cinema is next door to the Amsterdam Chinese Church; where pavements are festooned with cycles, salt herring is sold at street corner kiosks and carillons play anything from Bach to Scott Joplin.

This is also the city where it was not until we were filming that I discovered you apply the brakes on an Amsterdam bicycle by pedalling backwards and was almost pitched into a canal in the process. It is where, the last time I was there,

I heard music reeling from a bar and ended up playing a tambourine at a wedding party at 10.30 in the morning.

You can see Amsterdam from the bars and you can see it from a bike, but the best of all ways to see Amsterdam is from the water. Take a canal cruise the instant you get there. You will never begin to understand the place until you have. There are 75 miles of canals, more than in Venice. And whoever called Amsterdam the 'Venice of the North', I cannot believe saw either place. They are entirely different. For a start the canals of Amsterdam are not the city's streets as they are in Venice. Streets run along either bank of the Dutch canals. They are much more like leafy streams running through the middle of town.

On the map they look exactly like a spider's web, hanging beneath the River Ij (pronounced 'eye') and the Central Station on its artificial island. Now imagine the letter 'T' on which the river forms the crossbar. The leg of the 'T' is the Damrak, a big street that leads across a bridge out of the Stationsplein. It is from that square, in front of the station, that most of the tram routes start and where VVV, the excellent city tourist office, has its main information centre. From there Damrak follows the filled-in course of the River Amstel for half a mile to the Dam Square, site of the medieval fishing village from which Amsterdam grew, and still at the hub of the city today.

The canals spread from Dam Square in concentric rings. The first, and oldest, is the Singel. This was the moat which protected the original city, the part built before Holland's 'Golden Age' in the seventeenth century. From then on, as the city prospered and expanded, new canals were added, fanning out from the banks of the Ij: the Herengracht, the Keizersgracht, the Prinsengracht, thoroughfares of silky water settled between low, brick banks. My favourite hotel, the Pulitzer, imaginatively converted from old canal houses, overlooks the Prinsengracht.

From the cruise boats, with their big glass canopies and hulls so broad and so low they might have been got at with a rolling pin, you look up at the cars parked along every inch of the canalside and into the branches of the overhanging trees. The boats slip beneath small brick bridges with arched backs and stout iron railings and past the unbroken rows of houses.

Those houses ... other cities have pictures and prints to show off their past, some reconstruct it with fabricated façades in museum streets or fastidiously conserve the odd corner that has survived. In Amsterdam they have the real thing, all of it, the seventeenth century intact. It is as extraordinary as if nothing had touched the City of London since the last stone was laid at St Pauls. Street after street of slim brick houses stand without even a television aerial to bring them up to date. Their tall windows are so big that even by day they seem to emit light, house after house, packed along the canalsides like old books on library shelves.

They were built by the merchants whose ships by the hundred went trading in the Indies east and west. And they were homes — grand homes to be sure — but not palaces. That is why Amsterdam is such a practical city, never overwhelming, a place for living and working and not for show or ceremony. But rich though the house builders were, they could not afford to ignore the property tax which was levied on the width of a building's frontage. So the houses are slender — the smallest is no wider than its doorway — and the top floors had to serve as stores. The derricks which hoisted the goods from the quayside still jut from the high gables. And it was the gables which gave the houses their style. Until you reach roof level they are more or less uniform — another reason for Amsterdam feeling so 'together'. On the skyline, though, those sober businessmen let themselves go and decorated their homes with gables shaped like bells, or like triangles with steps up their sides, or made them ornate and Italianate.

The canal cruise is only an introduction. Having taken it, you will from then on do better by foot. You can get an idea of what life was like inside one of those patrician houses in the Willet Holthuysen Museum, a private house built in 1687 and comfortably furnished with pieces from the period.

Another house, evoking another period and quite another mood, is the Anne Frank Museum. The attic, where the Jewish family hid from the Nazis and where Anne wrote her diary beneath pin-ups of Deanna Durbin and Ray Milland, has been left just as it was when they were arrested.

Amsterdam was recently voted 'Cultural Capital of Europe'. It would have been almost enough to be sure of election to boast one of the finest symphony orchestras in the world — the Concertgebouw — and two of the greatest art collections in the Van Gogh and Rijksmuseum. Never mind the 40 other museums and the other music, from jazz to organ recitals; the theatre, opera and dance. Like everything else in the city it is all easily accessible. Even the Dutch seem relieved to lapse into the English virtually all of them speak as respite from the phonetic convolutions of their own language.

I hate to think what happened to the Van Gogh Museum's insurance premiums after just one 'Sunflower' painting sold for almost £25 million not long ago. The museum not only has another version of the sunflowers, but a quite astonishing collection of another 200 of Van Gogh's paintings and 400 drawings.

The Rijksmuseum is an even more fabulous treasury, possessing pictures by Franz Hals, Pieter de Hooch, Vermeer — whose luminous little interiors are so intimate that looking at them is almost like prying — and Rembrandt. 'The Night Watch', a canvas measuring almost 12ft by 14ft, shows a group of militia men setting out on their rounds — a sort of seventeenth century neighbour-hood watch scheme. The painting was Rembrandt's rejection of the conventional, formal portrait. I am sure the people who commissioned it thought they would get the oil paint equivalent of the group photograph. Instead, they were rewarded with a masterpiece of composition, painted with all the subtlety of light and character that made Rembrandt the greatest of all Dutch painters. 'The Night Watch' is reputed to be the most valuable picture in existence: £25 million would just about buy the signature and yet the Rijksmuseum has another half dozen Rembrandts in its collection. And Rembrandt's House on Jodenbreestraat, where he lived before his bankruptcy, contains more than 200 of his etchings.

Amsterdam long ago scoured its attics for 'new' Rembrandts so there's little chance of bringing home an Old Master with your souvenirs. You might pick up a piece of Delft china, though, from the antique shops along the Spielgelgraacht, less likely from the Flea Market which is now on Valkenburgerstraat. It moved there a few years ago and seems to have become even more junky in the process — alright for curiosity or if you are into battered trumpets or ancient light fittings. Safer, and cheaper, if you are in the market for antiquities, to settle for an old (not that old!) cheese. Go to the provision stalls on Albert Cuperstraat and buy one of the old, matured Edams. They are delicious and hard to find at home.

Shopping is one of the few things in Amsterdam which stops at night. Everything else carries on at full tilt. Even Rembrandt's memory is somewhat feverishly recruited to the cause of the city's nightlife. Rembrandtsplein is one of the two squares where the nightspots — bars, cafés, clubs and cabarets — are concentrated. The Liedseplein is the other. The entertainment can be as demur or as raffish as you care to find it.

At the demur end of the evening are the brown cafés. They are Amsterdam's pubs. The ones in the centre tend to be touristy, those farther out are places for the locals, where they go to meet, argue, flirt, read, play dominoes, even drink. All of them are old and individual, with sawdust on the floors, tables on the pavement. They are called 'brown' simply because they are painted brown.

Or there are the tasting bars, another Amsterdam tradition where you sip *jenevers* — Dutch gin. In the old days the regulars not only had their own glasses but their own barrels too.

If you economised at lunch with a bowl of *erwtwensoep* (porridge-thick pea soup) or an *uitsmijter* (open sandwich) from a *broodjeswinkel* (sandwich bar), or even if you ate at an *eetcafe* (bistro) or one of the three dozen or so restaurants offering three course tourist menus, you could treat yourself at dinner to an Indonesian *rijsttafel*. It is *the* Amsterdam speciality, a meal of perhaps 20 little dishes of tasty meats and vegetables all served with rice.

The canals keep going at night. The bridges are hung with hundreds of lights and the cruises take place by candlelight. It is like a ride in the ultimate theme park, the one where the theme is true. Even Disney has never woven romance from reality or made fantasy from a place where people live. If the canal cruise by day was the first thing you did when you arrived in Amsterdam, the canal cruise by night should definitely be saved for your last evening. In sunshine the place is beguiling; at night it is enchanted.

NEW YORK

The sight of that Manhattan skyline, whether it's for the first or hundredth time, always brings a kaleidoscope of emotions: excitement ... apprehension ... anticipation ...

From the airport expressway, it's easy to pick out the unmistakeable art deco lines of the Chrysler Building and the sloping roof of Citicorp. Once inside the island's canyons, you have to twist and crane to glimpse the garden-topped residential towers and the office blocks sheathed in black and copper.

New York landmarks tend to come and go for this is a city in a constant state of change. Today's parking lot is suddenly tomorrow's palatial atrium; a trendy discotheque tomorrow's cheap deli. Perhaps it is this overwhelming sensation of change that pumps the city with adrenalin, electrifying every molecule of air around you. There's no bland response to New York. There's only loving or hating it.

Some landmarks, of course, are here to stay, at least until the day after tomorrow, like the Empire State — still the best bird's-eye view — or St Patrick's Cathedral. Both are on Fifth Avenue and both, these days, are dwarfed by newer, towering neighbours. Old friends, like the Plaza Hotel, are saved by public protest while others are lucky enough to win renovation like the opulent Stanhope Hotel, reglossed, regilded and restored to its original grandeur, or the Radio City Music Hall, where I saw Bette Midler perform. I still have the red silk rose lit by a battery which I bought after the concert, and that says a lot about that lady's style.

Getting your bearings is most easily done from above. A number of buildings have observation platforms, or skyline cocktail lounges, while an incredible helicopter ride I took spins you over the whole incomparable scene, including bringing you eye to eye with that famous Lady of the Harbour herself, the Statue of Liberty. I was amazed to see real live people moving inside her crown as I flew around her. Do try to do that trip — it's sensational!

Gray Line and Circle Line tours are also a good introduction. It's simplest on foot, however, as long as you have that all-important map. With the exception of lower Manhattan, New York is laid out on a grid system with avenues running vertically and streets running horizontally each side of the central avenue — Fifth Avenue. New York is no mere sprawling mass but a collection of villages which are easiest explored and enjoyed individually. Although it is nowhere near as dangerous to walk as legend would have it, neighbourhoods do change with startling suddenness.

The bus routes are relatively easy to work out, but Livingstone would have been lost for ever had he ventured into the New York subway system. Its complexity is mind-scrambling.

Lower Manhattan is where New York all began and today it's a little world in itself. It was here that the city's first printing press was set up and the first street lighting introduced and it was this corner of New York which gave birth to the Stock Exchange. This is the most historic part of the city but its maze of tiny streets takes some careful following.

In Lower Manhattan is New York's newest attraction — South Street Seaport museum. In its day this area, around the foot of Fulton Street, was a hive of maritime activity and New York's commercial link with the Old World. Now once again, there are ships berthed at East River piers and the warehouses along Schermerhorn Row have all been restored. Once again, too, there is a Fulton Market — if a somewhat smarter one — where fish and fresh produce is sold.

Another unique part of Lower Manhattan is Chinatown, where even the telephone boxes are pagoda-roofed and grocery shops sell every possible Chinese delicacy. Not that long ago its brothels and opium dens made it one of the city's more notorious neighbourhoods. The area has now been 'spruced up' somewhat, though without losing its essential charm.

On the borders of Chinatown the scent of sweet and sour mingles with that of *linguini alla vongole*. Little Italy is another of Lower Manhattan's ethnic communities. Also downtown is Greenwich Village. It's hard to believe these days that this village held out longest against assimilation into the city. It was once a place where wealthy eighteenth-century landowners had country estates, but the estates were later split up and more modest homes built. And while the rich of the day built their homes in Washington Square, the Village became solidly middle class. Before long, the large houses were split into flats, artists moved in and Greenwich Village won its reputation as the city's bohemia. Today, Greenwich Village isn't quite as unconventional a place as it would like to think itself but it's still fun to browse in the bookshops and boutiques, drop into an elderly coffee house or take in a play at one of the off-Broadway theatres.

SoHo (the area *so*uth of *Ho*uston Street) took up where Greenwich left off. Artists and artisans, who could no longer afford Village prices, moved into the cheap lofts of SoHo's cast iron buildings when industry moved out. Suddenly fashionable, SoHo is the place for chic art galleries and trend-setting restaurants. Even more fashionable is the extension of SoHo now known as Tribeca.

Winos, weirdos, the glitz and the wits — that's New York and that's its charm. Tiffany's baubles are somehow bigger and sparklier than Asprey's and

Broadway's theatres manage to belt out the latest musicals more loudly than London's even though a lot of them originated in our own West End. The Helmsley Palace Hotel's chandeliers and panelling look more overdressed than elegant but New York thrives on being showy. Who, for instance, can resist a second glance at the golden statue of Prometheus backed by its fountain, the focal point of the Rockefeller Centre. Who can resist trotting through the perfumed halls of Bloomingdale's where the beautiful people buy their bread flown in fresh from France?

On the food front, you can, of course, find whatever you want in New York. Wherever you're staying there is a place to eat or drink close by that brims with local colour. Even the humblest diner is bound to be impeccably clean and once you've got the hang of the language — 'eggs over easy', 'tuna fish down' — feeding the family on a holiday budget is as easy as pie — Big Apple Pie.

The city is also a shopper's delight even if you're only browsing. The variety is extraordinary, ranging from stores like Macy's — which covers an entire city block — to the tiniest, chic-est boutiques. Certain areas are devoted to particular items — Sixth Avenue for diamonds, Seventh Avenue for wholesale clothes, Madison Avenue for art, and on the Bowery, in amongst the bums, winos and flop houses, there are two blocks of glittering shops selling nothing but lights.

And at the end of a week in New York as you flop into your plane seat trying to remember what sleep was like, the memories crowd in — munching warm brownies waiting for the Staten Island Ferry ... watching the tugs frog-marching the barges down a cold East River ... the bucking Yellow cabs and the bellow of fire engine sirens ... buying that handbag at Macy's and those shirts at Bloomingdales.

And I remember the wit, the wisecracks and the warmth of that exceptional being, the New Yorker.

HONG KONG

There may be a more dramatic approach to a city somewhere in the world but in my years of travel I've never found anything to match that breathtaking sweep into Hong Kong's Kai Tak airport.

You try to tell yourself you've seen it all before, it's just another city, just another airport. But it isn't and you're craning and twisting with everyone else, just to catch your first glimpse of that second most famous skyline in the world.

A low swing over the outskirts, a sharp bank and you're racing in over the water, lower and lower and yet still no sight of the runway you know is just a sliver of concrete jutting out into Kowloon Bay. As the wheels finally touch there is a sudden surge of adrenalin and the knowledge that over the next three or four days you are going to need it.

Hong Kong is often described as the New York of the East and perhaps this extraordinary colony is a distant eastern relative. But really the comparison does neither city justice. Hong Kong, for all its skyscrapers, is more British than American and more Oriental than British.

Where Britain ends and the Orient begins is impossible to tell, the join today is so well crafted. Perfectly uniformed British Sloanes slip out for a spot of lunch in a perfectly uniformed British pub while, ten yards away, a Chinese housewife harangues her butcher for the inferior quality of some delicacy that reminds one of nothing so much as an accident in the biology lab.

The pace is frantic and the atmosphere 240 volts day and night. We visitors wander about at a gentle 33 rpm while the rest of the world dashes round us at 78. Money is the spur. The same is true of all the world's great commercial meccas but here it's somehow different. Here you can taste it, smell it, breathe it.

Hong Kong was born British and has remained fiercely true to its origins. Unlike many cities, it grew not out of military or social necessity, but out of greed. Lured by the riches of China, Western traders appeared in Hong Kong as long ago as 1513 and began a merciless exploitation of the Chinese which lasted for more than 400 years.

Hong Kong flourished from the start primarily because of its opium trade with China. Backed by the superior firepower of our navy, we poured hundreds of tons of opium into China each year. In exchange, the prizes were silk and silver. Opium wasn't officially outlawed in Hong Kong until after the Second World War.

Hong Kong and its surrounding New Territories are theoretically leased from China and although the present Chinese government has never officially recognised the agreement, it has always found it expedient not to make too much fuss. On 1 July 1997, however, the lease expires and the colony will once again become Chinese soil.

Meanwhile, it's business as usual. Some indication of the bravado with which the end of the lease is viewed, can be gathered from the fact that the trendiest disco in town is called simply '1997'. A local businessman told me: 'Who knows what'll happen in 1997, but tell everyone in England that if they want to see the real Hong Kong they'd better get their skates on.'

Having got one's skates on and made the long flight, the next problem is where to stay. Whether you get the best from staying Hong Kong-side or across the bay in Kowloon is a continuing debate. Stay Hong Kong-side and you're in the heart of it. Stay Kowloon-side and you have views which rival those of Manhattan seen from Brooklyn.

There are few more beautiful cityscapes than Hong Kong. Through the day it changes constantly, light catching one facet and then another. At close of day, sunset splashes every one of ten million high-rise panes with rich gold and then blood red.

But it is when the day has finally died that Hong Kong is at its most spectacular. At night it has a still and almost icy beauty quite unlike any other city. At first you can't quite put your finger on it. And then you realise — all the lights are there, the neon is there, but nothing moves, nothing flashes. Because of the closeness of the airport, only still lights are permitted.

Perhaps Hong Kong's most publicised attraction, however, is its shopping — and with good reason. Shopping in Hong Kong is like shopping in no other city in the world. Shopping in Hong Kong is fairyland for grown-ups. It's not that the prices are that competitive — Singapore and South Korea are probably a better bet these days for most things — it's the unbelievable, utterly dazzling choice. Silks and stereos, designer fashions, carpets, antiques, cameras, jewellery — it just goes on and on. One moment you're in an ultra chic shopping mall, surrounded by designer labels, and the next you're up a tiny back alley having your own personal 'chop' or seal made with your name rendered in a single Chinese character. I've always found it interesting that every journalist's name, translated into Chinese, means 'great author'....

One of the great bargains of Hong Kong shopping used to be the made-to-measure suit, which not only cost a fraction of its London counterpart, but was of excellent quality. Today, sadly, it's not quite the same bargain. Good suits are, of course, still to be had but at more realistic prices. One of the bargains that is still around however is women's clothing — bought direct from the local factories who produce for many of the big designer houses. Almost indiscernable seconds and over-runs are available at a fraction of the price you would pay at home. Go to Stanley Market on the far side of Hong Kong Island and you will see racks of them. Linens and silks of all kinds are good value, too. The best are to be found at the large stores owned by the People's Republic of China.

The most popular buy for visitors, though, is jewellery — particularly diamonds which sell at about ten per cent below world-market levels. However, unless you're an experienced buyer, try to keep to the shops that are members of the Hong Kong Tourist Association. 'Solid gold' Rolexes at £45 may not be the bargain they seem.

But don't spend all your time fishing for your credit card — there's far more to see and do in and around Hong Kong than inside the famous department stores and chic boutiques.

Hong Kong is divided into two main areas — Hong Kong Island and the New Territories. Hong Kong city is on the island and Kowloon is across the water on the Chinese mainland. The two are connected not only by a tunnel but — much more fun — by the legendary Star Ferries that call constantly and mournfully across the water to each other as they pass. Some of the best and cheapest views are from these 7p ferry rides.

The most spectacular view of all, though, is from the Peak, the top of the mountain up which Hong Kong city climbs. The way up is by the 100-year-old Peak Tram, in reality a funicular railway.

Other corners of interest in the city include the reddish light district of Wanchai, home of the legendary — and, alas, mythical — Susie Wong; Causeway Bay, a particularly good shopping area; and the Tiger Balm Gardens — a Chinese view of the netherworld of spirits and home of some of the most garish and extraordinary statues you're ever likely to see. Chinese religions flourishing in Hong Kong include Buddhism, Confucianism and Taoism. The most popular is pragmatism.

Another 'must' is the floating fishing village in Aberdeen harbour, the other side of the island. Although the harbour is fascinating and the boats make a good show, few locals seem to rate the cuisine on the floating restaurants.

No visit to Hong Kong would be complete without a jetfoil dash to Macau, the Portuguese island colony 40 miles away. Here gambling is legal, casinos flourish and one of the sights not to miss is the Chinese trying their *joss* (luck) at the tables. Gambling for the Chinese approaches mania. One Hong Kong resident I know has made the return journey from Macau having lost his house — not once but three times!

The Citadel and the ruins of St Paul's — once the most magnificent church in Asia — are both impressive but the most beautiful spot on the whole island is the tiny and tranquil Old Protestant Cemetery, a 'corner of a foreign field' where the fading nineteenth-century tombstones record the often tragic fate of cabin boy and captain alike.

There is, of course, so much more to discover and explore in both Macau and Hong Kong. No matter how much you see or how long you stay, no matter how familiar it all seems to become, somehow you can never resist the chance to go back. Like an old vaudeville pro, they always leave you wanting just that little bit more....

LIVERPOOL

People living in the far flung corners of the globe, with just half an ear in tune to the sounds of the times, will know that Liverpool is synonymous with the Beatles. The Fab Four managed to turn a provincial city struggling with the decline of its maritime commerce into a place firmly on the pulse of the decade. They put the 'Pool' back on the map and Liverpudlians, as soon as they aired their vowels and consonants, never had to explain where in the world they came from.

But Liverpool as a holiday destination? Surely that's taking nostalgia for the Sixties just a little too far.

Liverpool, along with several other English cities, has been busy promoting itself as an ideal choice for a weekend visit. In competition with the more obvious natural attractions of the country's rural or seaside resorts, cities in general, and Liverpool in particular, are an open exhibition of man-made history. Believe it or not, Liverpool was alive and well pre-John, George, Paul and Ringo, and its story is both fascinating and still in high profile on the city streets and waterfront.

From humble beginnings as a tiny fishing village scattered around a muddy tidal creek (from which it takes its name), Liverpool grew to giddy proportions. By the eighteenth-century it had become the second most important city after London in the entire British Empire. Her fortunes have always been closely linked to the muddy River Mersey which wends its way south and east of the city. The first dock opened in 1715 and a string of others followed, trading mainly with the Americas in sugar, spices and tobacco; also in slaves, but they tend to play down that cargo.

The last era of international fame for Liverpool was intimately tied to the birth of the New World. Between 1830 and 1930 Liverpool was the principal departure point in Europe for emigrants to America, Canada and Australia and still retains more links with America than any other city in Britain. More than nine million of the 'huddled masses' passed through Liverpool's docks in this period, driven by poverty, hunger, unemployment, religious persecution or just plain ambition to a slice of the cake on offer across the water.

Although Liverpool is still one of Britain's principal commercial ports, the Cunard service to New York came to an end in 1966 and the last transatlantic giant set sail for Canada the following year, leviathans made obsolete by the jumbo jet. Now only the ghosts remain. The old floating landing stage has been cut down and today only plays host to Mersey ferry boats, immortalised in Gerry Marsden's song (which you'll invariably find yourself humming if you have the faintest recall for a tune).

The emigrants' last view of England was Liverpool's 'Big Three', a trio of magnificent buildings grouped around the Pier Head. The Royal Liver, one of the world's first multi-storey concrete buildings topped by the legendary Liver Birds; the Cunard building, now a regular office block, and the green-domed Port of Liverpool building, all of which are best seen from the deck of one of the Mersey ferries — and at least once during the day and once at night when they are all illuminated.

If you've already been to New York the scene will look strangely familiar. It is almost as though the architect who conceived these three landmarks drew up his plans, left one copy for the Liverpool city fathers to implement, took another copy across the Atlantic and used them as inspiration for the early skyscrapers of downtown Manhattan.

The decline in the city's transatlantic trade also left a legacy of huge redundant Victorian redbrick warehouses. But a remarkable restoration project has recently transformed the Albert Dock, the first to have been reclaimed from dereliction, into a superb waterfront showpiece. Opened in 1984 in time for the Tall Ships Race, these magnificent warehouses, the largest group of Grade 1 Listed buildings in the country, are now a world of wine bars, restaurants, smart speciality shops and exhibition areas that include an extension of London's Tate Gallery. It's like a satellite of Covent Garden in an infinitely more beautiful setting, the 'piazza' being a waterfilled haven for small craft.

The star of the on-going Albert Dock redevelopment is the Merseyside Maritime Museum, housed in one of the warehouses but also spilling over much of the quayside. There are ships and boats in wet and dry docks, rescued from the breaker's yard because of their one-time connection with the port, the restored Piermaster's house and other dockside buildings with displays of coopering, sailmaking and boatbuilding. Be sure to take the eerie trip back in time in the 'Emigrants to a New World' exhibition which includes a recon-structed dockland street, peopled with hawkers, porters, and drunken sailors, who grunt and curse as you pass, and a below-decks section of a packet ship to give a taste of the cramped travelling conditions. There's even an Emigration Bureau to give American visitors advice on how to trace their ancestors.

Set aside several hours of your weekend visit for a 'ferry 'cross the Mersey' to the Wirral peninsula, specifically to visit Port Sunlight, the nineteenth-century model village built by Viscount William Leverhulme, when he moved his small family soap business from Warrington to this then marshy, undeveloped site. The rest of the story is the Unilever saga (suitable material for a future soap opera?!). The most important building in the village, apart from the pub, is the Lady Lever Art Gallery, officially ranked as one of the top 200 galleries in the world. Built by William Lever as a kind of Taj Mahal in memory of his wife, it contains the Levers' magnificent collection of eighteenth- and nineteenth-century British paintings and other works of art including a superb collection of Wedgewood.

The gallery is no match, however, for the city's Walker Art Gallery which is the best of its kind outside London. Among its notable collection of European art dating from 1300 to the present day is a rich stock of Flemish and Italian works and paintings by the progressive nineteenth-century British artists like Millais, Leighton and Sickert. The Walker Gallery, along with neighbouring St George's Hall, a giant Parthenon of a building, reflect a civic pride and prosperity that seem utterly incongruous with these times of heavy unem-ployment and a city where local government has been in a state of political and economic turmoil.

Liverpool, as measured by its flourishing shopping centre, hardly gives the impression of a city struggling to keep up appearances. The long, tree-lined, boulevard-style Church Street and Lord Street make up the main arteries, both well-endowed with all the big-name chains and there's a massive undercover shopping precinct called St John — you can't miss it if you head for the tallest object in the city, the concrete tower. God is as well served in the city as mammon. The two modern cathedrals, one Anglican the other Roman Catholic, stand poignantly at either end of Hope Street.

There used to be a revolving restaurant on the top of the St John tower but at the time of writing it is closed and the tower is left just to perform its less romantic task as a ventilation shaft. But that doesn't mean going hungry. Since many emigrants failed to reach their 'promised land', either running out of money or finding that Liverpool offered alternative opportunities, there is a highly cosmopolitan mix of inhabitants and a variety of ethnic restaurants. Over 100 nationalities are said to live in the one square mile of Toxteth alone. Liverpool has its own Chinatown too (although the most interesting Chinese restaurant, Laus, is in fact unusually located in a large, residential Victorian house opposite Sefton Park close to where John Lennon lived).

But what of the Beatles, still the best public relations agents that any city could have? Well, the original Cavern is no more but there's a lively Beatles shop selling all sorts of Beatlebrac and you can take one of the Beatleguide mini-bus tours past Ringo's house, Penny Lane, Strawberry Fields (now a children's home), Paul McCartney's home and the Blue Angels pub where they played their first professional audition. At Festival Park, the site of Britain's first highly successful international garden festival in 1984 (which attracted over three million people) there's a huge recreation model of a Yellow Submarine.

But for a vivid journey through the Beatles era, visit Beatle City, a bright yellow former car-parts storage building which now holds a valuable collection of genuine Beatle memorabilia, including Ringo Starr's Mini Cooper, John Lennon's Steinway piano and Rickenbacker guitar, Brian Epstein's office, all backed by multi-media presentations, including a unique collection of rare live footage. There's even talk of Beatle City emigrating for a while across the Atlantic, so get there while you can. They play 'Imagine' just before you leave — a moving experience and a fitting way to end your city break.

BEACHES

Holidays come and holidays go but beaches go on forever. Or so it seems.
No matter how many new 'activity' or 'special interest' holidays there are to
lure people away from the beach, that old potion of sun, sand, sea and anything
else agreeable beginning with 's' is as powerful as ever.

It might not have been so. Holidays by the sea are one of our newer fads. It
was only 200 or so years ago that going to the seaside for pleasure was thought
of at all. Compared with wine drinking, horse riding or music, that makes it
positively new-fangled. And even 200 years ago no one was quite sure what to
do with the sea when they got there. For a short time they thought you had to
drink it. Not surprisingly that idea did not last long and it quickly became clear
that there was more of a future in swimming and sandcastles.

So the fashion might not have lasted. But today, for millions every year,
especially families, beach holidays are indispensable. Brave are the parents
who would dare to announce there will be no seaside this summer.

I have chosen beaches near and far, from the rugged coast of Pembrokeshire
to the hot swathes of sand in Brazil and the near-uninhabited shores of the
Seychelles. To these I have added the more popular places like the Algarve —
still my favourite for family holidays and where, despite the numbers who have
discovered it for themselves, I can still find beaches which I can have almost to
myself. Torbay is a resort to confound all those who would like to write off the
British seaside, and Benidorm will confound anyone who has never been there.

ALGARVE

Sooner or later, it always happens. It could be at an airport, during a party or simply in the street. Someone will pop the inevitable question: 'And where do *you* go for your holiday?' The implication, sometimes sounding more like an accusation, is that I have cracked that recurring 'where shall we go this year' dilemma and that I am keeping it a secret.

Well, I have solved the problem but it is no secret. Before I tell you about the place that has minted family legends, though, just bear in mind that one person's dream holiday is another person's nightmare. So please don't blame me if it doesn't fit your particular requirements.

Year in, year out, we have returned to Portugal's Algarve for our family holidays. Familiarity breeds content: the smooth buttery coloured beaches backed by honey-hued rocks, the hot sun and blue sky, the heady scent of salt-laden breezes, suntan oil and grilled sardines — these are what I dream of in midwinter, that no-man's-land between summer holidays. Then there are the dozens of little restaurants where you can eat well and cheaply; the unpretentious inland towns with their workaday markets; the sun-burnished country roads empty but for the high-wheeled, horse-drawn carts carrying elderly couples in black sitting bolt upright like stern Victorians. True, parts of the coast are becoming over-developed, — too many high-rise hotels and apartment blocks have been built and in the height of summer it gets very crowded — but you can still find a half-empty beach, rinsed clean by Atlantic tides, round the next corner.

Long after its near neighbour, Spain's Costa del Sol, became a high-rise holiday playground, the Algarve remained comparatively unknown. It still has a long way to catch up. The 90-mile, south-facing coast fairly sizzles in summer yet high temperatures are fanned by Atlantic breezes that also keep the sea refreshingly cool. In fact it can be quite cold, even in midsummer, and some exposed beaches thump to the resounding crash of boisterous rollers, big enough for surfing. Although scenery and atmosphere are Mediterranean, with a hint of Moorish North Africa, it is the cooler, cleaner Atlantic that gives the Algarve its individual character and temperament and places it apart from Spain.

Indeed, you might go to Portugal for the Portuguese alone. Polite, dignified and friendly, they remain among the most courteous people in Europe. It was typical that once, when I was hunting for fresh herbs in Portimao, I was guided to a shop in a tight warren of backstreets by a man who temporarily abandoned his own tiny store. And each year, when I return for the first time to shop in the local supermarket, Philomena comes from behind the till to give me a hug and a kiss. That *never* happens at home!

The Algarve stretches from wild and windswept Cape St Vincent, Portugal's *o fim do mundo*, (the end of the world) to the smooth, flat beaches of Monte Gordo, bordering Spain. The popular and most scenic stretch lies roughly midway. The first real tourist beaches with proper facilities begin around Lagos with the long curved sands of Praia da Luz, proceed through pretty coves like Dona Ana, and then march along vast Praia da Rocha, its superb, iron-smooth sands broken by oddly sculptured chunks and fingers of rocks, and edged by cliffs.

Praia da Rocha was for a long time the Algarve's largest resort, which meant it was as commercialised as Tenby or St Ives on a quiet day; now it is growing apace. Several hotels or apartment blocks are being built and work can start as

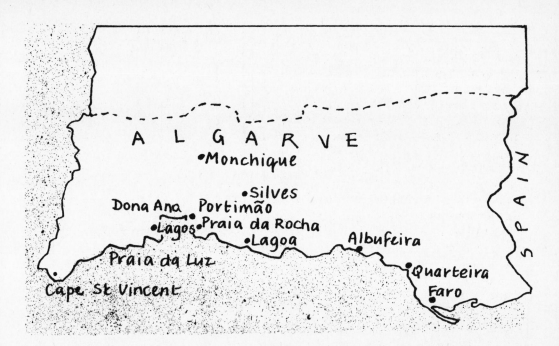

early as 6 am, so check carefully about surrounding development if you book at what is otherwise a good family centre on one of the Algarve's best beaches.

Today, Albufeira is the liveliest and largest resort. Despite its popularity, it retains its character and charm. The core is still a cliff-hanging fishing village, its few cobbled streets rising and falling above the town beach where rainbow coloured fishing boats are pulled up on the sands. A siren sounds when the fishermen land the latest catch in the tiny market, topping and tailing the fish on marble slabs so speedily that all you can see is the glint of the knife.

Above, a morning fruit, veg. and general market run by country folk spreads beneath the trees of the main square. The centre is packed and chaotic in high summer. Sir Harry's Bar posts up the daily news headlines on a blackboard and if you fancy a glass of port, the best place to head for is the Cave do Vinho do Porto in the Rua da Liberdade. The tangle of side streets is honeycombed with bars, restaurants and discos.

Albufeira's surrounding beaches are crowded, but move east or west along the coast and you'll find plenty of space on less frequented sands. Move out from Albufeira and you are gradually engulfed by hotels, apartments and holiday estates, similar to many parts of southern Europe. These soon thin out and the beaches on the way to Faro, which marks the end of the most scenic part of the Algarve, are uncrowded and undeveloped. With the exception, that is, of Quarteira, an unattractive burgeoning resort, in no way typical of the Algarve. There is one good reason for going there, however; it has one of the best fish restaurants in the area. Don't expect sophistication at the Central; it is large, brightly lit and noisy, often packed with Portuguese families. You eat off plain table tops but the food is fresh, well cooked and cheap.

Many Algarve hotels are built in a lavish style in their own grounds. They tend to be fairly expensive. Better value to my mind, and ideal for families, are the numerous self-catering villas, some on estates, others on their own, many with private pools, all with daily maid service. My favourite, to which I return regularly, is the spacious Vale do Lobo estate, about ten miles from Faro, spreading above a long, largely uncommercialised beach. Villas are secluded among trees or in Portuguese village-style terraces and furnished and equipped to a high standard.

Social life revolves around the square known as the Praça: bars, restaurants, discos, two stunning pools — one for children. It was here that my son, Mark, learned to swim, helped by a group he nicknamed the Penguins, after the way they waddled out to sea with flippers and snorkel masks. The disco is a magnet for the young and it's reassuring to know just where your children are at night.

Husband Neil, now joined by Mark, enjoys the superb golf course (golf is a particularly strong feature of the Algarve) and Emma and I — all of us in fact — play tennis at the Roger Taylor Tennis Centre, where you can play with or without tuition. The courts are superb, and floodlit at night, and it's a great meeting place for all ages with an outside bar and restaurant there too. In short, there is something here to occupy all the family, whatever their age. If you take a package deal, make quite sure that the price includes the club guest card, which entitles you to reduced golf and tennis fees, free internal bus travel and free entrance to the swimming pools — important, otherwise you pay hefty admission fees.

Eating out in Portugal is such good value that you sometimes wonder if it's worth cooking at all. (Incidentally, it's better to shop at the supermarkets local people use; those geared to holidaymakers tend to stock expensive imported items. British orange squash, for instance, can cost more than an acceptable bottle of local gin.) Nearby restaurants include Shepherd's at Quinta — that's Richard Shepherd of Langan's fame — with great food and an adjoining disco, but as far as I am concerned, nothing beats eating at the beachside restaurants. Joao Passos' at Ancao is the best. You reach it down an unmade road and there you'll find succulent shellfish and the T-bone steaks come with brown rice seasoned with bits of onion and bacon. It stands alone above the sands with the waves pounding on the beach and the air scented with salt and pines. In the heat of the day, you get the breeze from the sea.

Although holiday estates like the Vale do Lobo are self-contained, it's well worth hiring a car to explore the coast and country. To towns largely untouched by tourism, like Loule, where the market is now housed in a smart new enclosure. In narrow streets radiating from Dom Alfonso square, artisans beaver away in dark workshops, turning out handmade leather goods, copperware and furniture. They are said to be descendants of the Moslems who found refuge here after the mid thirteenth-century re-conquest.

To Faro, for its shopping: shoes are among the best buys. To Lagoa, the wine capital of the Algarve, where you can sample wines in traditional 'caves.' To Silves, a town of simple whitewashed houses crowned by an impressive castle. Further afield, drive through shady avenues of eucalyptus trees to hilltop Monchique, cool and refreshing on a hot day with panoramic cross-country views.

- But no holiday on the Algarve is complete without visiting Portimão. It's a pleasure to stroll around the hunched, white streets faced with brilliantly coloured tiles. But the big lure is the port. As the fishermen return, you can eat fresh sardines on the quayside, grilled to perfection with a sprinkle of salt to make them crunchy. When I first went to Portimão, they totted up the bill according to the sardine heads left on the plate. Now they make fish paté and a man in a boater and striped apron welcomes you to a table. Even so, nothing changes the taste of fresh grilled sardines and a crisp salad.

For me, nowhere has ever quite matched the Algarve for a family holiday. Now you know why we always catch an early morning flight from home and return in the evening: to squeeze the first and last out of the perfect holiday.

PEMBROKESHIRE

Places that don't go anywhere have an indefinable flavour. Cornwall is Britain's most popular no-through road; Pembrokeshire is another, less well-known but with a similar all pervading sense of times past. The coast of high cliffs and smooth sands are a kind of Land's End: next stop, America. The nearest motorway is 50 miles distant.

It feels remote. The world has somehow by-passed this corner of south-west Wales. So isolated was it in medieval times, that two pilgrimages to its cathedral at St David's were considered the equivalent of one to Rome. Today, it remains gloriously unsullied, surprisingly unchanged by fads and fashions: glistening sands edged with rock pools, pebbly coves bleached by sun and sea, gull-haunted and sea-wracked headlands, high-hedged lanes hung with roses and honeysuckle, lonely hills where curlews call. Modest villages hewn out of local stone retain a close-knit, community feel.

Pembrokeshire has a split personality. The south is known as 'Little England beyond Wales', a reference to the colonising of this part by Normans and, much later, Flemish immigrants. Here you'll find English spoken everywhere and also find the peninsula's two most popular resorts, Saundersfoot and Tenby.

Somewhere — and though local historians will quickly tell you precisely where, it has always escaped me — is an invisible cultural divide. The north has retained a strong Celtic identity and in the little village stores redolent of butter, bacon, sticky tonic wines, gum boots and coils of seasoned ropes, you'll hear the lilting, musical nuances of Welsh.

Even so, the north is fast becoming a modern 'Little England beyond Wales,' colonised by the numerous art and craft studios — 'too many to mention individually,' admits one defeated guide — mostly run by English refugees from the big town rat-race.

There are no big resorts in Pembrokeshire. Tenby, the largest, is small by any standards and has everything going for it — an enchanting walled town of narrow streets clustered on a rocky headland above great sweeps of sand. It was here while I was standing filming on the top deck of an open-top bus that I had to quickly duck as we went under a low bridge. On that occasion it was 'take two'.... And in the department of Trivial Pursuits, here's a piece of incidental intelligence: Tenby was the birthplace of a Tudor scientist, one Robert Recorde, who invented the sign = for equal.

From Tenby's captivating little harbour, you can sail out to Caldey Island in the summer. Here, Cistercian monks sell their main produce, Caldey Abbey perfume, made from fragrant herbs and gorse blooms, along with homemade chocolate, cream and even yoghurt, straight from their farm. Everyone can visit the old priory and churches but I can't tell you about the monastery — only male visitors are allowed inside.

For nature lovers, the sea-buffeted off-shore islands are paradise. From the top of Caldey, you can often see colonies of seals, breaking the water like benign and mustachioed old gentlemen; more seals and seabirds galore on

Ramsey; Manx shearwaters breed in summer on Skomer, sharing the cliffs with fulmars and puffins. Elsewhere, especially at Elegug Stacks, the cliffs are crowded with guillemots, razor bills, kittiwakes and cormorants; the air full of wheeling birds and the raucous, soulful cry of gulls. If, like me, you enjoy birdwatching, you'll find this a fascinating hunting ground.

In South Pembrokeshire there's a feudal legacy of medieval castles, largely used against the Celts: massive Pembroke, where Henry VII was born; Manorbier, overlooking sands; gaunt Carew, sacked by Cromwell; austere Roch, that seems to grow out of an inland rocky outcrop (and now, topped with a TV aerial, available for rent).

Cross that invisible border into North Pembrokeshire and all the castles disappear. The atmosphere subtly changes. The true Welshness of Wales comes to the surface.

Long before Christianity came to Wales, stone-age man farmed St David's Head. It's a mysterious, isolated place, its bare windswept heights studded with prehistoric relics, frowning outcrops of rocks and scattered, whitewashed farmhouses. Ancient trade routes crossed the headland for Whitesands Bay and the boat to Ireland. In Roman days it was known as the Promontory of Eight Perils, so deadly to shipping were the razor-edged rocks.

But it was from here that Wales's patron saint spread the message of Christianity. Into this bleak setting, St David was born on a headland. A ruined chapel, dedicated to his mother, St Non, is said to mark the spot. St David's became the centre of Christianity before Canterbury. Although warring Norsemen did more than their fair share of sacking and pillaging, Pembrokeshire escaped the later battles, sieges and invasions that afflicted other parts of Wales.

St David founded his monastery some 1500 years ago and today's cathedral dates back to the twelfth-century. At first, you can't find it. Standing in the little square, you are surrounded by a domestic huddle of small houses and shops, composing one of Britain's smallest cities. Then it comes into view below, nestling in a grassy hollow flanked by fields and stone walls.

Despite its hideaway location, there's nothing retiring about this cathedral: strong and angular, built from distinctive purple stone, storm-weathered and greying with age, it is a magnificent example of medieval architecture. The adjoining Bishop's Palace is now a ruin, thanks partly to Bishop Barlow, who lived there in the sixteenth century. He sold the lead from the roof to provide dowries for five daughters. It paid off — they all married bishops.

From St David's right round to Dinas Head lies a coast of wild grandeur. The coastal footpath spits flames of yellow gorse, climbing to clifftops and dipping to coves. Rare rock lavender grows out of the cliff-face and the little scented burnet rose flourishes, along with pink thrift and sea campion. Sunken lanes fan seawards like a spider's web. To Caerfai, where monks quarried stone for the cathedral; to Porth Clais, a steep-sided creek busy enough in Elizabethan times to handle timber from Ireland and wool and corn to Bristol; to St Justinian, where the lifeboat station stands on stilts and the boat will hit the water within 15 minutes of an alarm call.

There are some superb bucket and spade beaches. At Whitesand Bay, white-capped rollers cream endlessly up the glistening spread of sand. Traethilyfn is less busy in summer. Backed by Cornish-style cliffs, it can only be reached by the coastal footpath or by car through Barry Island Farm for a parking charge. Local knowledge and an Ordnance Survey map can turn up some hidden trumps.

Ghosts haunt Porth Gain. Gloomy ruins of a giant granite crushing plant dominate the tiny harbour. It's an eerie place. In the days before World War One it turned out 40,000 tons of stone and chippings a year for the quiet roads of Edwardian Britain. The plant closed one black day in 1931, throwing everyone out of work. When the old office on the quayside, now a café, was re-opened for the first time some 30 years later, they found a half-typed letter still in the typewriter, dated 1931 — a *Marie Celeste* of industrial archeology.

At Strumble Head, you peer down sheer cliffs into a devil's brew of seething water. The sea booms in scalloped rocks far below and thousands of gulls rise into the air with melancholy cries. Round the corner, Fishguard is the port that never quite made the big time. Destined as a major trans-Atlantic port, it is instead an Irish ferry terminal. Personally, I'm glad for Fishguard remains a charming little town set among headlands with corkscrew hills and narrow streets lined with lopsided cottages.

Another candidate question for Trivial Pursuits: where and when was the last invasion of Britain? Answer: in 1797 French troops landed at remote and rocky Careg Gwasted Point. The story goes that they mistook a crowd of Welsh women in national dress for British redcoats and promptly surrendered ... or vice versa.

Holidays here are old-fashioned in the nicest sense of the word. You'll find plenty of simple and spotless bed and breakfast places with lino polished to within an inch of its life and a Bible by the bed. Self catering is, quite literally, a cottage industry. There are scores to rent, from simple whitewashed two-up-and-two-down to those embellished with beams and inglenooks and furnished with antiques and dishwashers. Cheaper chalets and caravans dot the coast, mainly in the south.

Service is old fashioned too; it's even taken the self out of self-catering. You can buy takeaway crab and lobster salads from Mrs Phillips in Upper Solva and order gourmet dishes to your dining room table from the Fitzgerald's remarkable chef-on-wheels service, based at Mathry. Leon Downey's Victorian dairy at Llangloffan Farm — you can also stay there — churns out superb cheese in the traditional way. Stalls at Fishguard's Thursday market groan with flans, cakes and other fare. Some of the best and cheapest fresh fish (particularly mackerel) comes from boot sales in car parks, like the waterfront one in Goodwick.

Pembrokeshire, incidentally, doesn't even exist. Officially, that is. Back in 1973, the old counties of west Wales were amalgamated into Dyfed. But, as one local guide book puts it: 'We studiously ignore such administrative conditions'. Quite right. Pembrokeshire for ever . . . .

BENIDORM

'BENIDORM???' I can hear your horror. 'What's a place like Benidorm doing in a book like this?'

If that is your reaction I will lay a pound to a peseta you have never been there. If I had decided to write about Miami, say, or Acapulco or Surfer's Paradise on the east coast of Australia, and included them among the best beach resorts of the world, you would have read on unquestioningly.

The fact is Benidorm is up there among them, right at the top of Division One in the league of the world's big international resorts. Now you may not care for big international resorts in which case turn the page because what follows will not be to your taste at all. If you do like big resorts, read on because Benidorm is arguably the best in the Mediterranean. To begin to appreciate it you need to like places where you live it up most of the night and, if not exactly live it down, at least sleep it off in the day. It has two of the best beaches in Europe where you will not be alone in doing so, sleeping it off, that is.

Probably the most remarkable thing about Benidorm is that it was not built by chance. Other resorts have grown haphazardly; Benidorm was planned from the outset. I am not talking about the man who was going to take tourists there by stage-coach a hundred years ago (talk about someone having the right idea at the wrong time), but the architects of the town today. What you see now is pretty well what they envisioned in the early 1950s.

It was an uncanny achievement. Quite unwittingly they had put into practice a fairly advanced piece of social engineering. Back in the 1920s a German academic had fantasised in a scholarly sort of way about building what he called 'pleasure cities'. As a social scientist he had worked out that any formula made up from equal measures of population growth, increased wealth, shorter working hours and a good dash of human nature was bound to result in people wanting to give themselves a good time.

The way he saw those future tastes being satisfied was in a new design of city, purpose-built for enjoyment. Far removed from the old industrial and commercial centres which had provided the factories and offices where money was earned, these would be places of fun and entertainment where money was spent.

Sixty odd years ago that was fairly far-fetched even for a piece of theory. But in 1956 Benidorm's Town Council commissioned the blueprint for just such a city. When you think that the dawn of mass tourism had hardly broken, that Benidorm had only been declared a town three years earlier and that the population, mayor and corporation included, were for the most part fisherfolk, their foresight bordered on the visionary. They employed a planner to put a scheme on paper and today it is all but complete.

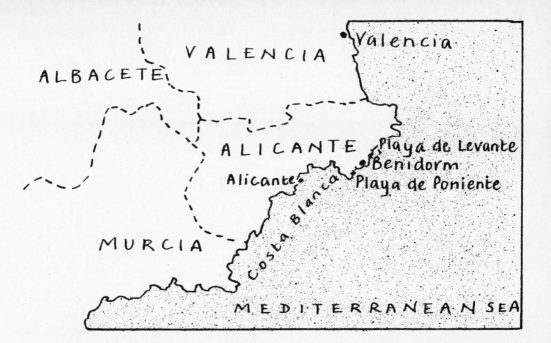

For the history of the packaged holiday is written 20 storeys high along the front at Benidorm. It is an inspired version of the classic tale you will find repeated the length of the Spanish coast: once there was a fishing village ....

In Benidorm it was crammed on top of a cliff sticking out like a beak between two enormous crescents of sand. Benidorm's city fathers may have shown foresight but the Almighty was positively munificent. Spain's east coast slants to the south west. But at Benidrom it turns sharp right so those two big beaches face due south. The sun pours straight on to them all day, from the moment it rises above the Sierra Helada to the time that it sinks behind La Cala. In summer the temperature burns in the 90s; in winter it can reach the low 70s. As rain is rare on the Costa Blanca a lot of elderly people take advantage of the cheap two and three month holidays and migrate there for the winter. So dry is this coast that Benidorm in the past has suffered from water shortages. Supplies are more reliable now.

Even Benidorm's most prescient villagers could not have known that a day would come when all the fish in their sea would be worth but an atom of the sand where they landed them and the sun they occasionally cursed.

Old photographs reveal how suddenly the changes came. In 1950 the scruffy sand of the Playa de Poniente, the western beach, drifted inland through scrawny bushes and across a faint road. Weed marked the high water mark and in the corner, beneath the village, a couple of dozen rowing boats lolled on their clinkers. Buildings were just beginning to spill off the back of the point, small rectangular houses with deep-set windows. No building was higher than the squat white church with the umbrella-shaped dome of shiny blue tiles. It dominated everything. Even today the Poniente is still the quieter of the two beaches, less developed and where the locals go and the holiday company reps escape their clients on their days off.

Tourism came earlier to the eastern beach, the Playa de Levante. By 1950 a gappy line of villas and small hotels straggled round the back of the bay. There was a dusty promenade and four forlorn palm trees planted in a row. Shelters against the sun — flat canopies of reeds on spindly legs — were set up along the sands like market stalls. Ten years later and the spaces between the villas had been filled by modest hotels the shape of up-ended shoe boxes five or six floors high but whose every room gave on to a balcony. The sea view had come to Spain.

Today, on that same front, a phalanx of towering apartments and hotels rears up in a white cliff of concrete, 30 storeys high and slatted with balconies. Buildings like that spread for perhaps three-quarters of a mile back from the beach. Benidorm has three million visitors a year.

It is not a place to go for retreat. The trouble — for Benidorm's reputation, that is — is that people equate popularity and crowds with the tawdry and cheap. Benidorm may be unashamedly popular: of its 120 hotels only seven have four stars; one has five; the rest divide almost equally between one, two and three star establishments. But Benidorm is not tacky.

What it does it does to a high standard. The Benidorm holiday is mass produced but is built for quality nonetheless. Those ranks of tall buildings, for instance, which extend back up the shore, are staggered like the seats in an auditorium so one does not look straight on to the back of another. And the height of any building is governed by the amount of land it has around it for gardens, swimming pools, tennis courts and so on.

The streets are much cleaner than London's; all three miles of sand are mechanically cleaned daily and the sea is tested for pollution at five separate points. And even the sea has been adapted for use by the mass market. Just off shore is a water-ski machine. It is a sort of marine version of the ski lift, tugging skiers around a half mile course at the end of cables which run between pylons set into the sea bed.

Behind the Levante Beach, overlooking the seafront Paseo, piano bars like the New Look, Bel Aire and Regine's are as smart as any in the Mediterranean with the clients, white wicker furniture, mirrored ceilings, perspex pianos and price lists to match. There are some excellent restaurants. I Fratelli is one of the best. That's Italian but you can find Swiss, German, Portuguese, Indian, Chinese and French cooking as well.

As you would expect in any big Spanish resort, there are some stylish, not to say extravagent discos. Nabab is in a Mediterranean garden; Star Garden looks like a flying saucer. In amongst the flashy nightspots, the transvestite shows and designer boutiques, there are the British pubs and bingo games, the cafés selling full English breakfasts (for a good deal less than you would pay in England) and covered bazaars packed with gift shops.

The range and sheer quantity of Benidorm's nightlife can be bewildering. On 'Wish You Were Here...?' not long ago we interviewed some young holidaymakers on their way home from Benidorm. Their only complaint was that there was so much nightlife that they felt almost cheated because they must have missed something. From the smallest pub or pizzeria to the clubs and cabarets, Benidorm runs pretty well round the clock. There are medieval banquets held beside the lists of a full-scale tournament in which half a dozen knights tilt at one another on horseback. The audience, sitting in the covered terraces, fuelled by red wine, cheer their champions while chewing barbecued chicken.

The Spanish dance show at the Benidorm Palace has the biggest production budget. Performed on an enormous, 130-foot long stage in front of several hundred diners, it is lavishly dressed and flamboyantly choreographed. The lighting is computerised and the sound system superb. Glitzy to the last sequin, the Benidorm Palace is where flamenco meets Las Vegas. To the clatter of clapping and castanets and much stamping of heels, haughty young men, shiny with sweat, put on a fiery and fiesty show. They curl their lips and hollow their backs, make-believe matadors taunting imaginary bulls. They have anguished jaws and trousers as tight as tomato skins. If anything the men are prettier than the girls in the troupe. And the girls, gipsy eyes a-smoulder and arms akimbo, are more macho than the men. Sexuality is turned on its head and a Cuban heel.

The biggest new attraction is for the daytime. Aqualand, in the hills above the town, is a water park designed and run by Texans. It is vast — 8000 people can swim and slide at one time. Aqualand is the kind of place where they work out how much water the average person takes with them every time they get out of a pool. (The answer is a litre and the Texans, quick on the draw with their calculators, ensure the system compensates.) The park's water, incidentally, comes from its own wells elsewhere in the mountains. They have also installed, along with a wave-maker, a 500-yard long artificial river and the 'kamikaze' slides, a number of fast food restaurants. Just as they would in Texas.

Unfortunately, I rejoice to say, there is no such concept as 'fast food' in the Spanish *mañana* culture. Or rather, no matter how fast you make the food, you will not make a Spanish family, on a day out in the sun, take less than two hours to eat it. Almost as soon as it opened Aqualand had to double the size of its eating areas.

That is something else people do not realise about Benidorm: underneath the neon it is entirely Spanish. When a festival takes to the streets and the men put on their best black suits, and the women wear lace *mantillas*, black blouses and full skirts, visitors, for all their numbers, can feel like intruders. And half the visitors are Spanish too.

The Horgueras de San Juan — the festival of St John — is held at the end of June. There are street parties, deafening fireworks, parades and ceremonial bonfires on which giant papier-mâché effigies are burned. Yet the whole festival — meat and drink to a tourist brochure — is strangely private. The people taking part seem quite unaware of the crowds of onlookers.

In the old village on the end of the point, the narrow lanes and small squares splashed with flowers, and the little white houses with heavy iron grilles on their windows are all part of a conservation area. Just in case the village did not look quite authentic enough, some extra touches have been added for good measure. The street names appear on decorative tiles and the street lighting is now by reproduction gas lamps.

Despite the tarting up, you will still find small *tapas* bars which could have come from a part of Spain where holidays have still to be invented. There are a couple of small hotels too in the middle of the original village, the Planesia and the Canfali, which overlook the sweep of the Levante beach. Like the festivals, they and the *tapas* bars are part of an engaging sub-culture which carries on oblivious of the tourists swarming round its doors. You will recognise the *tapas* bars because, to non-Spanish eyes, they are the least inviting in the street: ill-lit, no tablecloths, slightly seedy looking. But if you venture in you will be rewarded and not just by the miniscule prices.

I remember sitting outside in an alley, almost in darkness but for the neon pallor cast from the window opposite of a shop full of suitcases. Tourists in their colours milled in the light at the end of the' alley. But we ate stuffed octopus and mussels vinaigrette and ham carved from a joint still with its black trotter to show the pig had only been fed natural foods. There were sausages and cheeses — one, from La Mancha, kept in a glass tank of olive oil. There were *patatas bravas*, cold sauté potatoes in *all i oli* (garlic mayonnaise) and a piquant tomato sauce. There was a strong red wine from the Jalon Valley for 35 pence a litre.

Here you mix with the people of Benidorm, the ones who sit, fully clothed, in the shade of the palm trees at the back of the Levante Beach.

Properly you should devote an evening to a *tapas* tour, strolling from bar to bar and tasting rare cheeses, ham from the mountains and fish from what is left of the fishing fleet pulled up among the bodies bronzing on the Poniente Beach at the foot of the rocks below the village where Benidorm the phenomenon began.

THE SEYCHELLES

The take-off from Fregate was delayed, not for the usual, dull 'technical reasons' but because a hundred-year-old giant tortoise was sunning himself on the island's airstrip. His weight, girth and dignity were not to be lightly moved. While the engines revved on the little Islander plane, one of Fregate's 22 inhabitants — who are outnumbered three-and-a-half to one by giant tortoises on this one-and-a-quarter by quarter mile scrap of granite — came and tickled the aviation hazard in a sensitive join of his shell till he lumbered off under the coconut palms.

Fregate is not a place for timetables. Leave watch and the world behind and bring just shorts, T-shirt, swimwear, a wrap for evening, and plenty of books and suntan lotion. Fregate, the owner warns, is best for two or three nights maximum; most people cannot cope with utter peace and nothing to do for any longer.

You are certainly close to the wild: the guest rooms are set under high bread fruit trees or along the beach front facing the reef, and there just may be a lizard in the waste paper basket. Meals (fresh island fish, excellently spiced) and drinks (Mozambique, a cooling orange juice made from island green oranges) are taken on the verandah of the old plantation house. Birds come to share a meal under a vast banyan tree — the toc toc or Seychelles fody, blue pigeons, red cardinal birds and even the rare magpie robin (there are only about 40 in the world and most are on Fregate).

Days are spent beachcombing for violet shaded cowrie shells along the shallow, reef-protected waters or taking the two-hour round-island walk through a natural plantation of citrus trees, wild plums, bread fruit, cashews, cinnamon, mango and golden apple. A small, perfect sand bay is named Pirate's Beach after the first arrivals, the Madagascan pirates of the seventeenth century. Fregate is now a snippet of paradise, 20 minutes by air from Mahé, the Seychelles' 'capital' island.

Perhaps the 115 Seychelles islands are paradise because they have been so little destroyed by man. The total land of the Seychelles is only 44 square miles, scattered over 150,000 square miles of the Indian Ocean. The islands missed the Dark Ages altogether; Vasco da Gama only discovered them in 1502. They were first described by an Englishman in 1609 and first settled in 1756 when the French planted the stone of possession on Mahé. Even the inevitable English/French bickering for possession was gentle. The French commandant,

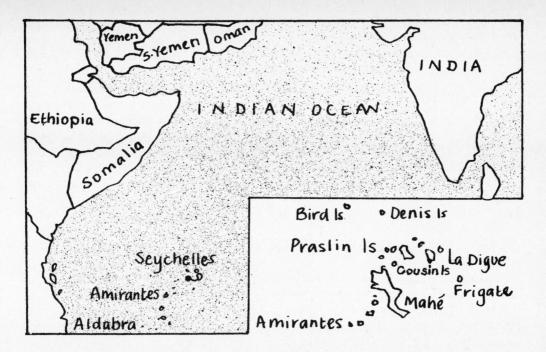

de Quinsi, meekly submitted to the British navy, flew the Union Jack and then raised the French flag once the navy sailed away. He repeated the deception whenever the navy inspectors arrived. In 1814 the Seychelles were ceded to Britain after the Napoleonic wars but de Quinsi was invited to stay on as the first British governor, which he did, tactfully anglicising his name to De Quincy. A street named after him in the capital Victoria is spelt both ways.

French character remains in the language, the cooking, the place names and the *joie de vivre*. There is little crime; the headlines in the tiny *Nation* newspaper are mostly about a new dredger for the harbour, and its tri-lingual features — in creole, the official language, French and English — discuss fishing and football. In spite of the fact tourism accounts for 60 per cent of the islands' income, the laid-back way of life persists, unspoilt and unhurried.

'It looks uninhabited,' remarked my companion on the British Airways weekly flight as we touched down on Mahé. The runway was completed in 1971 and only then could the islands open up to visitors. Even now it is difficult to see the houses and hotels snuggled into the lush greenery that cloaks the granite hills of the main island. Mahé, and the capital Victoria, have many hotels tucked into the endless coves that are edged with smooth, elephant-grey boulders the size of cottages. Beau Vallon Bay is a huge sweep of fine sand backed by soaring, often misted, mountains of the Du Morne National Park. Here there are the bigger hotels; the average Seychelles hotel is under 20 rooms. Fisherman's Cove on Beau Vallon is a glossy collection of buildings, the high thatched dining room and bar and little cottages descending to the sea. At the south end of the bay at Bel Ombre is the Auberge, an enchanting cluster of rondavel rooms slotted in amongst the tall trees, and smooth-sided boulders above a natural rock-pool on the sea's rim.

Full stopping the bay at the north end is the tiny Northolme, one of the oldest hotels and where Somerset Maugham stayed. It has a neat, modern room block facing down the bay but more secluded and spacious are the rooms up the steep steps in the tropical gardens. They look out to the sea and Silhouette island through a fringe of palm fronds and a rustle of sea grape leaves.

Not even earplugs will exclude the dawn squeaking of the perky yellow-eyed black birds. But why stay in bed? Below is a rock-surrounded cove where already a lady in a straw hat and cotton print dress will be gently brushing the beach rocks clean. The little tidal cove below the Northolme forms an exhilarating natural jacuzzi. After that, up the rock steps to the open-sided dining room for a buffet breakfast of tropical fruits — paw paw, pineapples and small, sweet bananas — passion and other fruit juices, cereals, eggs and bacon cooked on small heaters, fresh croissants or moist banana bread. The butter comes from Northern Ireland but the preserves are made from exotic local fruits. The Northolme's French chef produces set menu dinners, a blend of classical French cuisine and creole spicings. Lunch is just a salad on the terrace of the bar — perhaps heart of palm, typically Seychellois and known as millionaire's salad since to get the palm hearts the tree must be destroyed.

The Northolme is in the Seychelles Hotels group. Guests staying at one hotel in the group can dine and use the water sports of other hotels, as well as get into the casino. The casino is the pinnacle of night-time entertainment; otherwise there will be the occasional hotel disco and guitarists playing background music for dinner. The energetic might drive south for dinner at Chez Philos, the best restaurant on the island, or sample creole cuisine at Marie Antoinette's, an old house in the hills above Victoria.

Victoria is the 'big smoke' over the hill from Beau Vallon with its vine trendril curls of road. No larger than an English village, Victoria's heart is a crossroads signalled by a mini Big Ben opposite the colonial court house. Outside, souvenir stalls are set under huge, shady trees. A small museum shows off shells and wildlife, bric-a-brac from wrecks and *gris gris* (witch doctor's) equipment tantalisingly unexplained.

Mahé itself has 68 usually almost empty beaches. Driving a hired Mini Moke (an open-sided buggy) allows breeze-cooled tanning while touring, although on one visit when I had no choice but to go at the end of March, for several days I drove around in warm rain. I'd caught the end of the monsoon period. It's obviously best to check the weather out before planning any holiday. But back to the Mini Moke.... The narrow (left-hand-drive) potholed, storm-drain-edged roads are not for Grands Prix. South of the airport the houses thin out and the road swings round small deserted bays, each edged with mustard-light sand and a dump of curved boulders, ideal perches for watching the sea assault the reef. Then it's up and over a steep cliff rise and down into another empty strand.

But the best lies at the southern tip of Mahé. Grande Police beach is, I'd say, the most perfect in the Seychelles. It is reached down a steep, narrow track ending in a shimmy of sand pot-holes. A line of sea grapes and casuarina provide shade for parking and sleeping while below, the shelving sands sweep into the deep cobalt blue waters of the calm and cooling sea. On the south-west tip of the island are more such lovely bays, biting deeper into the land and backed by high hills. Here at Baie Lazare is the new Intercontinental Hotel, and further north is the Meridien-run Barbarons Beach. The road ends in a moke-wide path beyond Port Glaud in a national park area of islands and mangrove swamps.

Cool off from the coast by taking the mountain road from Port Glaud. It loops up and up, affording bird's-eye views from the terrace of the Tea House at the summit. More looping brings you through plantations of tea, vanilla and cinnamon and then indigenous forests of mighty trees, soaring, silent, and almost chilly with white water streams spluttering along beside the road.

Island collecting can be compulsive and the Seychelles have plenty to offer. For the adventurous, with 11 days to spare for a yacht trip, there's Aldabra enclosing the world's largest lagoon and the home of 50,000 giant tortoises. The Amarantes are just opening up, while Praslin, a 15 minute flight from Mahé, is the most popular island for both day or full holiday visits. In the centre of Praslin lies the lush, waterfall-striped, Vallée de Mai park where the rare black parrot can be seen and where the famous erotically-shaped coco de mer (sea coconut) grows. Believed by General Gordon to be the original Garden of Eden, the Vallée de Mai is like a prehistoric forest with its huge and ancient palm trees towering to heights of over 100 feet. The coco de mer themselves weigh anything between 20 and 40 pounds and it is hardly surprising that, given their rather suggestive female pelvic shape, they are considered to be a great aphrodisiac! The coco de mer is now a State-protected nut and the Seychelles' trade-mark.

The choice of nearby accommodation ranges from the small Indian Ocean beach club, consisting of casual native thatched huts along the beach, to the Château de Feuilles, a plantation house hotel on an air-cooled ridge with superb gardens. (It is a member of the Relais et Châteaux chain.) Newest is the Archipel, which you reach via a track through cathedral-like naves of casuarina leading to a fjord-indented bay. There traditional creole corrugated-iron-roofed houses have been recreated to provide cool, white rooms on the hillsides round a central dining pavilion.

If Praslin is too pacey, then a half hour's boat ride takes you to La Digue where nothing moves faster than a bike or the ox cart that supplies the island's transport. It will take you to Gregoires, a collection of thatched beach huts hardly formal enough to be designated 'hotel'. Or take another boat from Praslin (and little else — besides a swimsuit and sun oil), to Cousin, an uninhabited bird sanctuary owned by the International Council for Bird Preservation. From speedboats, visitors are transferred to inflatable dinghies driven by Rasta-haired creoles for a roller-coaster ride to the beach over and through the pounding breakers.

On Cousin you potter under the trees on a moving carpet of multi-coloured lizards. Occasionally you will encounter a giant tortoise who smugly bars the narrow track, while round your ears flutter fairy terns, birds so pretty they look as if they have inspired a hundred greeting card designers. They are pure white, the size of doves and have huge sooty black eyes. Above them soar white-tailed tropic birds taking advantage of the high air currents.

But I have saved two of the best for last. Bird Island has a charming thatched cottage hotel on the beach, run by a Seychellois and a lady from Liverpool. One can walk round the island in an hour sampling the beaches as you go. It is still big enough in season, however, to host two million sooty terns on their migration flights. Then the interior is covered with birds and while visitors swim, they watch from the shore for the flick of a fish.

And then there is Silhouette, a mysterious seducer. Seen from the west coast of Mahé it lives up to its name with a mountain outline, its brow usually clouded. Although it is only an hour and a quarter's trip by fast boat, *Le Cerf*, from Victoria, it has an inaccessible air. It was the home of a great and powerful *gris gris* witch doctor a decade ago and the rumoured hideout of Lord Lucan. Now it has its own little hotel of A-frame rooms set under palms along the beach. The local population of 125 grow passion fruit, go fishing, collect wild

cinnamon and send coconuts to Mahé. The most elaborate building is the
Grecian temple tomb of the nineteenth-century French owners. It nestles in a
shady hill over which you can toil in the sun to find yet another empty little
beach. This one has in-shore rock pools where snorkellers can view fish in
football jersey markings. (The Seychelles have 950 species of fish, rising from
tiny blue demoiselles to big game fish for which fishing expeditions can be
organised.)

After a buffet lunch of fish and salads the biggest decision of the day is
choosing the right palm on which to hang one's beach bag before dozing in its
shade and solitude.

TORBAY

There can't be many people who have not seen the ads, the ones with the palm
tree and the blue, blue sky, and wondered whether the English 'Riviera' is not a
figment of the copywriter's imagination. But the description is honest, decent
and truthful. Torquay — the self-billed 'queen' of the English Riviera — really
is warmer than the rest of the country. And, what's more, the tourist board have
statistics to prove it, including one that reveals January's mean average
temperature to be one whole degree higher than Nice.

But who needs statistics when you can see it with your own eyes? Torquay is
filled with hundreds of 'tickling sticks', those poster palm trees and other
sensitive sub-tropical blooms that flourish because of the warming caress of the
Gulf Stream. Strangely, for the leading resort of the west country, Torquay
faces every which way but west which means that it turns its back on the
prevailing westerlies while Dartmoor shelters it from northern savageries.

Frost is a rare visitor even in the depths of winter, snow even rarer. Normally
local families have to take their youngsters onto Dartmoor to show them what
snow even looks like. But they did have two days of snow in February '87 and
no doubt it will be a Torbay talking point for the next few years till they get
their next settling. Or unsettling.

Torquay is the closest you'll get to the Mediterranean without going abroad.
It actually looks like its French counterpart, a similarity that's more than a
question of thermometer readings. It's much more to do with colours and
contours. The vast majority of British seaside resorts consist of a long strip of
beach, backed by a prom, backed by a road and backed by a row of hotels. But
Torquay, because of its geology — an alternating mix of tough limestone and
soft sandstone — is a knobbly, up and down, in and out sort of place created by
differing rates of erosion by the sea. From the bedroom window of the Imperial,
Torquay's swanky five-star hotel for example, you not only look out to sea but
down to sea — it's right there below with neither road nor promenade between
you and the waves.

Even in winter Torquay seems a lot greener and more colourful than many
other resorts when basking in their summertime prime. In fact, thanks to a
certain Dr Russel's *Dissertation on the Use of Sea Water in the Diseases of
the Glands*, first published in 1750, Torquay began its claim to holiday fame as
a winter retreat. The rich came in small discerning numbers, often building
decorative Italiante villas which inspired Ruskin to call the town the 'Italy of
England'. In the archives of the Imperial there are clippings from newspapers
congratulating hoteliers on extending the season, referring to their success in
enticing visitors during the summer! And now the season is extended year-
round with highly successful gourmet weekends.

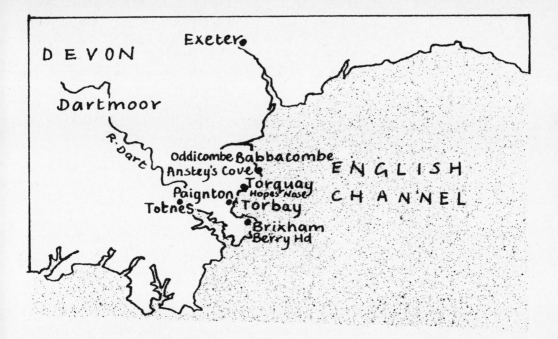

It wasn't until the coming of the railways in 1848 that Torquay became the great summer and winter resort of the south-west (in 1800 it was still primarily a fishing village with a population of less than a thousand). Today its marina, right in the heart of town, holds more pleasure yachts than it did fishing boats in their heyday.

But let's not get too carried away with Torquay. The town is just a part, a third, of this seaside story. The English Riviera means Torbay, an administrative grouping that also encompasses Brixham and Paignton and stretches for 22 miles around the bay between two promontories, Berry Head in the south and Hope Nose in the north. Together they attract a million visitors a year.

Brixham and Paignton are as distinct from Torquay as they are from each other. Brixham is an active, pretty fishing harbour built on a surrounding horseshoe of land that makes even Torquay's gradients seem like molehills. I didn't count them all, and I certainly didn't climb them all, but there must be at least a thousand steps linking the several narrow streets. The entire place seems to echo to the screech of herring gulls who mill above the fishing vessels and occasionally land on the head of William of Orange. His statue, just behind the harbour wall, commemorates his landing in 1688 with an army of 30,000 men intent on saving England for Protestantism. He wears a haughty expression (which looks a bit ridiculous when there's a seagull perched on his head). Brixham is also the most important port in the country for flat fish which means lots of excellent seafood restaurants. For good dining and the most romantic of views you'll find the Quayside Hotel hard to beat.

If Brixham is purpose-built for romantic interludes (as well as the place for plaice), Paignton is the traditional bucket and spade resort complete with whelk stalls, deck chairs for hire, wooden changing huts and, in contrast to the hills of its neighbours, everything on the level. Its highly accessible Paignton Sands, divided by the Redcliffe headland and backed by a grand swathe of lawn, is ideal for families with small children. They even have a special children's week in mid-August with a score of special happenings including a disco for the youngsters.

Torbay has 18 beaches in all, each with its own stamp of personality but all sharing clean, safe bathing whatever the state of the tide. Babbacombe, with its own jetty and pub, is rather like a mini-community, and is popular with the young, including some of Torquay's language students who spend several hours at a stretch in the sun with their ears tuned to the noun declensions and verb conjugations of Phil Collins on the Walkman. Neighbouring Oddicombe, because of its old-fashioned funicular, attracts a mixture of ages while Anstey's Cove is best approached by woodland walk. At low tide it is a rock pool potterer's delight.

Because of the shelter afforded by the bay, a range of watersports is available including sailing, windsurfing and water-skiing. There's also parascending from Torre Abbey sands, Torquay's most popular beach, but, unless you fall in, I never really understand how that counts as a watersport. They even held the yachting events of the 1948 Olympic Games here. There are also countless variations on the 'trips round the bay' theme, including cruises from Torquay up the pretty River Dart to Totnes. In addition, you can sail to the Channel Islands on board a ferry that looks as though it has just sailed out of the pages of a toy catalogue.

Torquay, Rudyard Kipling once observed, 'is such a place as I do desire to upset by dancing through it with nothing on but my spectacles'. Despite its conservative reputation, further underlined by its frequent choice as the venue for Tory party conferences, its officials now turn an unofficial blind eye to topless bathing as long as it is confined to the beaches (in the interests of road safety). The only really shocking sight on the shoreline is the 'beach feeding' that takes place in the winter. Topsoil and hardcore are tipped back into the sea to replenish those sections of beach being lost to erosion. It turns the sea blood red as if Jaws plus friends have been feasting on some of last season's holidaymakers.

If the weather isn't up to beach bumming there's an amazing menu of attractions ranging from the prehistoric caves of Kents Cavern to Oldway, the Versailles lookalike of a house that belonged to Isaac Merritt Singer, inventor of the sewing machine. Torbay also has more than 2000 acres of parks and gardens, the third largest zoo in the country at Paignton, a replica of the Golden Hind — Sir Francis Drake's galleon that thrice circumnavigated the globe — a model village and a steam railway that runs between Paignton and the River Dart. At an even more leisurely pace, horse-drawn carriages will lead you from the sea front to the immaculately preserved and heavily thatched village of Cockington.

It doesn't come as a surprise to learn that many visitors come back year after year. Some have never been anywhere else for their holiday. Some, according to manager Harry Murray, never even leave the Imperial Hotel, doing all their swimming in the two pools, their shopping from the showcases, their dancing in the ballroom or Le Pigalle nightclub and the rest of the time just gazing at ships at anchor in the bay.

But by the same token there are thousands of young people, born in the era of cheap package holidays to Spain, who have never set foot in the town. But no matter how familiar they are with the continent, Torquay would be the easiest of transitions to make were they to holiday at home. On the most glorious of days the scene is unique. You even have to pinch yourself to remember where in the world you are.

SALVADOR

Brazil is famous for its beaches. Who has not felt like a visit to the fabulous Copacabana beach, where the *Cariocas*, the people of Rio, love to spend every spare minute of their day? And who has not heard, if only in song, about the girls of Ipanema, that equally beautiful stretch of sand that lies just around the corner from Copacabana in the very centre of Rio de Janiero? These Brazilian beaches have a great buzz about them, with crowds of football-crazy youngsters playing soccer in the sand, the older folk playing cards on tables formed from flattened sand castles, the peddlars selling those amazingly brief bikinis to hoardes of beautiful girls ... this is beach-theatre, fascinating to watch.

The beaches are justly famous, but I prefer to get off the too-well-trodden track to find something a little quieter and therefore less well known. Besides, the beaches of Rio do have certain drawbacks. The water is very cold; the great waves off Copacabana conceal a strong undertow and petty thieves are all too common. No, nice as the Rio beaches are, my personal choice for a beach resort in Brazil lies somewhere else, a good distance to the north of Rio, along the shoreline of Bahia and close to the beautiful city of Salvador.

Like Rio de Janiero, Salvador was once the capital of Brazil. The Brazilians like to move their capital about from time to time. The present one is, of course, Brasilia, right in the centre of this vast country, a modern city, full of original and very striking architecture, and (just) worth a full day of your time during any holiday in Brazil. Salvador, on the other hand, could be worth an entire visit. It is a delightful, historic, fascinating city, full of things to see and do. Best of all, it has those beaches, which lie all around the vast island-studded sweep of the Bahia de Todos os Santos, All Saints Bay. There are more on the islands themselves, many of which can be visited.

Most holidaymakers, certainly all those visiting a beach resort, like to begin their holiday with a few days sunbathing, if only to relax and work up that essential holiday tan. Down in Brazil the sun is very fierce indeed, much stronger than anything you will experience around the shores of the Mediterranean. The temperature in Salvador hovers about the 84°F mark throughout the year, and it can be humid at times. To visualise it, imagine a lush, tropical kind of place, where long white sandy beaches are fringed with coconut palms and backed by shady little restaurants ... it sounds like paradise, especially if, like me, you like to sit in a pavement café and just watch the crowds go by.

The Barra district of Salvador, which contains many of the finest, most modern hotels, including the Bahia Othon Palace, has, as its centre, the busy Farol Praia, the Lighthouse Beach. As the name implies, there is a lighthouse at one end; at the other lies a fort erected in 1548 by the Portuguese explorer Francisco de Souza, and used subsequently to repel attacks by Dutch pirates on the fledgling port of Bahia. Between the fort and the lighthouse, the sand is white, the sea blue, and when the surf is up, crowds of youngsters gather to cavort in the waves. Other beaches are those on the island of Itaparica, far out in the bay, and the one at Bogari on the far side of the city from Barra. Bogari is an attractive fishing village, a very Bahian place, where the beach is backed by small bars and a long line of ramshackle shops selling everything from snacks to T-shirts, from bananas and coconuts to craft goods and jewellery. Itapoan is fringed with leaning palm trees, and could be in the South Seas.

In a place that offers so much to see and do as Salvador, it pays to get organised and plan your visit, beginning — after a day or two resting by beach

or pool — with an organised coach tour of the town. Coach tours may not
appeal to the truly independent traveller, but they are usually a quick, easy and
often inexpensive way to see the main sights. You can always return on your
own later, if anything in particular seems worth a second visit. Besides, it's a
good way to meet people and compare impressions.

Salvador falls roughly into two main parts. There is the modern area down
near the seashore, the *Baixa*, which ranges from the resort suburb of Barra to
the modern commercial port, and the old colonial upper city, the *Alta*, built on
the bluffs high above the sea at a safe distance from the once ever-present
threat of pirate raids. Today, these two parts are linked directly by a huge
public lift or elevator, the *Lacerda* lift, which rises for over 200 feet from the
shoreline near the port to the main square, the Praça Municipal.

Both parts of the city have their rival attractions. The lower city has the
beaches, the busy port and, something no one should miss, the newly-opened
Mercado Modelo, the Model Market. In here, it is possible to buy every kind of
craft from scores of stalls laid out on several floors, the perfect place for
souvenir hunters. There is lace or leather, or straw hats, or carved wood curios,
and those ever-present but immensely varied Brazilian T-shirts.

In former times, Salvador was the centre for the Brazilian slave-trade, and
the building which now contains the Mercado Modelo then contained the slave
market. Most of the present inhabitants of Salvador are descended from freed
slaves, which accounts for the spicy creole cooking and the lively music and
street-theatre, especially the *capoeira*, foot-fighting dances that were introduced by slaves from Angola.

The guides say that the Lacerda lift is never entirely free from pickpockets
and bag-snatchers. So walk up to the Old City, up the narrow, cobbled streets
called *ladieras*, which slant up steeply, making the *Alta* no place for visitors
with high heels or leather-soled shoes. Walking is the best way to see the centre
of any city and the benefit of walking up to the *Centro* is that you can see the

Bonifacio, the most spectacular of Corsican towns, perched high on sandstone cliffs.

From Merseyside to Manhatten ... Liverpool (above) and New York (below), cities linked by skylines and history.

Above: Albufeira, tourist capital of the Algarve: holiday developments have fortunately not yet marred the town's Portuguese character.

Below: The azure waters of . . . not the Med, but Pembrokeshire, one of the most attractive surprises of Britain's coast.

Above: Rydal Water, in the centre of Lakeland's most popular tourist area, remains tranquil and unspoilt.

Below: The Wild West at its most stunning: the awesome grandeur of the Grand Teton National Park in Wyoming.

Above: Abingdon, one of many pretty Thames-side towns and villages, perfect for leisurely touring.

Below: With all the experiences of the Nile at the water's edge, a well-appointed cruise ship is the most relaxing way to sight-see.

Above: The pantomime-like Barong dance performed on Bali is a spectacle of colour and rhythm.

Below: Typical of Val d'Isère, these ski chalets have been purpose-built to blend with their alpine setting.

Above: *It looks unreal but this is Africa, where exotic animals really do saunter across breathtaking views, like this one of Kilimanjaro.*

Below: *A new angle on the Taj Mahal: in India every sight assaults the senses, from the majesty of her palaces to the bustle of everyday Indian life.*

Above: The unmistakable sight of Istanbul, a city that offers rich rewards for the intrepid traveller.

Below: The solitude of Orkney's cliffs — remote to all except the nesting seabirds.

fine old buildings at close hand, while getting marvellous views across the heat-hazy water of Todos os Santos bay through the gaps between the houses.

The old city of Salvador is said to have no less than 230 churches, which is rather too many for anyone to visit. One, Nosso Senhor do Bonfin, is not only beautiful in itself but is surrounded by yet another street market where, apart from the street-vendors' stalls, you can find people still working at their traditional crafts — weaving, carving and lace-making. Groups entertain the crowds by dancing the *capoeira* to the music of pipe, drum and tambourine. It all looks very violent and skilful but nobody seems to get hurt. Another old African custom that flourishes in Salvador is the voodoo-like *candomble* ceremonies. These ceremonies are found in other parts of Brazil — in Rio they call the voodoo *macumba* — but the *candomble* ceremonies can be watched by the public, even by tourists, on Sunday nights and on any of the frequent Brazilian religious holidays.

Picture this old city of Salvador: a city full of colonial-style buildings and churches, each a riot of baroque or rococo architecture, and all tinted in ochre, yellow or pink. They are crumbling a little here and there, but beneath them the narrow, cobbled strets are thronged with a swirling, lively, colourful crowd. It's a place where the air is always warm and heavy, and scented with tropical flowers. If you can imagine that, you can realise why Salvador is so memorable, so different from the other cities of Brazil, a place no visitor should miss.

Since Salvador is a beach resort and a very popular holiday area for the Brazilians, there is no lack of after-dark activity, although modern pop groups are tending to replace the more traditional samba rhythms in many of the bars. The nightclubs lie in the streets behind the beaches of Barra and Itapoan, and there are discos under all the big hotels. As for the local food, it is delicious, international and very cheap. On one night you can eat creole, on another try the pool-side buffet at the hotel and for something special you can try the elegant Le Mignon, on the Avenida Marques-de-Leao.

Salvador is very much a seaside city. The *Alta* looks out onto that vast blue bay of Todos os Santos, and nobody should visit Salvador without taking a cruise out to the islands on one of the colourful Salvad schooners. The process of getting aboard a schooner is quite painless; you simply go to the harbour office by the Mercado Modelo, buy a ticket and then follow the surging crowds out onto the quay. The schooners look exactly like pirate ships, all long, raking and lateen-rigged, terribly romantic on the blue water. Everyone piles aboard their chosen ship and as each one fills up the crew cast off for the islands.

First stop is an uninhabited island where you are rowed in through the waves in small dinghies. Everyone gets wet and one or two fall overboard. An hour ashore, swimming or drinking wine cooled in a rock pool, and you set off again with the crew providing entertainment with music from a set of bongos. The big island of the bay, Itaparica, the Moonstone Island, is quite beautiful, green and tropical and full of whitewashed houses, each garden overrun with bougain-villaea and hibiscus.

Most British people holidaying in Brazil will take a tour round the country. Certainly, no one should go all that way and fail to see the great falls at Iguaca, or not visit the river port of Manaus, a thousand miles from the sea in the heart of the Amazon. Everyone wants to explore Rio de Janeiro and still there is Brasilia and bustling São Paulo.

Wherever you go though, be sure that your holiday includes a few days in Salvador, to lie on the beach, explore the old city, cruise in the bay and see a little of a city that is, by any standards, beautiful, friendly and unique.

LAKES AND MOUNTAINS

If you want to be 'in' these days you should be talking about the stress of your holiday. Never mind all the usual souvenirs, the out-of-focus snaps and the witty pottery conversation pieces. Don't even bother with a tan: stress is what to bring home with you this year. If you can't say your holiday was stressful, you haven't had a holiday.

Psychologists are producing treatises on the subject faster than the tour operators can turn out brochures; before long the pharmaceutical industry will be selling anti-stress potions at beachside stalls with a protection factor rated from one to six.

You notice I say 'beachside'. But why do we always think of sea and beaches when the topic of holidays comes up? We are forsaking whole regions of the holiday globe, places which still possess the antidote to stress, tension, aggression and all the other disorders of the post-industrial society.

Lakes and mountains — the two go together on earth as they do in brochures — are the holiday spots for people bored with holidays. They used to be more popular than they are today so the hotels tend to bask in old grandeurs and the resorts were mostly established in more spacious days. But the holidays are good for escape, exercise, scenery and the soul.

My selection of mountain holidays takes us from the humbling spectacle of the American West, which was once wild and is still wilderness, to out-of-the-way crannies in Italy and France. We go to Carinthia, which is southern Austria's lake district and to the English Lake District which is a cooler and greener version of Carinthia. And we go to northern Portugal. Nobody knows Portugal has a north, at least not one that extends beyond Lisbon. But then a little ignorance never did anyone any harm. No one in any of these places knows anything about holiday stress.

LAKE DISTRICT

When the tourists first began to stomp around his favourite piece of country-side, William Wordsworth was outraged, demanding to know whether there was 'any nook of English ground secure from rash assault?'. But even today, when the tiny populations of the Lakeland towns and villages are swelled by the invasion of summer pilgrims, you can still escape the crowds and wander 'lonely as a cloud' through some of the country's finest scenery — though, of course, by summer those fair daffodils will have long since faded away.

The Lake District hasn't always been so alluring. Before it was 'discovered' by Wordsworth and contemporary scribes the area was felt to be far too awesome for pleasure, a dark, almost satanic world where monsters were supposed to roam. It was certainly no place for the fickle or fainthearted and those who did venture into the mountains saw themselves as explorers rather than mundane tourists. Instead of shattering the myths they returned with tales about the hostile nature of the landscape in order to boost their intrepid reputations. When, for example, Daniel Defoe braved the journey in 1724 he described the area as 'a country eminent only for being the wildest, most barren and frightful of any that I have passed over in England.'

But the fashion for scenery was to change quite suddenly and radically. The same Lakeland landscape that had been so adamantly rejected inspired a great 'back to nature' movement for poets and painters who, in turn, gave birth to the so-called English Romantic movement. When Coleridge, Wordsworth, Southey and other men of words began to sing its praises and painters came to record its beauties, telling each other which 'stations' offered the best view of the 'picturesque', so the Lake District appeared on the map as a destination worthy of rest and recreation.

However, it was not until the coming of the railways that holidaymakers began to arrive in their thousands, seeking an escape from the harshness of their increasingly industrialised working lives. Several wealthy industrialists also came from their respective city grimes, building extravagant mansions and villas on the lake shores. Wordsworth even wrote one of the very first tourist guide books, a bestseller that brought him more fame and fortune than any of his poems (his groans about a rash assault were rather hypocritical since he did more than anyone to encourage the hordes).

The Lake District is the largest of Britain's National Parks but, even so, this most loved and visited patch is still surprisingly small, not only in size but also in stature, its mountains mere molehills compared with, say, the Alps. The actual lakes are no whoppers either. But that's not the point. The area is an expression of English countryside at its most beautiful and at its most diverse. It measures no more than 40 miles from either tip to toe or across its midriff. Drive up on the M6 and, if you happen to miss the flush of junctions you could find yourself fast approaching Carlisle without realising that the Lakes have been and gone.

Today, the Lakes are one of the most popular holiday destinations in the country and the main attraction is, of course, the scenery. Built upon one of the globe's oldest foundations and shaped by 500 million years of geological history, an enormous variety is heaped into one modest, 866-square-mile space. Wordsworth in his 1810 Guide summed it all up when he wrote: 'I do not know of any tract of country in which, in so narrow a compass, may be found an equal variety in the influences of light and shadow upon the sublime and beautiful features of the landscape.'

But don't try to rely on either the poets or the painters — ancient or contemporary — to recommend their favourite Lakeland scene. You can never come to the same place twice and find it looking the same. Cumbria offers landscapes that are all things to all seasons, highly sensitive to passing moods, colours and contours. In October the landscape is a rich pattern of autumn golds and browns; in February snow covers the mountain tops; and in March crocus, daffodils and wobbly lambs raise their faces to the spring sunshine.

'What is the name of Cumbria's only lake?' ask the local schoolkids. Ah, but there are 16 of them you confidently reply. Wrong. There is only one *lake*, Lake Bassenthwaite. The rest either have the suffix 'mere' or are called such-and-such 'water', so you never have to call them 'lake' as well. Of the 16 lakes, meres or waters, Windermere — at ten miles by one — is the longest not only in the Lake District, but in Britain.

Come by train, coach, or, as do four out of every five visitors, car, and Windermere is also likely to be the first lake you encounter. It has been utilised by its surrounding communities since Roman times, both as a means of transport and a source of food. In recent years, however, its pewter-shaded waters have been used almost exclusively for boating pleasures, and several of its traditional steam launches have, in fact, been rescued from a variety of ignominious fates (including the seabed, a compost heap and even a hen house) and mostly put on display in the Steamboat Museum. For the most authentic sense of Cumbria's maritime history, go for a ride on the National Trust's steam-powered yacht, *Gondola*, originally built in the style of a Venetian gondola and still plying the waters.

If you want to experience lakes unfettered by crowds you'll leave the shoreline spread of Windermere and neighbouring Bowness and head for the others. One of the most remote is Wast Water, which is also the deepest, its steep, grey scree slopes making it look quite threatening. Ullswater is many people's favourite, especially those wallowing in a view from the indolent comforts of the Old Church Hotel set right on the shore at Watermillock. Despite the miles of lakeside in Cumbria, the Old Church is one of very few hotels that enjoy an actual lakeside location.

There's a danger here of resorting to a shopping list of lakes — Derwent Water is the most photographed and Coniston Water, the most tranquil, barring water speed record attempts ... suffice to say, keep looking till you find the one that's right for you. After all, they say that the Lakes have 14 million visitors a year and that their reasons for coming are just as numerous.

However, you can still get away from the hordes that throng the Lakes' best-known touring centres. Indeed you don't really get the feel of the Lakes' natural, breathtaking beauty till you get out on your feet. Walkers are spoiled for choice. Every town and village is really a starting point for superb rambles — up bracken-covered slopes, through shady woods and past streams and waterfalls to the haunts of ravens and buzzards. Options range from easy-going dales, carved out by glaciers, signposted paths beside the lakes and, for the fit, routes that lead over the fells and up to dramatic Striding Edge or the famous summits of Sca Fell, Skiddaw and Scafell Pike, the highest peak in England at 3206 feet.

Most of Cumbria's high points can, in fact, be reached by the less-than-bionic stroller. In the most famous of all his *Pictorial Guides to the Lakeland Fells*, all written in long-hand accompanied by pen and ink drawings and all unique bestsellers, Arthur Wainright maintains that: 'The fells are not monsters but amiable giants. You can romp over them and pull the hairs on their chests and shout in their ears and treat them rough and they don't mind a bit.'

The same can't be said of the area's man-made attractions. Beatrix Potter's Hill Top Farm in Near Sawrey, by far the most popular, being also the home of Jemima Puddleduck, is one of few National Trust properties where they actually want to keep the numbers down. Each season some 75,000 people squeeze into her tiny home. Other obvious honeypots include Wordsworth's Dove Cottage at Grasmere, John Ruskin's Brantwood overlooking Coniston Water and the excellent National Park Brockhole Visitor Centre.

Small though it may be, it can take a lifetime of visits before anyone could honestly claim to 'know' the Lake District. Because of the diversity of its scenery and the enormous range of individual attractions, it will always be one of those all things to all people sort of places. But the words of one Father Thomas West still serve as a most fitting summary of the virtues of this corner of England. 'Anyone with a need to unbend the mind from anxious cares or fatiguing studies,' he wrote in the eighteenth century, 'will meet with agreeable relaxation in making the tour of the Lakes.'

LAKE ORTA

August is the best time to visit Lake Orta. Forget those cautionary tales about avoiding the peak season. Indeed, forget most of the advice you are given about Orta. Even Italians are likely to ask how you spell it. The truth is that few Italians, and even fewer tourists, know Lake Orta.

But that is not the reason for going in August. This is festival time when the string of lakeside villages hold their annual fling. On dark nights, dance music and bright lights pinpoint a celebration, oases of good humoured jollity. Pick the right fortnight and your holiday could turn into one long party.

In a tiny village near Pettenasco, they set up long trestle tables and an

impromptu dance floor by the lake. You jostle for huge mounds of pasta and sauce, salads and crisp, fresh bread. Gradually, the tables become top heavy with litre bottles of red and white plonk. The music is live and deafening.

A fireworks display is billed as the greatest pyrotechnic event of the century. An expectant hush follows the uncertain passage of a boat, transformed by lights into a passing imitation of a gondola — or is it a swan? It slides erratically against the night, as though pulled by wires. A cluster of fireworks fizzles unpredictably. Everyone laughs.

A night or two later, it is the turn of Pettenasco itself. Here, they hold a 'Grand Pesciolata'. It turns out to be a fish meal, served under a vast awning set up in the square. It is chaotic, confused and great fun. Arola is pure operetta. Act II, Scene I: under the shadow of the old church, villagers dance and an emotional tenor pines tremulously for his true love, who has disappeared, no doubt with the wealthy count.

At Legro, the railway station yard has been converted into an open-air dance floor. The band play polkas and waltzes, tangos and sambas. You can tell the local people from the few tourists: they know how to dance properly, even the teenagers. A young Italian girl asks a Londoner: 'How many animals have you? I have to milk 17 cows every day.'

Youths play pinball in the station café, steadfastly ignoring a group of giggling girls in dainty dresses. A diminutive Arab has set up a stall of watches and torches. There is much backslapping and handshaking but no sales. He smiles resignedly — a loser. As the warm night air eddies with the tang of a barbecue, passengers in occasional stopping trains pull down windows to stare disbelievingly at the unexpected scene.

This is Lake Orta in August. The atmosphere is vital and naturally alive, with a strong communal spirit. Foreigners are heavily outnumbered by locals, an encouraging mix of young and old, a genuine slice of Italian life untouched by tourism.

So just where is Lake Orta? In the southern foothills of the Alps and not so far from the beaten track as you might think. Over the high hills from Lake Maggiori, an hour's drive north west from Milan, it is neither as spectacular nor as large as Italy's more famous lakes. You could drive round its 34 kilometres of road in an hour or so.

The main town is Orta San Giulio. Virtually traffic free, it's like a stage set. Largely Renaissance, the patchy, colour-washed buildings glow with the mellow patina of age, tumbling down and along narrow cobbled streets to the grand square with its panoramic view of the lake.

Everyone gathers in the Piazza Motta shaded by venerable horse chestnut trees and the multi-hued umbrellas of the cafés. The sightseers depart in the late afternoon, leaving a vacuum of silence. Then, as the heat of the day recedes, the older residents emerge for an early evening stroll: a ramrod straight figure in a linen suit and a snappy panama hat; a clutch of dignified and upright, grey haired ladies. They perambulate, talk to the boatmen, take an aperitif at one of the half-empty cafés. Then they vanish, returning perhaps to their villas for dinner in darkened rooms heavy with ormolu furniture. A final postscript to a more leisurely age that still envelopes Orta.

For your own dinner, it's worth hiring a boatman to take you across to Isola San Giulio and its romantic waterside restaurant of the same name. The island's largely eleventh-century basilica and stately belltower is the hub of Lake Orta's history. Stroll round the narrow streets, past shuttered aristocratic villas flanked by scented gardens. The whole place has an atmosphere of eerie abandonment.

Orta could so easily be a fashionable place where yuppies socialise, like Portofino or St Tropez. It remains astonishingly uncommercial. Even its Wednesday market, held on the Piazza Motta since 1228, sells reassuringly practical things, like cheap jeans, leather sandals and ripe cheeses. On Thursday, the same market, much enlarged, moves down to Omegna, the lake's business town. To make a morning of it, catch an early boat from Orta or one of the resort villages, and head first for the President bar, where you can breakfast off the best brioches in town and sip strong, freshly ground coffee in the sunshine. Then it's into the fray, stall after stall stretching endlessly along the waterfront.

Holidays are unsophisticated. On the lake itself there are all sorts of watersports. But the chemist from Orta confided that swimming was a dubious proposition, looking darkly towards Omegna and hinting at pollution. Plenty of people do swim, but it's worth checking beforehand. And the surrounding hills make for good walking.

Tucked into an eagle's eyrie on a rocky crag overlooking the lake is the dazzling white shrine of Madonna del Sasso. It's a point of popular pilgrimage. Far below, Lake Orta spreads like a relief map in intricate detail. But more remarkable than the stunning view are the various legends attached to this precariously poised sanctuary. One has it that after boulders crashed down on a nearby village, miraculously causing no damage, a statuette of the Madonna, with real brunette hair, holding baby Jesus, also with real blond hair, was found at the spot where the chapel now stands. Another tells how Mary, an innkeeper's daughter, was pushed down the mountainside by her lover 'blinded with jealousy of an English brother in arms,' as a local guide book quaintly puts it. No doubt Don Antonio could elaborate. He is known locally as the 'priest of the open sleeves' because of his approachability and generous manner.

Even stranger is Sacre Monte of St Francis of Assisi, a stiffish uphill

20-minute walk from Orta San Guilio. Suddenly, statues loom among the trees, crowning rooftops, pillars and columns; cheeky cherubs and triumphal angels blow slender trumpets; robed figures rise, aloof and thoughtful. Embedded in thick woods and gloomy glades are some 20 chapels. Inside, tableaux of painted terra-cotta figures depict various events in the life of St Francis. Each chapel is crammed with lifelike statues, complemented by brilliant frescoes and paintings dating, mostly, from the seventeenth and eighteenth centuries.

Unless you go during the August festival time, you won't find much nightlife around Lake Orta. It's an ideal spot for peaceful holidays in attractive surroundings with just enough to keep you going. Hotels are few, mainly small and family run; book well in advance, whenever you go. In Orta, the San Rocco Hotel, with a swimming pool, is the best and probably the quietest, although the dignified and older Orta, in the same family for six generations, catches perfectly the period flavour of the town. Families would do better at Pettenasco where the lakeside Giardinetto, typically Italian, is run by the tireless Primatestas. The Approdo, an informal aparthotel with large pool, is also right on the lake.

Whichever you choose, you'll be won over by Orta's serene charm. And you'll be able to tell the Italians a thing or two — but then again, why not keep it a secret?

CARINTHIA

Imagine our Lake District transplanted to the sunny side of the Alps. Grassy lidos sprout forests of rainbow-hued umbrellas. Sunbathers reach for the suntan oil rather than the waterproofs. Water-skiers exchange wet suits for swimming trunks as they zap across the water leaving a plume of cooling spray. High up on hillsides hazy with heat, hikers in shorts and T-shirts sit on the sturdy wooden benches of open-air cafés, quenching thirsts and admiring the view. At night, there's dancing in the open air and music floats across a lake that laps a forested shore.

Carinthia is how the Lake District might be, given a geographical nudge south. It is Austria's sunniest region, locked into a protective ring of saw-tooth mountain peaks. The northern barrier keeps out the worst of the bad weather. Over the southern range lie Yugoslavia and Italy. The climate is influenced by the Mediterranean some two hours away. If it rains in Venice, they say, it will rain in Carinthia. And in summer, it doesn't often rain in Venice. Short spells of dull or wet weather cannot be ruled out, though.

Carinthia presents an entirely different face to the more popular Tyrolean holiday image of Austria. Popular with other Continentals, we British have ignored it since just after the last war, when it was temporarily placed under our jurisdiction. The name has much to do with that neglect. Though anglicised into Carinthia, it is Kärnten in Austria and printed that way on most tourist literature. So little is known about it here that many people assume it is in Greece. A less excusable geographic clanger was that of the American who once asked a local tourist office where the kangeroos were ....

Roughly the size of Yorkshire, Lancashire and Lincolnshire put together, Carinthia is a relaxed, sparkling world of warm lakes and eccentrically carved mountains. Industrialisation is happily absent, skyscrapers appear to have been banned. Despite its dramatic scenery, everything is neat and orderly — as though a giant landscape gardener, with a keen eye for proportion, had

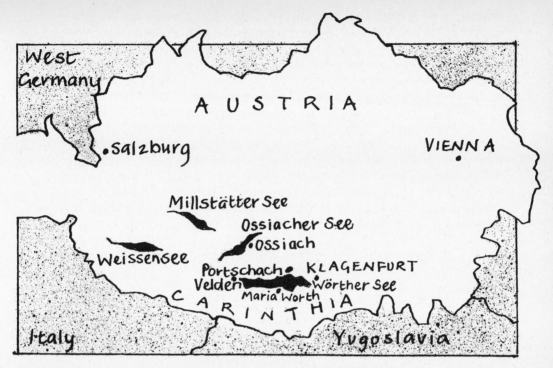

fashioned his own wonderland. There's a stunning view from the top of the Pyramiden Kogel tower near Maria Worth, with all Carinthia spread beneath you like a detailed relief map.

Wörther See is the largest of 200 lakes and, the locals insist, the warmest in Europe. Swimming in the near 80°F water in midsummer is like taking a lukewarm bath. Velden is the main resort. Far removed from the cosy Austrian mountain village image, Velden is smart and stylish, mainly modern, with a hint or two of turn-of-the-century elegance, brightened with razor-trimmed lawns and colourful flower gardens edged with trees. The whole place sparkles. Although only a little larger than a village, it offers more to do than many seaside resorts. From archery to windsurfing, there are more than 20 different activities. Swimming and sunbathing at the impeccably kept lidos is a pleasure, although rather on the pricey side.

It's fun to hire a cycle from the railway station and pedal along the lake to other, smaller resorts, like Pörtschach. Better still, some 25 well-signposted walks fan out from Velden deep into the surrounding countryside, well away from busy roads. You soon shuffle off holiday crowds as you strike into the wooded hillsides, fresh with the resinous tang of a thousand pine trees. You are never, though, too far from civilisation.

Walk number 12, for instance, skirts Saisser See, a limpid, hushed lake where the only building is a little, traditional-style restaurant that serves delicious fresh trout. Walk number three climbs steeply up through the scented pines to the isolated, 800-year-old hilltop church of St Georg at Gross Sternberg, before heading deeper into the mountains. Stop here for a snack and coffee at the church's adjoining bar. In all probability, you'll be served by Marcus, the parish priest, looking more like a pop star with his longish fair hair and open-necked shirt. However unlikely the spot, you'll almost always find someone providing food and drink in Carinthia.

Back down in Velden, afternoon tea-dancers waltz and quick-step their way on the lakeside terrace of the Schloss Hotel. The more expensive hotels have the advantages of private terraces, like the Leopold, where if you book early enough you can get a room with views of the lake. Back among the trees, prices in small family-run hotels drop sharply, while in the countryside, guesthouses and farmhouses charge no more than their equivalents in Britain.

The way to enjoy Carinthia is to choose a base near a lake and make daily sightseeing journeys. Most of them are natural beauty spots. Keutschacher See has well organised family lidos from which you can set off on a new sport — *shlurfen*. Wearing bulky lightweight plastic floats, you propel yourself with poles across the water; in short, skiing for non-water-skiers. It's cheap, it's easy, it's fun ... once you've fallen in a few times.

An air of mystery, rare in Carinthia, distinguishes Millstatter See, mainly because it is encircled by steep mountains that cast dancing distortions of themselves into the fathomless lake water, mesmerising to watch. Weissen See, highest of the bathing lakes, has a Norwegian fjord-like atmosphere. If anyone wonders where all the dragonflies have gone, they haunt the sedges of Faaker See in iridescent droves. A jubilant little lake, this, fringed by gently shelving beaches and spotlessly clean, traditional-style, family-run pensions in small villages with improbable names — Egg am See, Neu Egg and Faaker Strand. Ossiacher See is notable for glorious colouring: deep green wooded hillsides, changing blues of the lake, bright tents pitched at secluded camping sites along the shore.

Away from the holiday lakes, life is unhurried, changing only with the rhythms of the season. Rich fields of maize ripen under the sun, storks perch on wood-tiled houses, mountain streams trickle sonorously into hushed forest lakes. Wayside shrines, now carefully preserved, once doubled up as elaborate signposts. Each self-respecting village keeps a genial inn or two and its immaculate church.

Mostly a blend of Gothic and Baroque, the churches punctuate the landscape like exclamation marks. Kostenberg's is a perfect example of a medieval church fortified with narrow slits for archers. Farmers hid here when terrorised by the Turks. The simple exteriors give little idea of the treasure troves within. In Ossiach, gilded, painted and plastered, there's an unexpected and exuberant flourish of colour. Gurk's soaring cathedral, a monument to inspirational faith, is the most imposing of them all. But none is as romantic as Maria Worth, where two crown an enchanting toytown on a wooded headland; the view of it across Worther See no doubt inspired Brahms who composed his second symphony nearby.

Castles crown craggy hilltops. At Landskron, birds of prey dive, soar and hover over the gaunt grey ruins during daily shows. It is sensational to see a falcon, a giant eagle, the biggest in the world, or a stone eagle dive-bombing out of the sky against a forested backdrop with the emerald water of Osiacher See glinting far, far below. The stone eagle, for instance, can be trained to hunt foxes: there are ten to 15 pairs living free in Carinthia, an indication of its untouched terrain. Concerts are held at Finkenstein Castle in a vast amphitheatre surrounded by woods, fields and lakes.

Piled up on a rocky crag, Hochosterwitz is a cliché of a castle. Walt Disney used it as the blueprint for the one in his film 'Cinderella'. It was glamorised with a bit of Hollywood gloss, and is now immortalised in Disneyland. But the original, built centuries before 'Cinderella' was a gleam in Disney's eye, is made of sterner stuff. Fourteen gates, some with drawbridges, repelled all invaders and protected villagers who found sanctuary in the shady, hilltop courtyard.

After the steep winding climb, you can sit under the trees, sipping cool drinks. Unlike most castles, this was never the ancestral home. But it once housed 700 soldiers of Baron Khevenhuller, whose family still own it today.

Driving to Carinthia from Britain you'll need one night stop on the way. Or you can fly, via Vienna, to Klagenfurt, the regional capital. Since medieval days, it has been at the crossroads of trading. Salt passed through from the Adriatic, amber from north-east Europe. It still has a pervasive period flavour, with some 58 galleried courtyards, cobble-stepped alleyways, white and russet houses and the scarlet froth of geraniums at all possible points.

Although popular, Carinthia remains remarkably uncommercialised. Its lakes are unpolluted, its scenery untainted. There's plenty to see, lots to do. The quality of standard and service is high. Civilised simplicity is a nutshell summary of an oddly ignored holiday playground.

THE DOURO

The Tras os Montes ('beyond the mountains') area of Northern Portugal is, as its name suggests, a region cut off from the rest. Here big high ridges of harsh granite, like a gigantic rockery, are slashed by the River Douro, which gives the area its other name.

This is not a pretty, folksy, alpine area. There is no Swiss neatness, no clipped valley fields, fat cows or cosy geranium-swagged houses. It is a dour, bleak sweep of high ranges, blazing hot in summer and icy in winter. The people reflect the austerity of the place: sturdy, hard working, their relaxation is in fairs, feasts and *romaries*, pilgrimages — all fascinating for the visitor.

It is a place to go back in time, to escape from the bustle of everyday life and walk the high wind-swept uplands, where the granite boulders glisten with sun-sparked flashes of quartz. Pigs run almost wild in these hills; they once were worshipped here and that primitive time feels eerily close when one sees the tubby, pre-Roman, Thurberesque statue in the square at Murça, once the centre of pig fertility cults. (The term *'porca de Murça'* is now a Portuguese insult, meaning a political turncoat.) Pigs turn up in much of Portugal's traditional hearty food — in thick soups and *cozido* (stews), and especially in the sausages and smoked hams of the area; a slice of garlicky sausage is often added to flavour a soup along with a spoonful of olive oil.

All over the region, a variety of fairs — from produce markets to old-fashioned marriage fairs — act as meeting points. At Penafiel, the wide main street is terraced down to a fair-ground where the weekly horse and cattle market is held. Old colour-washed houses hang over the banks of the river by the Roman bridge at Amarante, whose patron saint, São Gonçalo, has the heavenly job of matching bachelor and spinster. The town is celebrated for its almond-based sweetmeats, particularly those made in phallic shapes. In the cathedral is the saint's tomb where, it is said, spinsters past their first youth and still seeking a husband have only to rub their naked bodies against the stone of the tomb to find one within the year. Bachelors still seeking wives presumably go to watch.

The fascination of this area is seclusion, secrecy, and splendid scenery. A clifftop view of the Douro gorge from Mesao Frio looks out over endless sharp ridges, their deep valleys wafting up scarves of mist, tinged by the morning sun, as haunting and intangible as an oriental painting. Or, on a hot summer's day,

coolness is found in the thick stone walls of castles and battlements around medieval villages.

Before the roads came, the Douro river was the way through the impassable mountains to the sea at Oporto. There is a slow railway along the Douro, and an old three-carriage wooden train from Vila Real to Chaves treasured by train buffs. The river was never an easy highway what with its boulders, rapids, falls and narrow granite gorges, where the opalescent water smashes its way down to escape into the Atlantic. In the mid-nineteenth century, a Scotsman, Baron Forrester, devised a flat-bottomed, square-sailed 'rebolo' boat to carry the casks of wine to Oporto. Today the wine goes unromantically by road tanker but the occasional 'rebolo' is preserved as a public relations gimmick by port wine producers. But the wine must still be sailed over the sandbar at the Douro's end to earn its name.

And that prized name is for the brew nicknamed 'the Englishman's wine' — port. For out of such unyielding granite hills comes the richest and sweetest of drinks for which collectors have paid up to £1250 a bottle. The British still drink 90 per cent of the vintage port produced. That port is produced at all is witness to man's mind over nature; crowbars and explosives had to be used to chisel out the terraces of the mountains on which the vines grow.

Using direct flights to Oporto, an easy tour of the area can be made driving the width of Portugal — about 160 miles — to see the extremes of Portuguese life from the bustling, hill-piled second city, Oporto, to the lonely crumbling stones of Bragança in the north-east corner or Miranda do Douro on the eastern borders with Spain. The region is close to patriotic Portuguese hearts — they say Oporto gave the country its name and Bragança its king.

The region's proximity to the Spanish border is the key to the toughness of both its people and buildings. The River Minho forms the frontier in the north and the mountains and Douro river the one in the east. These natural defences have kept Portugal cut off from the rest of Europe ever since the Portuguese, under the Duke of Bragança, fought off Spanish rule in the seventeenth-century. The thickly-fortified towns and villages of the Douro are testimony to the region's turbulent history.

Before heading into the mountains, the visitor can make a detour north from Oporto up beyond Viana do Castelo to the lush pastures of the Minho valley. Apple orchards, duck ponds, sleek cattle and white-washed farms surround small towns like Ponte de Lima on the Lima river, Barcelos on the Cavado and Monçã on the Minho. Barcelos is a worthwhile shopping stop. If you miss the big market on Thursdays, there is a permanent display of crafts in the Torre de Porta Nova castle on the steep banks of the Cavado river. Here you can buy a variety of decorated pottery, including the famous Portuguese cockerels, as well as other local crafts: carved candles, blue and white spun flax table linen, white pulled-thread bedspreads and even carved oxen yokes that make unusual bed heads.

The Minho is also the richest area for tasting Portuguese food, and the tourist office is producing a guide to the best Minho valley chefs. Many are women who casserole lamprey, trout and salmon with local wines, or shred tall-stemmed couve cabbages (often seen instead of fencing round a cottage) into heart-warming, thick *caldo verde* soups. They also make the most delicious egg custards and caramel puddings, scattered with cinnamon, from old convent recipes that start with a Mrs Beetonish 'take a dozen eggs ...'.

The Douro soon embarks on its rock-cut way eastwards from Oporto, passing through lines of hills with exhilarating views. Just south of rugged and rural Regua is elegant Lamego, a sparkling-wine producing town with old baroque, episcopal palaces. North of Regua is Vila Real, Portugal's leading table wine town with the famous Mateus palace nearby. Vila Real is the centre for *vinho verde*, the light and lively 'green' wines (green in the sense of young). The vines for these form a garden-like feature of the landscape climbing over pillars, arches, canopies, and pergolas to raise the grapes from late frosts and provide room underneath for other crops. North of Vila Real are spa towns founded by the intrepid Romans (who thought the Lima was the river of Lethe, of death and forgetfulness), Vidago and Chaves, the latter noted for its hams.

On into the more remote region there's Murça of pig fame then Mirandela, as its name suggests, softer and set in a mountain dip where almond and citrus trees grow. Then it's a climb up into granite horizons, heath clad moors, to Bragança. In spite of its regal name, this is a rather scruffy and dirty spot. Its upper town, on a hill with a castle surrounded by walls and old narrow streets, is crumbling, but it does have the twelfth-century pentagonal council chamber, Domus Municipalis, to admire. Opposite the Santa Maria church is another ancient pig statue, this one with a curious spiral on its back; two more pigs are in the local museum. Bragança is well north of the Douro valley, but a road leads south-east to Miranda do Douro where the river enters Portugal from Spain. In the sixteenth-century, Bragança was so remote that many Jews came here to escape persecution. Miranda was even more cut off, to the extent that it still retains its own dialect and customs. However, the town is more accessible nowadays, since a river dam has been built.

In such a harsh and undeveloped area, you may wonder where you will manage to stay. In the 1930s the Portuguese government, wishing to encourage motorists to make sorties into the more inaccessible corners of the country, set up subsidised *pousadas*, or inns, and the Douro area has several of these. *Pousada* means 'to perch' and the idea is to use the inns as a touring overnight stop. The *pousadas* are often in old palaces or convents, or they may be custom-built, but they are furnished with regional antiques and crafts and serve traditional recipes. The choice includes the 15-roomed Sao Gonçalo crouching 4600 feet up in the bare hills between Amarante and Vila Real. At Bragança the 2150-foot Serra de Nougeira *pousada* is on a hilltop looking out to the medieval walled town. At Alijo, between Regua and Mirandela, is an 11-roomed, superbly situated *pousada* named after Baron Forrester, with views of the mountain vineyards from its garden terrace. At Miranda do Douro the *pousada* de Santa Catarina has 12 rooms in a modern building with a terrace for viewing the river and mountains.

You can now also stay in a *quinta* (old farmhouse) or *casa antiga* (manor house), living with the owners and eating their cooking. Minimum stays of four nights are arranged from Britain by specialist operators. Many of these old country houses are found in the northern areas. Furnished with antiques they make beautiful bases from which to explore an area rich for explorers.

THE AUVERGNE

It sometimes seems that France is a country overburdened with advantages. It has attractive towns and cities, a good climate, wonderful food, famous wines and lots of varied coastline along the Atlantic and the Mediterranean. As if all that was not enough, it also has the Auvergne.

The Auvergne is not one of the best known or most popular regions of France, which might indicate a rather limited appeal. The Auvergne's attractions are subtle, and not easy to define, but I must add that they grow on you. All true Auvergne-ophiles — if there is such a word — become possessive about the place and tend to go back there year after year. They are also very discreet about exactly where they go and what they do, so in describing this green heartland of France I am breaching that secret code which says, simply, that the Auvergne is a place you must discover for yourself. Its appeal is personal, not universal.

First of all though, where is it? Look out your maps, look to the centre of France and find the city of Clermont-Ferrand, a little to the west of the river Allier and set beneath the long mountainous spine of the volcano country which runs north to south down Central France. This, and the jumbled land that stretches out on either side for 50 miles or more, is the Massif Central, the Auvergne, the very heartland of France.

This land is very old. It was created aeons ago, even before the earth began to cool. On the Monts Dômes, west of Clermont-Ferrand, the rounded, forested cones of extinct volcanoes lie everywhere, long-exploded time capsules from when the world was young. Volcanoes apart, steep hills, or *puys*, are typical of the Auvergne, but this region has a very varied landscape of mountains and forests, deep river valleys and high windswept plateaux.

The Monts Dômes in the north are round, green and attractive, but the southern peaks, the Puy de la Tache and the Puy de Sancy in Cantal are higher, soaring up to 1886 metres; that's nearly 6000 feet, so it is not surprising that in winter this area is popular with skiers who come up from the cities below to the resorts of La Bourboule and Le Mont Dore. Alpine downhill skiing is growing in popularity hereabouts, but the main winter activity is still cross-country skiing or, as the French call it, *ski de fond* — which I rather enjoy myself.

Any area which is suitable for *ski de fond* in winter is likely to be a popular

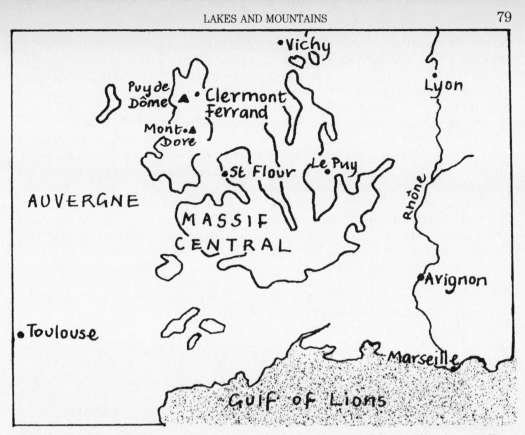

walking area in summer, and so it is with the Auvergne. It's a walker's paradise, seamed both with local footpaths and the long, long trails of the *Grandes Randonnées*, a nationwide network of footpaths that now totals over 25,000 miles of waymarked trails, reaching into all parts of France. Some of the finest of these criss-cross the Auvergne, and those who enjoy walking, could do no better than walk the famous *Chaîne des Puys* footpath or, for something a little gentler, try the *Tour de Vélay*, which circles the city of Le Puy.

So much for the country, although one could write a whole book about the landscape, about the Truyère or Loire gorges, about the beautiful lakes, like the Lac de la Corsine or the gem-like Lac Pavin, which actually lies in a volcanic crater — or indeed about every part of this green and beautiful country. The best thing is to go down there and see it all for yourself. If possible, go in the late spring, at the end of April or early June. This is mountain country, where the snow can lie on the tops of the hills until well into summer but the spring is my favourite season and the one to recommend.

Spring is also the time when the clichés come true. There really *are* flower-filled meadows, full of daffodils and wild narcissi, poking their heads through a thin crust of snow. You still can see the local people doing the spring ploughing, with oxen pulling the plough rather than the modern tractor. It is not impossible that you might even see a shepherdess in the hills near Arlempedes, playing her pipes to a small circle of attentive sheep — not something you expect to see in a Western European country in the last quarter of the twentieth century, but the Auvergne is like that. This is a village region, full of small hamlets where the people tend their flocks or run their farms much as they always have, keeping their traditions alive, even if all too many of the young folk are leaving to work in the towns.

The towns, too, are many and varied, mostly small but with something for all tastes, from the spa town of Vichy and the fortified town of St Flour high on a hill — a spectacular sight — to my favourite city of all, Le Puy, which is one of the start-points for the road to Compostela. Le Puy is a fascinating city, very typical of the Auvergne, and quite unlike any other town in France. It is notable for two *puys*, sharp spikes of rock which jut up from the centre of the city. One of them supports the small chapel of St Michel de l'Aiguille, while the other bears a huge statue of the Virgin, Notre Dame de Le Puy, which was forged from the bronze of Russian cannon captured at Sebastopol during the Crimean War — and fairly hideous it looks too. Le Puy stands on the infant river Loire, here a rushing torrent, and is surrounded by a tumbled green countryside. North, across the wild green country, is the great abbey at La Chaise-Dieu and further on lies Clermont-Ferrand.

Clermont may be best known today as the home of the Michelin Man, but it is an historic place, where the Pope preached the First Crusade to the chivalry of France in 1095. The modern commercial centre of the city has the considerable compensation of excellent restaurants, especially the Clave in the Rue St Adjutor, or La Retirade on the Boulevard Gergovia, which owe their success to the support of the local businessmen. Traditionally, the people of the Auvergne, the Auvergnats, provide barmen to the bistros of Paris. The ones who are left tend to be good trenchermen and enjoy their food immensely. Typical dishes include the *Potée Auvergnat*, a blended stew of port and sausages and vegetables (very filling!) and *tripoux*, veal and mutton served with herbs and potatoes. Local delicacies include *cèpes* (wild mushrooms) and ham, especially the ham from Ussel, *jambon cru* or mountain ham. All manner of home-cured ham and sausages make a visit to an Auvergne *charcuterie* an essential part of any visit — and then there is the wine and cheese.

The *bleu d'Auvergne*, a veined blue cheese, is (almost) as good as Roquefort, but the typical local cheese is the pressed variety from Cantal known as the *fourme*, a soft cheese made from rich cream and curds with a great variety of texture. Cantal is the best known, but there is *fourme* from the Monts du Forez in the east and from St Nectaire, while the *fourme d'Ambert* is said to date back to the time when Julius Caesar passed this way to fight Vercingetorix.

The Auvergne is not — to say the least — among the notable wine regions of France, but there is a Côtes d'Auvergne produced from the vines grown on the hills near Clermont-Ferrand, and a rather nice picnic red from the vineyards of St-Pourçain.

By now you should be able to visualise the Auvergne and take some measure of its charm. It is not a touristic region and has no serious intention of becoming one, whatever the local tourist offices may attempt from time to time. This is the *real* France, stubborn, insular, self-sufficient and very beautiful. It is a country where what you get out of it is very much related to what you are prepared to invest in time, effort and attention, the perfect country for Britain's ever-growing band of independent travellers, a place to remember and return to, again and again.

THE TETONS AND THE BIGHORNS

America is a wonderful country for a holiday. The United States is so big — the whole of Britain could fit quite comfortably into Nebraska, one of the smaller states — that it might take years of travel to see even a small part of it. Most

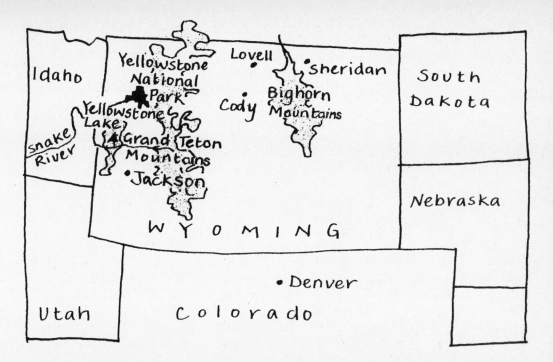

visitors begin with a trip to Florida, the Resort State, or to New York. But once you have sampled Disney World, seen the EPCOT Centre and the Everglades, or made that almost-mandatory excursion on the Staten Island Ferry to see the Statue of Liberty, the time has come to head West.

Beyond the Great Plains, on the fringes of the Rocky Mountains, lie the two cowboy States of Wyoming and Montana, each with a mountain range small enough to explore, yet beautiful enough to remain in the memory. In Wyoming, it is the Tetons; in Montana, the Bighorns. In both places the scenery is spectacular, the welcome warm, the food usually steaks and the dress simply jeans. That alone will make a visit fun — and besides I love those cowboy hats and boots. I bought a pair of boots as a present and stupidly thought that American sizes were the same as at home. They weren't! They were much too small and I had to keep them for myself — tough!

The journey from the Tetons to the Bighorns begins with a flight from Denver, Colorado, to the little town of Jackson in Wyoming. Jackson stands in the middle of the huge basin called Jackson's Hole, carved out of the mountains by the Snake River, just to the south of Yellowstone National Park. This really is the Old West; a memorial to those cowboy soldiers who left Wyoming to fight in the Great War stands in the Central Park. Tall gentlemen in Stetson hats and western boots throng in the Mangy Moose or The Million Dollar Cowboy Bar. Jackson's Hole was the place chosen to make the film of the classic Western 'Shane'. If Hollywood says this is the real West, who are we to argue?

Jackson's Hole was discovered by the *voyageurs*, French fur traders, who came here every summer from the end of the eighteenth century to camp and trade with the Indian tribes, the Utes, the Northern Cheyenne and the Teton Sioux. Most of the mountains therefore have names which are not only French but reflect those rough and tumble frontier days. 'Teton', for example, means breast, while 'Gros Ventre' — those mountains which lie to the east of the Hole — means fat belly.

The ranchers arrived in the early 1880s and from that time until today, Jackson's Hole has been cattle country. In the last 20 years many of the ranches have 'gone dude', i.e. opened up for tourists, and ranching now takes second place to tourism. Jackson's Hole has also become an established ski centre in the winter and is very popular with walkers, climbers and white-water rafters in the summer, who come here to walk along the valley, climb the rock walls of the Tetons or ride the rapids of the Snake River.

The town of Jackson is certainly worth a few days of anyone's time to stroll, heels thumping on the wooden sidewalks, and take a look at the National Elk Reserve. Some 10,000 elk take shelter there each winter. I suppose that is why antlers are so plentiful in Jackson. The town is awash with them, so if you want to buy a hat-rack, this is the place to do it. (How you get it onto the aircraft for the flight home is your problem!) After a day or so here, relaxing on a dude ranch and slipping into those slow Western ways, the time has come to head north along the edge of the mountains, towards Yellowstone Park, one of the natural wonders of America.

Yellowstone Park was established in 1875, the first National Park in America and, be it noted, one established while the West was still Wild. It was founded a full year before the Sioux wiped out six troops of General Custer's cavalry on the banks of the Little Bighorn River a few hundred miles to the east. Perhaps that's why conservation is so important in America: it has deep roots. These National Parks are very beautiful, well-protected and closely-patrolled places where you drop litter at your peril.

Yellowstone is vast. It straddles the border between Montana and Idaho, a home for buffalo and bear, the elk, the beaver, and all manner of wildlife. The park also contains a thermal area with great geysers which draw the crowds. The most famous is Old Faithful, which spouts steam and scalding spray high in the air at regular intervals. There are camper sites and motels throughout the park, good roads to drive around on, and guided trails through all this marvellous mountain scenery. The only real rule (apart from 'no litter') is 'don't feed the bears'. The black mountain bears are in danger here because if people feed them they cease to forage for themselves, come into camp sites, become aggressive and have to be shot. However one success story in the struggle to save America's wildlife is that of the American buffalo. These wonderful shaggy, placid creatures used to be killed for their hides; now they are once again on the increase and in no danger of extinction.

A car is almost essential in America, even for a visit to the mountains, which are far too extensive to cover on foot. A fine road, Route 20, runs east across Wyoming from Yellowstone, along the banks of the Shoshone River, past a series of dude ranches. Most of these were once proper ranches and made a fair living by rearing cattle, but the beef market has declined and tourism is their main occupation today. These ranches are always open, even to passing visitors. Some of them, like the Crossed Sabres Ranch at the western end of the Shoshone canyon, are very luxurious indeed. This road runs through the Shoshone National Forest, through quite outstanding scenery, before leading eventually to the town of Cody.

Cody is a town which no true Western buff should miss. It was founded around the turn of the century by Buffalo Bill Cody, the Indian scout and showman, and it still has echoes — if a little faintly now — of those Good Old, Wild Old Days. Apart from many Western shops and saloons, it contains the Buffalo Bill Museum, a complex which includes the Museum of the Plains Indians and a fine collection of Winchester firearms, 'the gun that won the

West'. A good place to stay in Cody is at the Irma Hotel, built by Buffalo Bill and named after his daughter.

The town, even if much modernised, is still built on Western lines with long, straight streets wide enough to turn a Conestoga waggon in, and plenty of those broad, shady side-walks where the visitors can shop while sheltering from the scorching Western sun. I recommend at least a day in Cody, then perhaps a day or two at a dude ranch, one by the pool and one in the saddle. You can't possibly come all the way West and not want to ride the range on a cow-pony in one of those high-cantled Western saddles. In the West, horseback is the only way to travel.

Mountains are the theme for this Western journey, but west of Cody the landscape flattens out for a while. Not for too long though, because after an hour or so of rolling and dipping across the prairie, past Greybull, we come to the town of Lovell, cross the Bighorn River and begin to climb, winding up and up into the beautiful Bighorn Mountains. In late June, when the sun scorches the prairie grass, there is still snow on the top of the mountains, reaching down long pale fingers to great drifts of purple sage and blue-bonnets. The road across the Bighorns is virtually empty of traffic and I doubt if there is a more beautiful or spectacular mountain journey. The blue mountains surround you and far below the prairie stretches far away out of sight to the south, the grass bleached golden by the summer sun. Up here in the mountains it is still spring. If there was anywhere to stay, you would happily stop for a day or so in the Bighorns, but the mountains are empty and it is already dark as the road winds down the eastern slopes and into the town of Sheridan.

Sheridan is named after General Philip Sheridan who fought for the North in the Civil War and was later to command an army fighting the Sioux on the Western Plains. General Custer was one of his subordinates. Although the town is a tourist centre and full of motels, it lies in the centre of the Indian War battlefields. The Custer battlefield lies just to the north, the Fetterman Massacre happened just to the south, and various other forts and sites lie within easy distance. When you have seen these places so many times in Western movies, it seems curious to find that they actually exist.

The Little Bighorn is a tributary of the Bighorn River, which runs across the Bighorn Mountains. It is a muddy, winding stream about 20 yards wide, the high banks lined with cottonwood trees. Follow the minor road beside the river north from Sheridan, ignoring the modern Interstate Highway, and you eventually come to the site of the Custer Battlefield. It lies on the *right* bank of the river, and is still very much as it was on 25 June 1876, when General Custer attacked the huge Indian camp that lay along the *left* bank — his fatal mistake.

Those interested in the often sad and savage history of the Old West will find the Battlefield Museum, which is just beside the site of Custer's Last Stand, an interesting and evocative exhibition, full of maps and dioramas and relics gleaned from the battlefield over the last hundred years. Those who find battlefields of only limited appeal can meet real Indians down at the nearby trading post where the snackbar serves 'Coke 'n' Custerburgers'.

From the porch of the museum, the details of the Custer fight are quite easy to follow, for the whole battlefield would fit quite easily into London's Green Park. The Americans are very good at presenting history and a lecturer, dressed in Cavalry regimentals of the period, complete with revolver and sabre, gives a vivid talk on the events of 1876 and life in the cavalry during the last century. Standing in the sunshine, looking down to the green tops of the cottonwood trees beside the Little Bighorn River, the years just roll away.

WATER

It has always been supposed that the British take to water like ducks. Nelson is called down from his column as an example ... an example of what? How Dad is cut out to swing the tiller of a hire boat as he scatters dinghies on Wroxham Broad on August Bank Holiday? We boast of being an island race as if the only way any of us travelled was by ketch. And the amount of salt there is meant to be in our veins would be enough to concentrate a saline drip.

And it all turns out to be a nonsense — 22 carat, clinker-built baloney. The legend of our seafaring prowess is a myth. The imaginary man in the British street — or stuck on the M1, more like — has no more affinity with the ocean wave than a contra-flow system has to do with a tidetable.

The truth came out in some research carried out for the hire boat industry. The boat hirers wanted to know why more people were not taking their holidays. The pollsters came up with the reason: there are not that many of us who like being on the water. We are suspicious of boats; we don't think we shall be comfortable in them and we are frightened of falling overboard.

Yet for those who do enjoy holidays afloat, there is a tremendous range of wind-blown and spray-stung holidays to choose from. Take cruise ships. They come in all shapes and sizes and offer totally different experiences. Cruise regulars will nevertheless argue furiously over their respective merits. I have picked three sea cruises: the one with the most exciting itinerary (*Pearl of Scandinavia*); the one that has the best combination of high quality service and value for money prices (*Ocean Islander*); and the ship that offers the ultimate in seagoing luxury (*Sea Goddess*). For good measure I have added a river cruise: the incomparable Nile. Of the British waterways, I have selected the Thames — liquid history someone called it, and a river that can be cruised almost as easily by car as by boat. Finally, there is one of the newer waterborne holidays and one which again the British have made their own: flotilla sailing. Now that is an idea which might entice Nelson back to the helm and even discover a successor or two.

FLOTILLA SAILING

The weather forecast said it would be a *thelassa lega* sort of a morning, meaning a duck pond of a sea. Since it was Day One of the flotilla sailing holiday, and the first time that most people had set foot aboard a yacht, there were several audible sighs of relief. 'We'll just have to chug-a-lug-along,' said the genial flotilla leader from New Zealand, which he translated as 'main sail up and engine on, nice and slowly'.

Flotilla sailing has brought yachting in the Med, once a mere daydream for all but the mega-rich, within reach of the ordinary holidaymaker. With up to a dozen yachts sailing together under the watchful but unobtrusive eye of a skipper, engineer and hostess on the lead boat (the one that answers to the name of Mummy) this 'sail in company' approach is ideal for people with insufficient funds either to own or charter a crewed yacht, yet lacking the experience to go 'bareboat', the nautical term for self-drive yacht hire (not, as landlubbers might assume, a boat crewed by naturists).

Sailing days invariably begin far later than planned. With a wiggle, twist and a few bone creaks you rise from your bunk feeling your age, poke your head up through the hatch, sniff the breeze and grab a first cuppa before the skipper's briefing. This daily ritual usually takes place in last night's taverna, now this morning's breakfast café. Coffee cups and yogurt pots are shifted to make room for the chart on which the day's passage is plotted, places of interest highlighted and navigational hazards underlined. Hidden rocks, shallow waters, restricted military areas and blobs of honey dripping from your toast must be avoided at all costs.

Although you sail in the company of other boats there are no rigid follow-my-leader rules. Individual yachts are more or less free to make their own way to the late afternoon rendezvous, usually ten to 12 miles away, or four to five hours of sailing. During the day your floating home demonstrates its great advantage over all other means of transport — it allows you access to the inaccessible.

You can anchor for a midday swim, snorkel, windsurf or lazy picnic in lonely coves that simply cannot be reached from the land side. Apart from the frenzied simmering of the cicadas and the distant tinkle of goat bells, these remote worlds are blissfully quiet. Such daytime havens are combined with umpteen tiny overnight harbours, timeless places far too insignificant to draw the tourist crowds. If you have any doubts about whether paradise really exists, a flotilla sailing holiday is as good a way as any of restoring your lost faith.

Most evenings are shared with the rest of the flotilla in a taverna, eating yet another moussaka and watching waiters lift tables in the air with their teeth. If you're anchored in a large town, the horn-pipe revellers among the flotilla will probably set course for a disco. Few on flotillas are ever seasick but there are plenty of green faces on the mornings after the nights before.

Most of the flotilla companies that cruise in the Med require that at least one person on board knows the ropes (or rather the sheets, shrouds, halyards, warps and painters) before letting their clients loose on their £20–30,000 vessels. After that a couple of agile shipmates will come in handy. Some companies also offer weekend primers on the English coast so that gravel pit admirals can get some practice on what will at first seem like a battleship, while the rest of the family can learn the finer manoeuvres that life in a sardine tin entails. But there's no reason for even the inexperienced to feel at all apprehensive about taking such holidays. Even if you haven't any old salts

among your friends to make up a competent boatload, you can take pot luck on a 'mix 'n' match' holiday on which the flotilla company pairs up inexperienced singles or couples with dabber hands.

Once you have learnt how to handle the boat, most flotilla companies will let you deviate from the main itinerary for three or four days of independent sailing, lone passages which make you feel like Messrs Drake, Cook, Columbus and Chichester all rolled into one. Just to be on the safe side, each yacht in the flotilla also has a VHF radio, a 'sailie-talkie' device enabling you to summon assistance in the event of a nautical hitch or just 'roger and out' your well-being at occasional intervals.

The Greek seas are the most popular flotilla haunt in the world, the sailing equivalent of the nursery slopes in the winter ski resorts. Dawn till dusk swimwear replaces the Michelin-person padding and wet weather outfits generally needed by British sailors. In the Med the only protection needed against the elements is likely to be a sunhat and an all-over coating of Factor Six. And with negligible tides and currents, even-tempered winds, clear visibility and no magnetic variations to worry about, a Greek flotilla holiday is plain sailing.

Well, almost. Winds can, and do, whip up the Beaufort scale faster than you can say jolly boating weather, turning the Greek seas very curly-headed indeed. On occasions, when violent storms seem to erupt from nowhere, bringing horizontal rain, Zeus lightening and zero visibility, you can feel like some ancient mariner straight off a sardine tin. It is usually all over and back to sunny bliss in half an hour — and what a tale to dine out on! In fact, although winds do vary according to the sailing area (the Sporades, for example, are likely to offer a point or two more on the Beaufort scale than, say, the Ionian islands), the most likely disappointment in these waters is the absence of any lively winds and the all too frequent need to motor between ports of call.

Greece by no means has a monopoly on flotilla sailing holidays. The southern Turkish coastline is an obvious alternative — its recent growth in popularity as a holiday destination has in fact largely stemmed from its discovery by British sailors. The stretch of coastline between Bodrum and the Kekova Roads in particular offers a beautiful, unmolested backdrop for a sailing holiday, being a blend of broom and thyme-covered mountains, wooded inlets like over-ripe Norwegian fjords and occasional fishing villages lying in the sun like tired dogs. Although a Turkish sailing holiday initially costs more, once there the prices are among the lowest in the Med. The coastline is dotted with one-rickety-jetty-and-two-taverna villages where it's virtually impossible to spend more than £5 on the fullest meal — with wine.

Don't be surprised to find on your Turkish flotilla people from as far afield as Australia, Canada, South Africa and Florida who have heard about the delights of these waters and, more important, were not disappointed by what they found. Turkey offers the last wholesome stretch of Mediterranean — but it won't stay uncommercialised for ever. Already several resorts have begun to attract the tourist masses but, since many of its finest parts can only be reached by yacht, sailors will continue to enjoy an exclusive membership of the coastal club for several years.

The Yugoslavian coast, with its chain of 750 islands, fair to middling winds and innumerable safe anchorages, is also a relative newcomer to flotilla sailing. The pine-covered, serrated limestone shores of the Istrian peninsula, the most northerly hump of the country, is a port hopper's paradise. Several of the towns share a distinctive Venetian stamp of design, a legacy of past Italian rule. Rovinj, for example, is an architectural gem dramatically poised on a rocky promontory, its silhouette sharply defined from several nautical miles away by its eighteenth-century cathedral and pencil-thin bell tower. On closer inspection you'll find several classical buildings, narrow streets, cobbled alleys and relics of its medieval town walls and gates. Further south hundreds of islands, all tailor-made for sailors, pepper the Yugoslav horizons, as do naked Germans on speedboats, sailboards, lilos and even barer rocks; naturism is enormous in these parts and so, it has to be said, are many of the people who practise it.

If you've never been to sea in anything smaller than a cross-Channel ferry you will obviously have your doubts about flotilla sailing. 'Holiday' will probably seem like the last word you'd use to describe an activity that you've previously associated with heartiness, drowning, throwing up or getting very wet. Most people like their holidays to be relaxing — not that easy if you're in constant danger of being asked to tie knots or being washed overboard by a freak wave.

But being on a boat (provided you enjoy sailing) is better than lying on a beach. It provides just as much opportunity for indolence and sunbathing but gives you a sense of achievement as well. Look down and you may find porpoises swimming alongside. When it's someone else's turn on the tiller, its yours to sunbathe, book in one hand, bottle of cold beer or glass of wine in the other. Tax, mortgage payments, career, and anxieties about whether you left the frying pan on the stove cease to exist. Cut off from the cares of everyday living your only real worry is whether that splash was the bottle opener.

OCEAN ISLANDER CRUISE

We may have lost the Empire and our balance of payments can sometimes look a bit sick but we still lead the world in the export of hairdressers.

Every cruise ship seems to have a British crimper and, as when ashore, they are an excellent source of inside information. So, when an experienced seagoing hair stylist insists that the *Ocean Islander* is the friendliest ship she has worked on, it is a recommendation well worth repeating. She is not alone. It is clear that all the crew and cruise staff on the *Ocean Islander* are happy in their work. When that happens, it is the best possible news for passengers.

The ship is only 5000-ton, carrying no more than 250 passengers and 140 crew, so there's no need to spend days trying to find your way around. And, with just a couple of bars and lounges to relax in, the staff soon become familiar faces. Too much formality on a ship this size is out of place so the service is friendly and relaxed rather than stiffly efficent. Your pina coladas are less likely to be delivered in respectful silence by a fast-vanishing waiter than with a flourish by someone you have come to know, with an enquiry about your day or a tale about theirs.

I have always been fascinated by the characters found working on ships. It is all those old romantic stories about people running away to sea, I suppose — and *Ocean Islander*, with its cosmopolitan complement, has more than its share of those. Order a drink in the main lounge bar and the chances are it will be a Korean taking the order, a Colombian mixing it and a jaunty Jamaican who brings the drink to your table. It will be a grave disappointment to admirers of Esperanto that the staff manage to communicate easily with a bizarre amalgamation of English and Spanish and more than a dash of jokes. In fact, everyone has a smile on their face and the stoniest-hearted of passengers would find it hard to resist the atmosphere of jollity that fills the ship.

It is not just the crew and staff that are cosmopolitan. Too often, these days, cruise ships have either 95 per cent American, German or British on their passenger manifests. It is so much more fun to have a mix and that is certainly true of the *Ocean Islander*'s passenger list on the European and Scandinavian cruises. There are British, Europeans, South Americans and Mexicans, and Americans with no one group dominating.

This has had its impact in the galleys, too. There is no giving in to the North American fad for bland food on the *Ocean Islander*. French and Italian cuisine are the mainstay of the imaginative menus with more basic 'prime ribs'-type fare as an optional back-up. There is, though, a separate weightwatchers' menu for those passengers who don't want, as the old joke goes, to leave the ship as cargo.

Food is always important on a ship and that means presentation as well as quality. The *Islander* scores top points on both counts. Meals are an event, with different themes every night from French bistro to Scandinavian smörgåsbord. The waiters and busboys seem to enjoy these as much as the passengers, throwing themselves into their 'roles' and costumes with gusto. There are a couple of formal nights every week, in keeping, I am glad to report, with a definite return to dressing up on cruises. For a while in the Seventies it became fashionable to go casual all the time but long dresses and dinner jackets are making a comeback. Cruises may (thankfully) no longer be the stuffy preserve of the rich and snobby, but it certainly adds to the romance of an evening at sea to see everyone in their finery, and *Ocean Islander* cruises are full of glamorous evenings.

The ship is small enough to ensure that passengers are aware most of the time that they are on a cruise. On some of the huge ships now being built for cruising, you can go for days forgetting altogether that you are even at sea, especially if you spend your time in darkened discos and casinos. This has its good as well as bad points. If you are prone to travel sickness then the *Ocean Islander* is probably not for you. On the odd occasion when there's a heavy sea running, passengers know all about it. But, as with all cruise lines, Ocean Cruise Line picks out the most suitable (i.e. calm) cruising areas and seasons for its ships. For the *Ocean Islander* this means winters in the Caribbean and cruising up the Orinoco in South America, and summers based in Copenhagen for weekly cruises alternately to the Norwegian fjords and to the northern capitals (including Leningrad) and the Baltic.

Cruises in these northern waters are becoming increasingly popular but OCL is the only line to offer regular weekly departures, since most lines concentrate on longer cruises. It means that *Ocean Islander* cruises work out at eminently affordable prices. In 1987, they started at £697 for a two-bed, inside cabin (including return flight to Copenhagen from UK airports). At those prices, and with the quality of food and service on board, the destinations come almost as a bonus.

Cruising is definitely the best way to see the fjords and, unlike some parts of the world, when it is easier, cheaper and more rewarding to find your own way ashore, on this particular cruise the organised excursions are the best and often the only practical way of seeing the sights. Prices are on the high side but that reflects the high cost of living in Scandinavia. Do-it-yourself tours in the fjord ports are difficult to organise and likely to be even pricier.

The ship's first call, after a fast haul from Copenhagen, is Gudvangen in Norway. It is a strangely proud moment to be on deck, at the prow of what, within a few hours of boarding, has come to feel like *your* cruise ship, as she ploughs a dramatic solitary furrow into port. In this case it is a port at the end of an awesome 4000-foot deep fjord. Tenders take passengers ashore where coaches are waiting to take them to the top of the Flam Railway, some 2700 feet above sea level. The train ride down is spectacular with pauses for picture-taking of huge waterfalls along the way. The train has five sets of brakes, so steep is the descent.

In the meantime, *Ocean Islander* has chugged the 19 miles around the arm of the fjord to meet the passengers again at Flam. Another day, another fjord but you can't have too much of this kind of scenery. Sognefjord on the second day is just as breathtaking and the tour even more seat-gripping. It is a day of extremes from the heights of mist-shrouded Mount Dalsnibba, and the towering Hellesylt waterfall, to the depths of Lake Hornindalsvannet, Europe's deepest at 2000 feet, and the sheer vastness of the Jostedalsbreen Glacier.

Once again, the ship moves on, this time to Geirangerfjord passenger-less. Once re-boarded, she steers a calm and steady course back through the fjords towards the busy port of Bergen. Here and in the next port, the Norwegian capital Oslo, the shore excursions are less essential although they do make interesting trips — to the composer Greig's former home and burial place near Bergen and to the Viking Ships and Kon Tiki museums in Oslo.

This is not a cruise for inveterate shoppers. The cruise staff make this clear to passengers at their first get-together on board. But in the Bergen fishmarket, although prices are fairly steep, there is a huge range of Norwegian and Icelandic knitwear, far greater than we see back in Britain. Hefty Nordic sweaters make impressive presents.

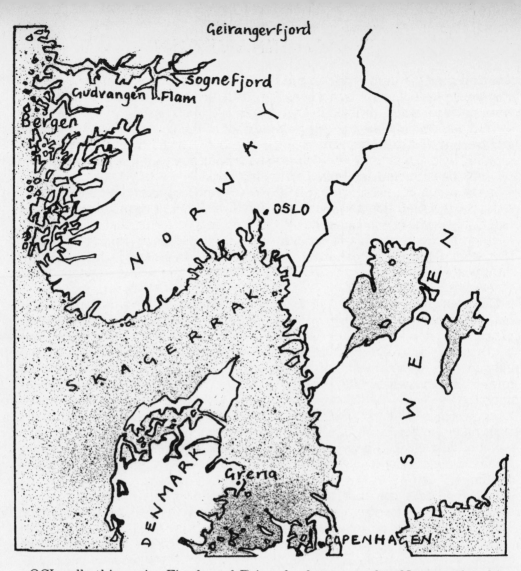

OCL calls this cruise Fjords and Fairytales because, after Norway, the ship makes a call at Grena in Denmark before returning to Copenhagen.

The Northern Capitals cruise, incidentally, costs the same and looks equally attractive, but then the *Ocean Islander* is so friendly and comfortable that it almost does not matter where she goes. The ship was completely refurbished when OCL bought her in 1984 and she has clearly been well looked after since then. The cabins are not huge but they are comfortable, most have an outside view and all have their own tiled bathrooms. There is a decent-sized swimming pool on deck (which obviously gets more use up the Orinoco than off Oslo) and a smallish fitness centre with a selection of instruments of self-torture plus a sauna. The main lounge converts into a cinema most days but get there early if you want a reasonable view of the video screen.

Organised entertainment is kept fairly low-key. Study the daily events sheet in your cabin to find out where to go for your daily fix of aerobics or, occasionally, bingo or trapshooting. There is some of the traditional cruise ship-style cabaret after dinner (one restaurant, two sittings) or there is the piano bar that converts into a disco late at night.

For high quality cruising which doesn't break the bank, the *Ocean Islander* is hard to beat. Just ask the hairdresser.

PEARL CHINA CRUISE

The first time the cruise staff on the *Pearl of Scandinavia* went to China and saw their passengers on to coaches for a three-day excursion to Peking, they were not sure when, or even if, they would see them again.

That was seven years ago when the terrors of the Cultural Revolution were still fresh in the memory. Although the Bamboo Curtain had been opened to tourism, no one was quite certain just what was in store for those who had only recently been reviled as 'capitalist running dogs'.

In the event, the passengers from the *Pearl*, the first ship to cruise regularly to China, returned safe and sound, if weary from a hectic round of sightseeing. Since then, cruising to China has got better and better as the Chinese have adapted to the strange ways of their visitors. But although the frisson of fear that went along with those early forays into post-Red Guard China has now disappeared, it remains the most exciting and stimulating country for a Westerner to penetrate.

The country is changing fast as it strives towards its 'four modernisations' but its internal transportation system and range of habitable hotels still leaves plenty to be desired. To undertake a land tour to see even a tenth of this vast land's attractions requires considerable time and patience and even if you are blessed with an abundance of the latter, there is usually not enough of the former. This is where the cruise comes in. The *Pearl of Scandinavia* is operated by Pearl Cruises, which has recently been taken over by Ocean Cruise Lines, which is re-naming the ship the *Ocean Pearl* early in 1988. She has been cruising in the Far East throughout the 1980s and has now developed a cruise to China that ensures passengers see plenty of the country in just two weeks (plus the flight time to and from Japan and Hong Kong where the cruises start and finish).

If anyone tells you that this is cheating, seeing China the easy way, the answer is simple: they're absolutely right. But refer them to the backpackers' 'Bible', the *Lonely Planet* guide. It acknowledges that even longtime enthusiasts for roughing it have been terminally frustrated by the problems of travelling in China. The guide recommends against staying too long because of the very real danger of ending up hating the place with its inexplicable bureaucratic barriers and its primitive travel and lodging conditions.

Having a cruise ship as a base, especially one as welcoming as the *Pearl*, gives the best of both worlds: days full of the sights, sounds and smells of China, nights back on board in a warm, comfortable bed; Chinese banquets for lunch, top quality international cuisine for dinner.

A China cruise provides such a kaleidoscope of memories that it is dificult to know where to start. When the country first opened to tourists, cruise lines and holiday companies were given set tour itineraries from which no deviation was allowed. Visitors were taken from factory to factory, commune to commune, pausing only to hear interminable and poorly-translated speeches from local officials. This was no propaganda campaign, simply a lack of understanding of why people were coming to China and what it was they wanted to see and do. But the Chinese have learned fast and now there is a wide choice of tours. Factories (apart from silk ones, of which more later) are right off the list of attractions and the Chinese are quick to seek advice on ways to improve their service to tourists. In the cities the only restriction on doing your own thing is the fact that 99.9 per cent of the population do not speak or understand any European language.

The welcome is warm, even if it is sometimes still mingled with curiosity. As the police forge a passage for the tourist buses through massive jams of bicycles, women hold up their colourfully dressed toddlers to show you. Everyone is smiling.

One of the most interesting tours is a 'meet the people' arrangement. There are countries where this can be disappointing, not to say embarrassing: a family may be putting up with hordes of gawping strangers just for the money, or it may be a 'show' house designed to give you a false impression. In China, take the visit at face value. The home you visit will be basic in the extreme, by Western standards, but the family will be proud to show it off and answer even the most banal questions with a smile. The rest of the neighbourhood will also turn out to provide a colourful and often musical welcome.

A silk factory is another eye-opener with its Dickensian working conditions and a design department unashamedly scanning European and American fashion magazines for designs. This is the cheapest place to buy silk, too, with prices from less than £2 a metre. Silk is almost as cheap in the Friendship Stores, in which visitors are encouraged to shop. They take Western credit cards and are in all the main towns and cities. Despite their generally gloomy interiors and uniform range of stock, they are packed with bargains in cashmere, silk and crochet blouses, lacquer work and porcelain. If you can face carrying it, a beautiful tea service is yours for less than £10. Incidentally, don't let anyone in Hong Kong tell you that prices of Chinese handicrafts are cheaper there; they're not.

Other unexpected highlights of a China cruise include the scenes of Shanghai's famous Bund (waterfront) as hundreds of Chinese exercise by shadow-boxing in the misty mornings or half-light of dusk. From Shanghai, there are trips to the garden city of Suzhou, a blaze of colour from the spring onwards. Not far away is Wuxi where a cruise on the Grand Canal that bisects it is an unmissable experience. All Chinese life is there: laden barges criss-crossing perilously close to collision and life going on as it must have for centuries for the families living hugger-mugger in the whitewashed riverside houses. It is vibrant, colourful, busy, noisy and squalid all at the same time.

Even if you are not a train buff, the chance to sample Chinese railways on the way to Wuxi and Suzhou is a rare treat. There are two classes, soft and hard (perhaps a more honest description of first and second class that BR might care to adopt). In soft, there are lace tablecloths, endless supplies of Chinese green tea and even the chance to buy silk scarves and other gifts from some real travelling salesmen as a little private enterprise creeps into Chinese society. Don't be surprised if you keep seeing the same man selling T-shirts at each sightseeing point on the tours. The routes are well-known to these would-be Arthur Daleys who seem to be tolerated, if not actively encouraged, by the authorities. In fact, there is some danger that before too long the unacceptable face of capitalism will be spoiling China's most famous 'sights'. There is already a rash of unsightly souvenir stalls at the main entrance to the Great Wall and on the road to the Ming Tombs.

Completely unspoilt however is the Summer Palace, a short drive from Peking. This is a stunning collection of temples, lakes, gardens and follies like the Marble Boat which the Empress Dowager Ci Xi had built with funds meant for the rebuilding of the Chinese Navy. Perhaps the most impressive of Peking's sights is the Forbidden City, which covers 175 acres with its ornately carved halls and gates. These are all part of that three-day trip to the capital, a city of

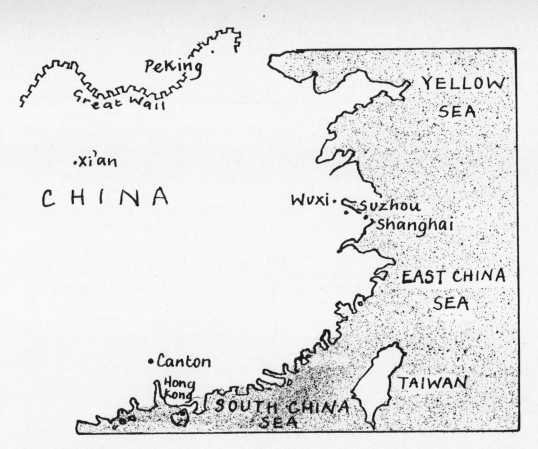

broad avenues, little motorised traffic, and a useful and recently-extended Underground system.

The Peking tour, like all the other excursions, is included in the fly-cruise price (from £3390 in 1988) but there is one optional extra tour, to Xian to see the Terracotta Army, an extraordinary collection of hundreds of larger-than-life-size clay warriors which lay undiscovered for 2000 years.

But your memories of China will be of the sights they don't write about in the guide books: the children flying kites in the huge Tian An Mien Square or the sight of Shanghai, the world's most densely populated city, at rush-hour.

Two pieces of advice for anyone embarking on their first trip to China: firstly the food will not resemble anything ever bought from the local takeaway. There is a saying that the people of Guangzhou (Canton) will eat anything with four legs except the table itself. It is worth bearing in mind. Banquets will be an endless series of courses, most of which are served up without adequate, if any, explanation of what they are, and a few dishes will be an acquired taste that most of us will never acquire. Secondly, what the Americans call 'comfort' stations are anything but. Once outside those few deluxe hotels, it is best to hang on until you are back on the *Pearl*. There are some experiences most of us can live without: Chinese loos are one of them.

In 1987 the China Explorers cruise itinerary went from Kōbe to Nagasaki in Japan, and then on to Dalian, Qinhuangdao (for Peking), Yantai, Qingdao, Shanghai and Xiamen in China before arriving in Hong Kong ready to do the same journey in reverse. For the first time, the ship also made a couple of cruises that included *both* Chinas, with a call at Taipei in Taiwan. But it is the

People's Republic of China that holds most fascination and it is now at a stage where it is either going to change very fast or the barriers are going to go up again. Either way, go and see it now. You won't regret it or forget it.

SEA GODDESS CRUISES

It was once said that the world is divided into those who dream of having their own private yacht and those who dream of being a regular passenger on somebody else's. If that is the case, then count me among the latter. When it comes to life on the ocean wave, how much more fun if someone else is doing the driving and the worrying about tides, winds and the crew's wages.

There is, though, another way to indulge your fantasies and its name is *Sea Goddess*. In fact, there are two ways as there are two *Sea Goddess* ships. On board, the atmosphere is like no other cruise ship. Everything is designed to make the passengers (116 at the most, with 80 crew and staff to look after their every need) feel just like guests on a private yacht. This begins before they even step on board. Everyone receives a personal preference form on which, as well as requesting either a queen-sized or twin beds, they can list the drinks they want stocked in their cabin fridge. These, along with any replenishments required as the cruise proceeds, are provided for no extra charge, just as drinks and wine in the bars and restaurant are free.

The catch is the cruise price which is currently about £3000 for one week. But, as they say, if you have to ask the price, you can't afford it. If you can, it is worth every penny.

For once, calling the cabins 'suites' is no brochurespeak. They really are something special, not so much in size — they are large without being huge — as in their furnishing and contents. The bedroom with its bed(s) and dressing table is curtained off from a living area with couch and coffee table. Floor to ceiling wardrobes for once actually allow long dresses to hang properly, and smart units house the sound system, TV and video, and, of course, your very own combination wall safe. The bathroom is a revelation with thick towels and bathrobes (His and Hers) provided along with designer toiletries. The suite has tasteful decor, all pastel shades, and those extra touches like French crystal champagne glasses automatically added to every guest's fridge order.

When you retire to bed after a sumptuous meal with a new movie from the ship's extensive video library, accompanied later by a midnight feast of caviar and champagne delivered by the 24-hour cabin service, you will begin to understand why people sincerely want to be rich.

Part of the *Sea Goddess* concept is the choice of itineraries the ships operate. Their small size (4500-ton) and shallow draught allow them into ports other cruise ships cannot reach and give the captains the flexibility to add stopovers almost at whim. As the captain on one cruise explained to passengers surprised to find themselves making an unscheduled stop at a tiny island — they were there because he 'liked the look of it'.

In the Caribbean, the scheduled itineraries concentrate on the islands that do not have cruise ships stacked up ten deep in their harbours — places like Virgin Gorda, Mustique, Isles des Saintes and Gustavia on St Barts. Often honorary membership of their exclusive golf and tennis clubs is open to *Sea Goddess* guests.

Recently the ships have moved on to newer routes to Alaska and the Far East, but the Mediterranean is still a natural habitat: not just any old

Mediterranean cruises, though, but ones that pick out the places where the Beautiful People go. In fact, when the ships were operated by the Norwegian consortium that conceived and had them built in 1984 and 1985, the idea was not to package the cruises in any way. The assumption was that *Sea Goddess* guests, in search of Beautiful People doing Beautiful Things, would be catching the ships almost like an exclusive bus service midway through a Grand European Tour. Since Cunard took over in 1986, the brochures have included optional flights to join the ships but only first and business class fares are quoted. If you want to travel economy, you have to ask — if you have the nerve.

Monte Carlo is a key departure port and not just because *Sea Goddess II* was named there by Princess Caroline. The place has style, discretion and wealth — a *Sea Goddess* mixture, if ever there was one.

A typical cruise from there will take you to St Tropez, Portofino, Collioure, Barcelona, Ibiza and Puerto Banus, a genuine Riviera route. Arriving at these places is an eye-opener for anyone who has cruised on other ships. The *Sea Goddess*es slip in quietly with none of the usual hullabaloo ashore or on board. There are no tannoy announcements, no rushing to the gangway. There's no need as there are no shore excursions. The ships' staffs are happy to help out with individual arrangements, ordering cars or taxis, booking restaurants and arranging temporary club memberships, but *Sea Goddess* guests know places like St Tropez intimately or have friends there to meet them. Just like passengers on a private yacht, in fact.

It's the same at sea. There's no list of endless activities. The ships have well-stocked libraries (books as well as videos), chess, backgammon and other games; a health spa with sauna, gymnasium and jacuzzi; a swimming pool and whirlpool on deck, and a stern ramp which, when the ships are at anchor, lets down into the water so that a bronzed Adonis can supervise water-skiing, windsurfing and snorkelling. Guests are left alone to choose how they want to spend their time even if, for some, that means monitoring the stock exchanges of the world — information comes through the ships' satellite links, and there is direct-dial telephoning all round the world for a mere £10 a minute.

In the evenings, a small but plush casino, and an occasional cabaret, provide the sum total of the organised entertainment. One of the nicest touches is the cocktail pianist whose playing, at the bottom of an atrium in the reception area, filters through as you walk and dine. The cabaret is not exactly end-of-the-pier stuff but, as everyone is a guest, there is no gulf between performer and audience. It is a little like one of those Hollywood movies where someone is called up on stage from the audience and they turn out to be Judy Garland. One minute, you are having a drink with someone, the next they are up on stage singing 'Feelings'. It is that kind of ship, that kind of intimate experience.

Dinner on a *Sea Goddess* is a main event. Just about the only firm rule on board is that guests dress for dinner. Only a couple of nights a week are designated 'formal' but every night offers the chance to show off your wardrobe. More or less anything goes by day, although casualwear, however skimpy, will always have room for a designer label. Dinner, though, remains the only real chance for that popular cruise sport of oneupman(or woman)ship. Without the need to pay for drinks and with tipping forbidden, there is none of the competition on the lines of 'my cocktail party was bigger and better than yours' that can bedevil the best of other cruises. And, since the Captain and officers are in the ship's only cocktail bar before dinner most nights, there is no contest over invitation lists either.

Nor is there that unseemly rush to the restaurant. Guests are encouraged to treat it as they would a restaurant ashore, to turn up when they want (between 8–10 pm) and sit where and with whom they like. Menus are in the *nouvelle cuisine* style with just a nod in the direction of larger American appetites.

Most of the sailing takes place during the early hours of the morning so the ship is free to stay in port throughout the evening and well into the night should guests want to try out the local casinos and nightlife. It is no reflection on the quality of *Sea Goddess* food if guests occasionally dine ashore. The kind of people these ships attract are quite unconcerned about missing a meal they have 'paid' for!

There must be a drawback, I hear you thinking, but apart from the cost, it is hard to think of one. Perhaps the only word of caution should be that, as the ships are so small, they are not the best choice for transatlantic or other ocean voyages if you are the sort who gets sick just looking at the Woolwich ferry.

NILE CRUISE

The Aga Khan knew a thing or two about the good things in life, so the attractions of the Nile could have no better endorsement than his decision to build his mausoleum on a hill behind his villa on Kitchener Island on the river banks. If he couldn't take it with him, the Aga was determined that his freehold in eternity should include his favourite view. He is not alone in his admiration. People have been taking packages to cruise along the Nile since the action-packed days of General Gordon (Thomas Cook made the travel arrangements even in those rebellion-quelling times) but never in the pleasure-seeking numbers they do today.

Cruise boats of all shapes, sizes and standards ply the route between Aswân and Luxor. Some of the best are those operated by major hotel chains such as Hilton, Sheraton and Marriott but there are many — often cheaper — alternatives. As everywhere, you tend to get what you pay for. The beauty of a Nile cruise, though, is that everybody sees the same historic marvels and soaks up the same unique atmosphere along the way. The usual holiday concerns and irritations pale into insignificance: cruising the Nile is like seeing the pages of the Bible fall open and come to colourful, teeming life.

Some of the cruises — notably those of the Presidential Line — continue past Luxor right down to Cairo. But even if the boats don't go there, the traditional Nile holiday includes a few days in the Egyptian capital before or after the cruise. It is a city that everyone ought to see at least once. For some, once is enough. It is a chaotic madhouse of a place. Traffic — motorised, horsedrawn, two-wheeled or two-footed — battles for supremacy with the only rule of the road being the survival of the fastest and the noisiest. It is a place for the quick and the deaf.

The Egyptian Museum in Cairo is packed with extraordinary treasures even if they are displayed with little flair. No human touch is needed to show off the pyramids, however. It doesn't take much effort to go and see them either, as they are just on the outskirts of the city at Giza and Saqqara. Everyone wants to sell you an excursion to the pyramids. In fact, it can be cheaper and a lot more comfortable to do this part of your sightseeing independently. The usual tour of Giza, Saqqara and Memphis (one of the Pharaohs' ancient capitals, founded 5000 years ago) is offered as a full-day excursion. In reality, it is easily manageable in less than half a day.

Ask your hotel to recommend a reliable taxi-driver and fix the price before

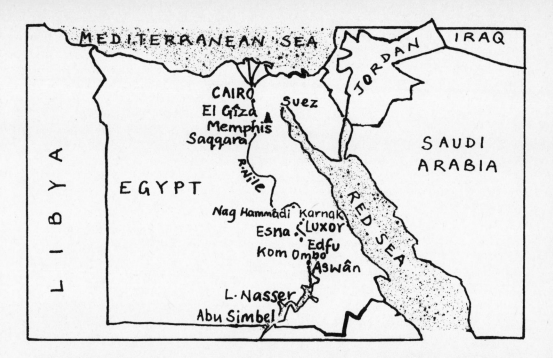

you depart. The drivers, as you might expect, are the usual selection of heroes and villains but even the latter can be unconsciously entertaining. There is the story of one, Ishmael, who was so keen to show off his popularity with his passengers that he kept a visitors' book. Unfortunately, he didn't read English nearly as well as he spoke it so he could not know that the entries he proudly indicated to prospective clients included many such enlightening statements as, 'spent a delightful day with Ishmael including three hours at his brother's carpet shop and one hour visiting his mother'.

A good driver will take you only to what you want to see and that will inevitably include those three giant pyramids at Giza and the awesome Sphinx nearby. If possible try to be there around sunset — not only will the temperature be more bearable, but the sight of the sun dropping slowly and then suddenly out of sight behind these extraordinary feats of human engineering helps roll back the years to those Pharaoh days. Also distractions of the souvenir sellers, beggars and camel-drivers seem that much more intrusive in the heat of the day. If you want to ride a camel this is definitely the place but, again, ask your guide or driver to negotiate so that you pay the right price and avoid arguments with the hordes of camel-drivers vying for your custom. The ships of the desert provide a high, if none too comfortable, platform from which to view the pyramids and a shot for a million photo albums.

After seeing Memphis, and its Pharaonic burial ground at Saqqara with the giant Step Pyramid, the mood is set perfectly for the Nile cruise. The flight from Cairo to Aswân leads straight into some serious sightseeing with a visit to the Aga's mausoleum. It is a splendid way to start the cruise part of the holiday because it involves a *felucca* ride. This basic sailing craft has served the Nile Egyptians for centuries and the leisurely voyage across to Kitchener Island is the best possible introduction to the Nile. Some intrepid visitors have imaginatively (if bravely) hired *feluccas* to make the entire journey upriver to Luxor. It has to be the best way to get closest to the river and its communities but it is certainly not an experience for the fastidious. *Feluccas* are not over-endowed with mod cons.

Back on the regular tour, it is time to see Aswân's modern claim to fame, the High Dam which was completed at huge cost in 1971. On an island between it and the old dam, there's Philae Temple which was moved to preserve it from the impact of the new dam. The most famous 'removal' was that of Abu Simbel and there is usually the option of taking a flight to see the temple in its new surroundings. It is a tiring trip as its distance from Aswân means that you end up seeing it at the hottest time of day. Even so, everyone who goes recommends it.

If you decide against Abu Simbel, it does mean there is time for a stroll around the local market before the cruise boat leaves in the evening. As the market is essentially run by the locals for the locals, there is none of the pestering that is normally the lot of tourists visiting 'sights' in Egypt. Because of their comparative affluence, cruise passengers tend to receive more than their fair share of attention when they arrive at each port of call.

From Aswân the boat moves up-river to call first at Kom Ombo for a tour of the ruins of a Ptolemaic temple to which the Romans added a few touches of their own. There's no town or village by the ruins but there are still plenty of boys selling you everything from the ubiquitous *galabiah* (a sort of unisex nightshirt) to postcards — the clean variety! Sending the postcards is a typically unorthodox Egyptian process. The shops where you buy them offer to stamp and send them for you — an offer you can't refuse as finding anywhere else to buy a stamp is impossible. They then proceed to toss them in a drawer that is permanently full of other unstamped cards. Amazingly the system appears to work.

After Kom Ombo, it's Edfu and Esna; they sound like a double-act but are, in fact, the sites of more temples. The one at Edfu has been superbly restored and is probably the best example you will see along the Nile. A nice touch is the transport used to take you from ship to temple: a horse and carriage. Luxor is the next stop but, on most cruises, by no means journey's end. There are temples to visit at Luxor itself and at Karnak nearby. Lines of ram-headed sphinxes used to link the two but now only those at the entrance to Karnak remain, an awe-inspiring reminder of the grandeur that once was there.

Most cruise boats now take you on to Nag Hammâdi for the temples of Abydos, a settlement dating back even further than Memphis. The temples are from more recent times and boast some fascinating wall paintings and cartouches. Dendera Temple at the next port of call is especially lovely with its staircase leading to the roof and an unusual view of the Nile.

The longer cruises sail on to Cairo at this point but most turn back to Luxor for what, in showbusiness, they would call 'the big finish': the Valley of the Kings and Tutankhamun's Tomb. They are on the opposite bank of the Nile to Luxor but there is a regular ferry. Going down into the tombs themselves is very popular but it is not for anyone with even the merest hint of claustrophobia. The stairs are very steep and difficult to negotiate. Cameras have to be left outside and since modern cameras can all look the same, it pays to tag yours so you can identify it among the huge jumble that piles up on busy days.

Even this briefest of descriptions of the archaeological splendours awaiting passengers on a Nile cruise might give the impression that this is 'another day, another temple' type of holiday. It is not. All the excursions are optional and, even if you take them all, because they are timed to start very early and finish before the sun is too far up, there is still plenty of time for relaxing, sunbathing, or just taking in the overwhelming sights, sounds and smells of Egypt. The sight of mysterious women in *purdah*, with just a speck of nose and tiny feet showing; of babies being carried on their mothers' shoulders as the washing is taken down to the banks of the river, and of the expressive faces and gestures of the street vendors as they haggle as though for their very lives ... these are as much a part of the Nile cruise experience as temple-viewing.

Shopping is an experience on its own with bargains to be had in alabaster vases, gold cartouches, tablecloths, rugs and perfumes, provided you understand which currency you are haggling in and realise that they'll start off at at least treble the price they're really asking. Also, since 'change' never seems part of a vendor's equipment, you need to have lots of small coins so as not to lose out on the deal.

The only other word of warning is about avoiding 'gyppy' tummy. Saying 'no' to salads and ice in drinks will give you a better chance but the changes of climate and style of cooking are so great that even those with the strongest of constitutions can succumb. On the brighter side, it is usually only a 24-hour bug. At Karnak, there is a large stone scarab on a plinth around which tourists are invited to trot three times and make a wish. Few wishes do not come true on a Nile cruise, including relief from Pharaoh's Revenge.

JOURNEY DOWN THE THAMES

I have always loved the Thames, ever since those days in the Sixties when I first came to work in London and would take a stroll down by the river between announcing stints at the BBC. My pleasure in London's river has never palled, and I don't think it ever will. I still love walking across Westminster Bridge, looking at the light on the water and the skyline far downstream towards the City. The Thames is a romantic river, full of life and interest and following it downstream from the source to the tideway will take you through some beautiful and typically English scenery, the perfect route for a holiday journey, especially in spring when England always looks at its best.

Although you can make most of this journey without stepping out of the car, the preliminaries have to be made on foot, for the source of the Thames is not all that easy to find. Besides which, the exact point is open to dispute. Most people concede that the river rises by Thameshead Bridge on the A44 near Tetbury, south of Cirencester. The actual source of the river is a spring. This tends to dry up in mid-summer, which is why a springtime visit is recommended. The site in a field is marked by a small plaque, but those who want to photograph something a little more striking can group themselves in front of the statue of Old Father Thames by St John's Lock on the river at Lechlade. Our journey can begin at Thameshead Bridge from where we set off east, towards the distant London Town.

From Thameshead, the road east and the river go through or close to some pretty places, most notably Ashton Keynes. The Thames runs down the main street. A series of bridges spans the river to give the villagers access to their houses. Cricklade, the first main town, is a very old market centre. Here King Alfred thrashed the invading Danes who had rowed their ships up the river, while little Kempsford has a church built with funds donated by John of Gaunt. There is history all the way down this historic river, but this quiet upper part is the ideal area for a picnic, and full of sheltered spots.

At Lechlade one of the Thames' seven tributary rivers, the Leach (or Lech)
flows in, the river widens, and the first pleasure boats appear as, with ever-
increasing frequency, do the first of a long series of Thames-side inns. Then
comes Radcot and the famous Swan Inn, then another tributary arrives, the
Windrush. This is memorable because at the point where the Windrush joins
the Thames at Newbridge there are *two* famous inns, The Maybush and, on the
opposite bank, The Rose Revived. The Newbridge is in fact the oldest bridge on
the river, although some say that honour belongs to the bridge at Radcot, built
about 1270.

Minor roads weave all over the valley now, perfect routes to follow as the
river swings around towards Oxford, but no wise traveller will miss out the
Trout Inn at Godstow. Back in the twelfth century King Henry II kept his
favourite mistress, Fair Rosamund, at Godstow when what is now the Trout Inn
was the guesthouse of the nearby nunnery. Today the Trout is a popular spot
with the students who walk out here in the evening from Oxford, and also with
those travellers in urgent need of a good meal or a pint of ale during a journey
down the river. It's a very pretty spot, the perfect English inn with a wide,
stone-flagged terrace beside the river, and great trout finning quietly in the
waters below the weir. This is also the place to turn off for a visit to Blenheim
Palace, home of the Dukes of Marlborough, or nearby Bladon, to see the grave
of Sir Winston Churchill who was buried here in 1965.

Oxford has been described as both 'a city of dreaming spires' and 'a terrible
waste of time' (though why the latter I shall never know); either way, you have
to go deep into the old college quadrangles to escape the modern accretions of
the successful commercial centre. A college tour is always well worth while, but
if you only have time for one stop, then the Magdalen College deer park is the
one I would choose. Otherwise, just wander about 'The Broad' or 'The High',
and wish you could spend a few years here, with little to do but study.

South and east of Oxford we leave the Upper Thames behind and come to

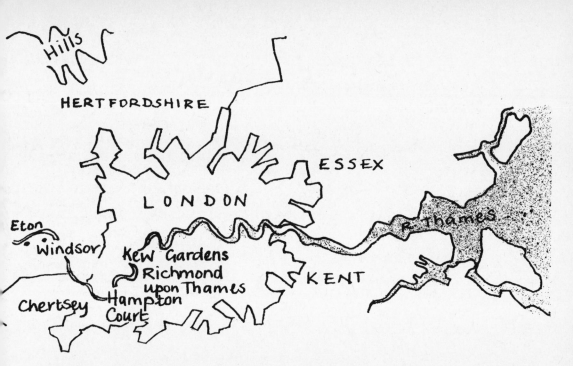

the Middle River, the Thames Valley proper, which will carry us east as far as
Staines. This part of the river has two major towns, Abingdon and Reading, and
a number of smaller ones, like Wallingford, Henley and Marlow, plus a countless
number of small, delightful Thames-side villages. To find them all you have to
do is wander, driving gently around narrow lanes, which will certainly lead to
somewhere that is both very English and quite unspoiled.

To come down the Thames without taking to the water would be a waste and
from now on a day afloat is always possible. You can rent a boat for a day on the
river from any one of a score of boatyards, or take a cruise on one of Salter's
Steamers, which have been plying the waters of the Middle Thames from
Windsor to Oxford since well before the First World War.

With such a vast choice of places to visit, one can afford to be selective.
Abingdon has a fine Town Hall and the beautiful St Helen's Church, as well as
some very good hotels (including the Upper Reaches) and restaurants. On the
way there the Norman church at Iffley with its Romanesque west door is very
photogenic, as is Nuneham Park, which was laid out by 'Capability' Brown.

Clifton Hampden has the 600-year-old Barley Mow Inn, where Jerome K.
Jerome wrote parts of the River Thames classic, *Three Men in a Boat*. The
author is buried at Ewelme further downstream.

Past Clifton Hampden the countryside changes yet again. The long beech-
wood escarpment of the Chiltern Hills looms ahead, the river curving to breach
it at the Goring Gap while, off to the south, the rolling Berkshire Downs block
off the sky and most of the Harwell cooling towers. The place to stop
hereabouts, either for lunch or a night, is at The George Hotel in Dorchester, an
old coaching inn just across the road from Dorchester Abbey. The Abbey is
newly restored. It is a beautiful building, and houses the shrine of St Birinius, a
strange find in a straggling Thames-side village otherwise full of antique shops.

Past Dorchester the main road cuts off right into Wallingford and Crowmarsh
Gifford, but I recommend following the river for a while before turning off left

through Benson to the little village of Ewelme. Ewelme is a real gem, with a fine Perpendicular church, a medieval almshouse, and a church school, all erected in the fifteenth century by the Duchess of Suffolk, granddaughter of Geoffrey Chaucer. Her tomb in the church is quite magnificent, but even those who — like me — find history of finite appeal, will still enjoy Ewelme. The local industry is the cultivation of watercress, which grows in great shallow chalk pools all over the village, so the tinkle of water is everywhere. Linger here, then take a very minor road which will lead you back to the river at the twin villages of Streatley and Goring, deep in the Goring Gap.

Although they lie on separate banks, these villages can be enjoyed together by wandering across the linking road-bridge above the lock and weirs. There are several fine pubs, notably The Miller of Mansfield, and a good hotel, The Swan, as well as one of England's finest cheese shops. The Ridgeway footpath, which emerges from the Chiltern Hills on the river bank before climbing the steep slopes of the escarpment, can be followed for a mile or so, but these two Thames-side villages are really built for relaxation. They are places for riverside picnics, to sit and watch the river-craft passing through the lock, or just to lie back in the long grass and sunbathe.

Skirt Reading, which has nothing much worth stopping for except the ruins of a Cluniac abbey, turn off the A4 road just east of the pretty village of Sonning, pass Shiplake and you come to the town of Henley, home of the Royal Regatta. In many ways, Henley is the most Thames-side of all Thames-side towns. Here you feel the river is really important, the focus of the whole place. Apart from the river and the regatta, Henley has a quite remarkable range of ethnic restaurants as well as a famous inn, The Red Lion, where King Charles stayed in 1632.

Leaving Henley, our road runs along the left bank of the river past Medmenham to Marlow, a Georgian town with a fine bridge spanning the river and leading to the village of Bisham. Bisham Abbey, now a sports centre, was once the home of the Hoby family and the site of a Thames-side legend. In the days of the first Queen Elizabeth, Lady Hoby, lady-in-waiting to the Queen, was a noted disciplinarian. When her small son blotted his copybook, she beat him severely and locked him in a dark cupboard. When she was suddenly summoned to the Court at Windsor she forgot to release him. Unknown to the servants the child was left in the cupboard and died. They say that the weeping, remorseful ghost of Lady Hoby still haunts the Abbey. That is as may be, but her tomb — and that of her son — are certainly in the nearby church.

Cookham, a few miles away, yet another beautiful village, was once the home of the artist Sir Stanley Spencer. Sights to see here include the church, the Stanley Spencer Gallery in the main street, and for lunch or dinner, the famous Bell and Dragon hotel. On the hill above Cookham is Cliveden House at Taplow. The former home of the Astor family is now owned by the National Trust and leased as an hotel. The grounds of Cliveden are magnificent and from the terrace there is a particularly fine view up river towards Marlow.

From here a short drive by-passing Maidenhead brings us to Eton and Windsor, together worth a full day of anyone's holiday. You should see the Castle and Eton College of course, wander the narrow streets and perhaps take a trip on a Salter's Steamer.

This wandering riverside holiday can go on, to Chertsey and Hampton Court, up to the start of the tidal waters at Teddington where, some say, the true Thames ends and London River begins. On the tideway there is Richmond and Kew Gardens and Syon House and, if you keep going, the Houses of Parliament and Big Ben, as good a place as any to end a famous journey.

WINTER

I have never understood why the holiday calendar hasn't been turned upside down and winter made more important than summer. Summer seems a silly time to go away: it is in winter we are really in need of escape.

Ask the swallows. They don't muck about waiting for the pipes to burst and the gas bills to swell. First sign of a nip in the air and they're off, no messing, direct flight to the sun. But what do we do? Just when Britain is at its greenest and warmest, when the days are long and the flowers are out and there is a considerable chance of sun, we up and off. Whereas in winter we sit it out, slithering about on icy roads, trussed up in our thermals, cursing the cold and the damp. If ever there was a need for palm trees, surely it is then.

So here are some ideas to change the habits of a lifetime. In January the sunshine is only four hours away, hibernating in the Canary Islands. There's sunshine in Bali too but it will take more than four hours to reach it. But then there is more than sunshine when you get there.

There is more to winter than simply sunshine — snow, for a start. My three winter sports centres are all quite different. Stylish St Moritz puts the ritz into skiing. Nowadays there is always so much else going on there that it sometimes seems the slopes are incidental. At Val d'Isère skiing is all. Val d'Isère is to snow what Bordeaux is to grapes — a place of earnest pilgrimage — while Söll, in Austria, combines something of both worlds. It appeals to funseekers and skiiers alike.

And then, after all that, where is my final choice for a holiday in winter? Why, Britain, of course. Brilliant mornings, brittle with frost, comfortable country hotels, roaring log fires and old habits all die hard.

THE CANARY ISLANDS

The Canary Islands form a scattered archipelago off the west coast of Africa — which is less than 70 miles away at its nearest point. This ensures winter sunshine, but the mildness of the islands' climate is helped by the influence of the Gulf Stream. The islands are not all *that* hot, though; winter temperatures hover between 60°F and 70°F, whilst in the summer it rises to the 80s. There is usually a breeze; the mountain tops can attract cloud cover, and the air is fairly humid and generally mild. The word that comes to mind about Canary Islands' weather is 'pleasant', but a tan, even in December, is practically guaranteed.

The Canaries archipelago actually consists of seven islands: Grand Canary, Lanzarote, Tenerife, Fuerteventura, La Palma, Gomera and Hierro, plus some islets and scattered rocks. The islands vary considerably, from the somewhat barren, like Lanzarote, to the green and lush Grand Canary, but they all offer ever-improving scope for tourism, especially for winter holidays. It also helps that there are no local taxes or Customs charges. Duty-free shopping is just one good reason to visit the Canaries because apart from cut-price cameras, watches, tape-recorders and jewellery, the islands can also offer a good range of local crafts, embroidery, pottery, ceramics and basket-work.

Catering for an international clientele, the Canaries can offer an equally wide range of cuisine, but one with strong Spanish overtones and a bias towards fish and the fresh local produce. Those who always like to try local dishes rather than over-familiar 'international' cuisine need not be disappointed, because the Canaries do boast their own distinctive dishes. Most common, apart from watercress soup, is *sancocho canario*, a fish salad served with a hot sauce, or *salmorejo*, rabbit stew, and of course, bananas and tomatoes, which the islands export in great quantities, but keep the freshest and finest for local consumption.

Tenerife is the largest island and has a varied climate. The rugged terrain is marked by a central mountain range now preserved as a National Park and rising to the peak of Monte Tiedé, which can hold onto heavy cloud and give you a sunless day. Choosing a resort here is dependent on whether you prefer the attractions of a big city, like the main port and capital Santa Cruz, or prefer to laze on a beach. In Tenerife you even get a choice of sand — golden or black. The main tourist centre in Tenerife is Puerto de la Cruz, which has several beaches, and an elaborate park of public bathing pools along the Avenida de Colon. Puerto de la Cruz is a real tourist town with bars and boutiques, discos, pavement cafés, restaurants ... and cranes. New hotels and apartment blocks are going up all the time, so cranes tend to dominate the skyline. But if you like a lively holiday, with all day in the sun and half the night in the disco, then Puerto de la Cruz could be just the answer.

Rather quieter are Playa de las Americas, (although on one visit, in the early part of the year, holidaymakers were packed sardine-like by the swimming-pool), and Los Cristianos, on the south coast. The latter is an attractive town which is being steadily transformed into a major tourist centre. Since Tenerife is such a large island several days can be devoted to excursions: to Monte Tiedé, to the wine centre of Tacorante, or to the beaches at El Socorro.

Fuerteventura, although next in size, is a total contrast. A much quieter island, it is best known as a centre for sports fishermen who fish for tuna or swordfish in the deep waters between the island and the African coast. The opening of the new airport at Fuerteventura may soon change this idyll but for the moment Fuerteventura remains one of those islands virtually untouched by

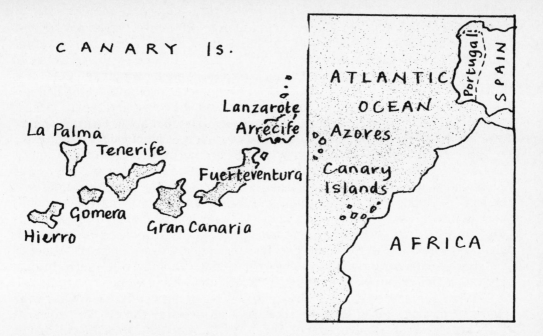

tourism, although there are plenty of hotels for the present number of visitors and some good seafood restaurants.

Grand Canary is a very agreeable island, much less brash than Tenerife. The interior is green and beautiful. There are lots of places worth visiting, some excellent beaches and a very varied terrain which includes an expanse of desert as well as high mountains and deep valleys, the mountain-sides cloaked with banana plantations. Las Palmas, the capital, which lies on the northern tip of the island and is one of the most attractive cities in the archipelago, is flanked by two beautiful beaches, the Playa de Las Cantaras to the west, and the Playa de Malpaso to the south. Grand Canary has a long tradition of winter tourism and is very popular with the older, more sedate visitor.

Before I move on to my favourite Canary island, Lanzarote, we might pass briefly over the smaller ones, La Palma, Gomera and Hierro. La Palma soars up from the sea to the peak of Roque de los Muchachas. The capital, Santa Cruz — an old Spanish colonial town with parts which date back to the sixteenth century — actually lies on the edge of the vast Caldera de Tarirende crater. The crater is the largest in this volcanic archipelago, and is now a National Park. La Palma is the most attractive of the smaller islands, very green, covered with pines and banana trees, and well worth a visit. But those who prefer something really small and right off the well-beaten track are sure to find it on either Gomera or Hierro.

And now Lanzarote. Lanzarote grows on you. Driving across the island from the airport at Arrecife, or even looking down as the aircraft flies in, many first-time visitors are appalled — it looks so *barren* — but give it time. After a while the very starkness and the contrast it offers with beautiful flowers, white houses with emerald-green doors and window frames, becomes very appealing — and that's without any help from the sea and sun and sky.

Lanzarote has been developed all of a piece, thanks to the influence of Cesar Manrique, an artist who has exercised a strong but largely benign influence over the island for many years. It is Manrique who has decreed that no tall buldings should be erected — though one was put up while he was absent abroad — and Manrique stood firmly against the erecting of roadside advertisements, garish neon, or all the other touristic excrescences. As a result, Lanzarote is an unusually clean, neat and charming island.

Arrecife, the capital, is a small town of about 20,000 people and, as the name implies, is built on a reef. Apart from being a port it has a number of hotels and many good restaurants. The island is intensely cultivated with black volcanic soil proving rich enough to produce great quantities of melons, tomatoes, peas, grapes, corn, even tobacco, all grown in small fields all over the island. Beaches are plentiful (with some catering for nudists) but the main sights on the island are the great caves at Los Jameos, which now contain a restaurant and a deep emerald-green pool, and the still hot volcano on Timanfaya, the Mountain of Fire. Evidence that this volcano is still awake is provided by the steam that gushes back when a bucket of water is dumped down a crevasse in the rocks, and by the fact that the mountain restaurant grills its steaks on volcanic heat — although the last eruption took place nearly 200 years ago.

Near Timanfaya visitors can go on another popular Lanzarote excursion, a camel ride. Scores of patient camels wait beside the road, ready to take tourists on long caravan trains up the black slopes of the nearby mountains. Otherwise, the main touring can be done by car. There are plenty of places to visit, mostly for the fine views over the coast. One particularly beautiful viewpoint is on the Bateria del Rio, the most northern point on the island, from where you can look down on the little island of Graciosa far below.

Lanzarote, quieter than the bigger islands in the group, offers visitors a good mixture of sunshine, beaches, interesting excursions and reasonable food. As a winter sun destination the Canaries are a good choice and Lanzarote remains one of my own favourite winter islands.

ST MORITZ

Once upon a time, and not so many years ago at that, skiing was generally accepted as an upper-class or, as we now say, an up-market activity. That was never entirely true, but certainly until the early Sixties it was safe to assume that anyone sporting a suntan in February was a young English mi'lord just back from the snow-slopes.

All that has changed. Well over half a million Britons, drawn from every social group, go skiing every year and some resorts, Söll in Austria, Sauze d'Oulx in Italy, Formigal in Spain, Méribel in France, have become almost exclusively British. If we take the word 'exclusively' in its second sense, the same is true of the world's first and most stately ski resort, the Queen of the winter season, St Moritz. St Moritz is different. St Moritz is fantastic. St Moritz has style. St Moritz is simply a different world, a place where the moon's a balloon, full of pretty people. St Moritz comes alive at the first whisper of a settling snowflake, summoning the Beautiful People from all over the world to ski on the Corviglia or the Corvasch, or simply to sit about, seeing and being seen, on the terraces of the Palace or the Kulm or the Carlton, those famous watering holes for the international jet-set. Even if you can't join in, St Moritz is a fun place to visit but, and I have to say it, some aspects of St Moritz are bizarre.

Before that last comment raises hackles at the Swiss Tourist Office, let me add that as a resort, for a quiet winter holiday or some super downhill skiing, St

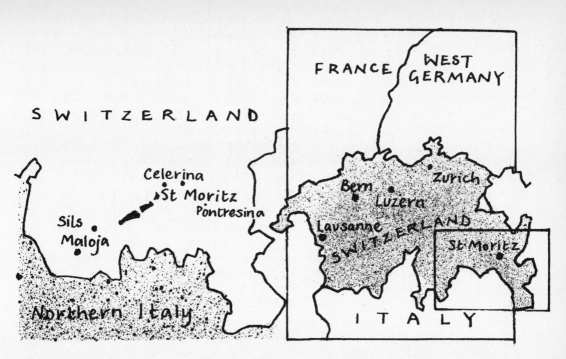

Moritz must be listed among the best in the world. I don't mean that the resort is bizarre — I mean the *people*. It's hard to believe that poeple can still flash carats of gold jewellery about, wearing a ring on every finger and a snow-sweeping fur coat, dark glasses and a constantly-maintained Riviera tan — at ten o'clock in the morning — but they do hereabouts ... and that's only the men.

Sitting in any café or slope-side bar, watching the St Moritz parade go by is one of the pleasures few other ski resorts can offer. For that you must go to St Moritz, or — so rumour has it — Gstaad, but Gstaad is said (at least in St Moritz) to be a bit flash and *nouveau*. St Moritz still caters for old money, and those with a certain style; surely we must all fit in there somewhere?

The first fact to bear in mind about St Moritz is that it is not just a ski resort. It's a winter sports resort. In fact, St Moritz is *the* winter sports resort, with a whole host of things to see and do, apart from large amounts of downhill skiing. It caters for the young and not-so-young, for the family party, and the roving single, but most of all for the well-heeled. St Moritz is not cheap, but it does give value for money.

Unlike most ski resorts, where the lift system and the ski runs are the focal point of interest, here it is the ambience which counts. St Moritz is an old Swiss town set above a long series of lakes fed by the Inn River in the long and beautiful Engadine Valley. It has been a ski resort almost from the moment that Alpine skiing was invented about a hundred years ago, and rose to its present celebrity in the years between the wars when the rich and famous divided their winter between the slopes of St Moritz and the shores of the Mediterranean.

Today the town has expanded and falls into two parts, the *Bad*, the old spa on the floor of the valley, and the *Dorf*, up on the hillside. These two parts are divided by the tracks of the railway line which runs the whole length of the valley and gives the roving skier access to a number of other resorts like Pontresina, Maloja, Celerina and Sils, which lie up and down the Engadine. St

Moritz is still very much a hotel town where much of the activity centres in or around one of the major, long-established hotels. The Palace is the best known, the Suvretta House is coming up fast, and the Kulm and Carlton are ever popular with the British. All these hotels are stylish, but the Kulm can act as a model for the rest.

It is big and Victorian, built on a splendid scale, with vast lounges and a long mirror and crystal chandelier-bedecked dining room, catering for the après-ski revels. It was built in the middle of the last century and has always been a deluxe five-star hotel, which is another way of saying that it isn't cheap. In fact, well over half the accommodation in St Moritz is in four- or five-star hotels. At the Kulm a four-course dinner is served each evening, with gala nights at least twice a week, when black tie for the men and long gowns for the ladies is definitely *en-tenue*. On other evenings a suit and cocktail dress is the very minimum you can get away with. Like the Palace and the Carlton, the Kulm is very smart. Those who want a change from the main dining room can divert to the Rôtisserie des Chevaliers, which is strictly *à la carte*, but if you fancy going native and trying Swiss or local Engadine specialities, then it's off to the La Stuvetta which is *Gast-Stube* in style and good for a cheese or beef fondue. Later, you can dance the night away in the Sunny Bar nightclub which has live bands until the small hours. By no means are all the Kulm's regular guests keen young skiers so the hotel arranges bridge tournaments, has a playroom for the children, an ice-rink for the more athletic, plus that ever-more essential pool, sauna and massage parlour. Throw in a wide selection of guests, drawn from every nation with two gold coins to rub together, and there you have it — the lot!

The town itself is pleasant, pin-bright and very lively with plenty of tearooms, piano bars, restaurants of every kind, and a vast quantity of very smart boutiques and jewellers. Nightlife is often centred on the hotels, like the Kulm, with the King's Club disco at the Palace as the main hot-spot, though the Steffani is less expensive and therefore more popular with some.

But what about those winter sports that made St Moritz so famous in the first place?

Let's start with the skiing: it is excellent. As usual in Switzerland, the bulk of the runs are intermediate 'reds' so the degree of difficulty rather depends on the line you choose to take from top to bottom. There are around 250 miles of downhill piste on slopes well supplied with bars and restaurants. Top slopes are the Corviglia, a south-facing mountain, excellent in the morning sun, with good runs down from the Piz Nair, the Trais Flours (or Three Flowers) and Glund, and good runs down to the *Dorf*, the *Bad* and the little village of Celerina. This last run depends on the snow cover and can be quite tricky if there is ice about. The Corvatsch is excellent between the top and middle station and has one very fine run to St Moritz Bad. The lifts are a mixture of chairs and drags, with cable cars for the long uphill hikes. Other areas well worth visiting — and make an effort to do so, because at St Moritz there is a tendency to get on one slope and stay there all week — are those of Furtschellas, above Sils, the Morteratsch glacier above Bernina, and the long, heavily mogulled Lagalp. In short, there is plenty of skiing, especially for those of the intermediate-to-expert ability. Facilities for absolute beginners, on the other hand, could justify some extra attention. But there's more sport in St Moritz than just skiing.

The day might begin with a stroll from the Kulm down the road to the Cresta Run. This icy slide is now over 100 years old but still drawing dare-devils from all over the world. Beginners can try it out if they are really keen. Those who fail to negotiate the narrow, icy trough that plummets towards Celerina and fly off their sled — or skeleton — at the Shuttlecock turn, even earn the right to the special Shuttlecock tie. The Cresta Run hearties gather on the Kulm terrace from about noon, so that is the place to make contact.

Across the road from the Cresta Run is the Bobsleigh course. One of the more alarming sights in St Moritz is the sudden appearance beside you of a bobsleigh on the snow-wall turn beside the road. A four-man bob hurtles round the bend, glued to the ice-wall by gravity just feet from the roadside. Life is never dull in St Moritz.

To those violent pastimes can be added curling, ice-skating, toboggan and ski-bob rides, horse-riding, hot-air ballooning, hang-gliding and, almost as important as downhill skiing, cross-country skiing. Cross-country skiing, or *Nordic* or *langlauf* or *ski de fond*, may be a sport with a multitude of names but it is much older than Alpine skiing. Man has been sliding about the winter world on Nordic skis for over 3000 years. Compared with that, downhill skiing is a very *parvenu* activity. The Engadine Valley is seamed with cross-country ski trails and there are probably as many Nordic skiers in the resort as there are the downhill variety.

St Moritz and the neighbouring villages of the Engadine Valley comprise something of a mecca for Nordic skiers. Once a year it is the setting for the 26-mile Engadine ski marathon which draws up to 15,000 skiers from all over the world. The time allowed to complete the course is six hours, but the winners usually finish in about an hour and a half.

Every skier will want to visit St Moritz at least once in his or her lifetime, for it really is the culmination of everything that a ski resort should be. It has a long season, good snow, a well-thought-out lift system and a great deal to do apart from skiing, both on and off the slopes. These days that may be true of many other resorts, but St Moritz also has style — and that is getting a good deal harder to find.

SÖLL

Austria has always been popular with British skiers. That uniquely Austrian combination of clear air, good snow, pleasant pin-bright hotels, good food and cheerful nightlife, hits just the right chord with the British, even if improving skiers find the Austrian slopes a little limited after a year or two.

Austria is a great ski country, but the skiing is particularly suited to beginners so, as a first piece of advice, if you have never been skiing before, choose Austria for the first trip. Amongst all its other advantages it has good ski-schools where the instructors speak English, a variety of not-too-testing slopes, and plenty to do in the evening, or even in the daytime, if you go off the whole idea of sliding down mountains.

That is not to say that only beginners will enjoy Austria — far from it. Choose the right resort and Austrian skiing is unmatched. Even keen skiers will want to visit Kitzbühel, St Anton, Schladming or, if they did not go there the first time, Söll.

Söll is the ideal resort for those young skiers who like a lot of skiing mixed with plenty of noisy nightlife. With the five other villages of the Grossraum circuit, Brixen Ellmau, Going, Hopfgarten and Scheffau, Söll offers the closest Austria can get to the great ski areas of France, such as the Trois-Vallées and

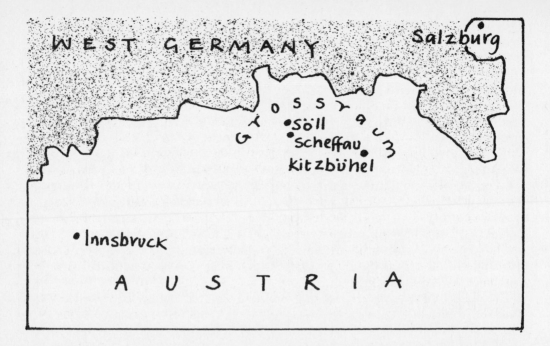

the Portes du Soleil. And what the area lacks in skiing capacity it more than compensates for in friendliness, nightlife and a wide choice of things to see and do.

Söll is by far the largest of the Grossraum villages and, if the voices in the streets are anything to go by, the one most popular with the British. Practically every major British ski holiday operator includes Söll in its winter programme. Although the really wild spirits are said to gather at Sauze d'Oulx in Italy, Söll still attracts large numbers of the exuberant young who find the local nightlife just as attractive as the steeper slopes of the Hohe Salve. Older skiers might just prefer to stay somewhere a little quieter, like the pretty village of Scheffau, from which access to the Grossraum circuit is just as easy. The nights are much less noisy without the young folk trooping home from the discos in the small hours.

The Grossraum skiing is ideal for beginners and improving intermediates, even up to the first stages of the expert level. In other words there is plenty of it but much of it is not too demanding. The Söll slopes are the most difficult and include one very tricky black run from the steep slopes of the Hohe Salve (1830m). These slopes face north and therefore hold the snow well. As always the degree of difficulty on any run depends on the visibility, the snow conditions, and the line the skier takes, so that many otherwise pleasant reds in the Grossraum circuit can turn a little black when the cloud comes in or the snow turns icy.

The links between the lift systems of the various resorts are fairly good and steadily improving. New lifts and T-bar drags are being added to cut out or reduce the amount of walking between lifts. That used to be the major snag with skiing in this otherwise well-planned area. The one walk that really cannot be avoided, since the ski-shuttle buses are far from frequent, is the one from Söll itself to the foot of the main Hohe Salve chair lift. Although more ski buses are promised, the crowds continue to grow. Beginners can find this a problem, for although the nursery slopes are beside the main lift, they hardly slope at all and are often without snow. Most of the classes therefore take place on Salvenmoos plateau above which is much steeper than the valley floor. The long blue run down the road back to Söll is often icy and a really crowded ski-motorway in the late afternoon.

As in any ski resort as popular as Söll, large crowds can mean long lift queues, especially at weekends when the locals come up from Innsbruck or Salzburg, but with new lifts being added all the time, this problem is at least being contained. Beginners will probably find the local Söll skiing perfectly adequate for their first two or three weeks. Second-year skiers, or better, will certainly need the full and more expensive Grossraum pass which will let them explore the region during the day before returning to Söll for the obligatory *Glühwein* before dinner and the evening frolics. Access to the Grossraum circuit is actually easier from Scheffau, but Söll is much livelier after dark.

Söll is a very Austrian resort, scrupulously clean, very friendly, and still very much a village although many new hotels and a large sports centre with swimming pool and saunas have been built recently. Like most Austrian resorts, the accommodation is mainly in hotels — chalet and self-catering holidays have not really caught on yet in Austria. The Hotel Post is the oldest hotel, right in the centre of the village and close to the nightlife, but beginners might prefer the Ingeborg or the Eisenmann, which are close to the nursery slopes. Staying in them cuts out a lot of walking — and that's something you'll be glad of if it's your first time in those heavy boots, which have given me some of my most uncomfortable moments.

The nightlife is a mixture of the traditional Austrian and that preferred by the British abroad. This means that the evening starts soon after ski-school in any one of half-a-dozen cafés, or the hotel coffee shops, where creamy coffees, hot chocolate, *Schnapps* or *Glühwein*, plus the odd sticky cake or two go down well to the sound of music from a group or juke-box, while the skiers shout about their exploits during the day and lay plans for the evening. After a bath, dinner is taken either in a local restaurant or at the hotel. Austrian food is popular with the British. Typical hotel fare would be a soup and a main course, often veal or a stew, followed by a rich, sweet pudding, aided by plenty of good Austrian wine. Most of the hotels offer a fondue evening at least once a week. All the tour operators arrange evening events and excursions for their guests. After dinner, it's out on the town, possibly for the obligatory Tyrolean evening. No ski holiday to Austria is complete without sight and sound of the '*Vood-Choppers' Tanz*', or the '*Iron-Vorkers Tanz*', both complete with stamping, yodelling and thigh slapping; many of the dancers are instructors at the ski school. It's all very jolly and a definite must for any family party.

Söll has no lack of discos, notably the Whisky Mühle, which is the one with the latest music and the most space. Austrian discos must be the only ones in the world where the hard rock stops now and again for a Viennese waltz. Even the young Brits soon join in and whirl their partners about the floor.

Folklore and fondue evenings apart, there is no lack of outdoor après-ski activity in Söll in the hours between slope and disco. A visit to the sports centre for a swim (you will need a bathing hat) or a sauna is one way to ease muscles tired by skiing. If you need more outdoor activities, or want to try other winter sports, there are toboggan runs, moonlight sleigh rides, and an ice-rink for skating or curling. Those who find that downhill skiing is just that bit too exciting can try cross-country skiing along the valley floor. Cross-country skiing is very popular at all the Austrian resorts and the facilities at Söll are excellent with good equipment for hire and plenty of waymarked *loipe*, or tracks.

Instruction in downhill and cross-country skiing is provided by the Grossraum ski-schools which are all very good. As I said earlier, most Austrian instructors speak more than adequate English and in Austrian ski-schools an increasing number of instructors are BASI (British Association of Ski Instructors)-trained teachers from the UK, New Zealand or Australia. The schools offer four hours instruction per day, six days a week, and those beginners who stick at it can expect to be getting along well by Thursday afternoon.

However, unless the skiing proves totally absorbing, a day off the slopes for an excursion to one of the nearby cities is always a good idea. Here Söll is particularly fortunate because it lies almost mid-way between Innsbruck and Salzburg. Of the two, I would choose Innsbruck. Salzburg may have Mozart but Innsbruck is much more lively, with good shopping, good restaurants and a fascinating old town, all narrow, cobbled alleys and dark arcades. It is perfect for exploring on a cold winter's day.

And that is Söll, an attractive, typically Austrian resort, ideal for lively, enthusiastic younger skiers, especially beginners, or anyone who will enjoy a fun-filled winter holiday.

VAL D'ISÈRE

Anyone who has worn a pair of skis for as long as two minutes will realise that skiing, for all its speed and grace, is certainly not as easy as it looks. Most people persevere with lessons until they can ski to their own personal satisfaction, after which they retire to the slope-side bar to watch the crowds whizz by, and are more than happy to ski the less challenging slopes in the pauses between frequent coffee stops. That's the general picture, but that is not the case with the skiers who flock to the resort of Val d'Isère.

Val d'Isère is the ski resort for *serious* skiers. Other well-known resorts or ski areas, like the great inter-linked networks of the Trois Vallées, or the Franco-Swiss Portes de Soleil, may have more lifts and runs but when it comes to seeking the hard stuff, the ski-buff and the ski-bums flock to Val d'Isère.

Glamorous names for ski areas, like the Trois Vallées and the Portes du Soleil — the Gates of the Sun, no less — are becoming ever more popular in the ski world. The people of Val d'Isère, ever eager to take up a good idea, have adopted 'La Planète Blanche', the White Planet, to describe that vast expanse of steep slope powder snow that now, with lifts, links Val to the neighbouring — if not exactly twin — resort of Tignes. Since the famous Olympic downhill champion Jean-Claude Killy lives in Val d'Isère, the sub-title of La Planète Blanche is 'L'Espace Killy' — the Killy Space — and the wearing of Jean-Claude Killy ski gear is almost *de rigueur* in Val, at least when the great man is around. Picture Val then as the most dedicated, state-of-the-art ski resort in the Alps. You don't go to Val to enjoy yourself — you go there to ski.

Famous as it now is among ski buffs, Val did not begin life as a ski resort. It is not one of those high mountain places created after the Second World War simply to exploit the rising winter holiday market. It's an old, very old, village of the Tarentaise, sunk deep in a steep-sided valley beside the rushing river Isère, and it first took an interest in skiing as long ago as 1932. The Solaire cable car was installed in 1943, during the dark days of the Second World War. Since

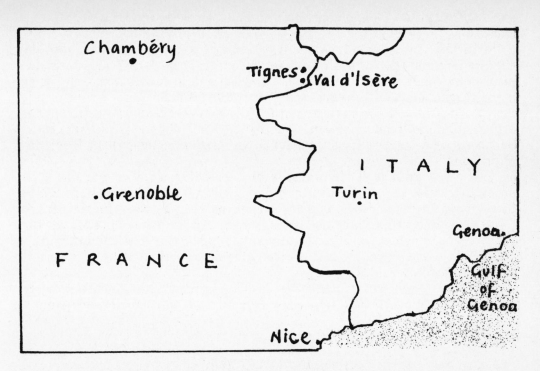

then the snowfields beneath the peaks of the Pissaillas glacier, at 3000m, and the Grande Motte, 3650m, have slowly been enriched, if not enhanced, by a spreading interlocked series of lifts which now link Val and Tignes into one ski area. This is nice timing for the 1992 Winter Olympics, which will be held in various resorts in and around the Tarentaise with the most spectacular event of all, the Men's Downhill, taking place on the famous OK (Oreiller-Killy) run at Val d'Isère.

If this paints a broad outline of the Val d'Isère–Tignes ski area, keen skiers will be interested in some of the practical details. The resort's ski area runs at between 1800 and 3350m, which ensures a long ski season, certainly from December to April, and plenty of varied runs on- and off-piste. The total ski area is given as 10,000 hectares (say 26,000 acres), laced by 300 km (180 miles) of marked piste, which should keep even the most dedicated ski-buff busy for a day or two. Although the runs are constantly being extended and upgraded, the current division of the 125 runs is that ten are black (difficult, and for experts), red, 32 (for keen or improving intermediates), and green, 83 (for beginners and the less enthusiastic). What has happened to the blue (easy) runs, I cannot tell.

Off-piste skiing is ever more popular, though skiers should only venture off-piste if they are very good or accompanied by a guide, and even then not if the chequered avalanche flags are flying. Val and Tignes offer great scope for off-piste skiing and ski-touring across the Tarentaise. Those who prefer to stay on-piste can get round the slopes and runs quite easily on a network of no less than 115 varied lifts and poma-tows, of which 59 are from, or on, the Val d'Isère side. This number is being added to constantly, and will no doubt have increased by the time you read this, or arrive in Val d'Isère.

Since Val is trying to attract more beginners and intermediate skiers, as the seed corn of future custom, the ski-school also merits inspection. Jean-Claude Killy is consultant to the Val d'Isère ski-school, which can muster 180 *moniteurs* on a good day, including three world champions and no less than 15 former coaches of the French ski team. There is also a Snow Fun Ski-School for the less dedicated, which tends to receive more than its fair share of British beginners, eager to learn not just the snow-plough, but how to ski-surf or mono-ski, those ever more common snow sports, which they claim to teach in no less than five languages. All French ski instructors now have to speak — or at least instruct in — a second language, and most of them opt for English. I must add that students hoping for an in-depth discussion on exactly what is wrong with the carving of their parallel turn may be doomed to disappointment. The bulk of the English instruction stops at the 'Toin on ze bomps an ben yor k-k-neez' level, but at least it's a start, and there are now fewer complaints about incomprehensible or impatient instructors. Besides, most of the people who come to Val d'Isère can ski already.

Like Val d'Isère, Tignes has to be visualised as a modern resort, somewhat over-commercial, but highly organised with a very definite bias towards the better skier who likes to ski all day and is not really very interested in the snugness of the houses or the ambience of the resort after dark, although a certain amount of nightlife never comes amiss. This is a good thing because neither place would score many points on the architectural beauty scale and Tignes is almost an eyesore ... although, like most of these high-mountain resorts, it looks a lot better when draped with snow. On the other hand, there is a reasonable amount of après-ski in Val. It has some good restaurants, and excellent if expensive shopping, notably for the latest ski-wear. You can eat oysters, chilled on a bed of snow, in a small restaurant half-way down the main street of Val. Since there are over 50 restaurants to choose from, including seven perched high on the slopes, no one need go hungry or miss out on that delicious cooking which you expect in France. Those who like to go on after dinner can choose from a couple of piano bars, eight discos and two cinemas in Val or, if they stay across the mountain in Tignes, from three 'pubs' and three discos. Val has a number of bars inhabited almost exclusively by the British, notably the famous Dick's Tea Bar.

To complete this survey of the skiing at Val d'Isère, we must also look at the facilities of Tignes, for the two resorts are so closely linked that anyone skiing from the one place will spend a great deal of time among the runs and lifts of the other, a point to bear in mind when purchasing a ski-pass. Tignes has 98 marked pistes, two black, ten red, five green and (I'm happy to say) 22 blue, with the steep Tovière Black run as the one which sorts out the men from the wimps. The less macho go for La Sache or La Grande Motte, which are said to be red, but keen skiers reckon there are really three kinds of red run — red 'reds', French 'reds', and Val d'Isère/Tignes 'reds' — which are somewhat black ... you have been warned!

On the entertainment front, Tignes has one famous restaurant, Le Ski d'Or, an hotel-restaurant, about four miles from the resort at Val Claret. It is not cheap but it is very good and worth a long lunch stop or an evening excursion. Besides that there is a host of 'snacks' or bistros where the usual range of Savoyard dishes, mostly of the ribsticking fondue or stew variety, are just the thing to round off the skiing day.

An area lift pass covers both resorts at some cost, but the beginners' slopes have some free lifts and their own, cheaper, lift pass. The transfer time from Geneva airport is about four hours, although this time is likely to diminish as the roads are improved for the 1992 Olympics. The two resorts lean towards self-catering, although Val, which draws many French skiers, has plenty of small, simple hotels. Most of the major British ski holiday companies, especially those offering chalet parties, have villas, chalets and apartments to let. Those who fancy something more *soignée* can choose from one or two up-market hotels, and family groups can make use of the ski-kindergarten or the ski-nursery.

But will you enjoy it? If you are a good, keen, even aggressive skier, the answer is almost certainly yes. Val, in particular, is a very French resort, so if you like the French and can get along in their language, so much the better. The ski facilities are first-class and constantly improving, so for these people for whom the only thing that matters about a ski holiday is the skiing — and lots of it please — I can unhesitatingly recommend the Val d'Isère–Tignes area for the ski trip of a lifetime. Those who are less committed might choose to go somewhere else first, but when that parallel turn on steep ice has finally been perfected, Val d'Isère will still be there, with as much skiing as even the keenest skier will want to handle on his or her winter holiday.

BALI

It's like one of those word association tests: say Bali and most of us (at least those above a certain age!) immediately pipe up 'South Pacific'. The famous film musical created a lasting impression of an exotic tropical paradise, and 'Bali Hai' was the most evocative song, sung to the backdrop of a brooding volcanic island.

In fact, South Pacific was filmed mainly in Hawaii and, at the last count, at least three countries were laying claim to one of their islands having 'played' Bali Hai in the movie. The truth of the matter is, though, that the Indonesian island of Bali (it's not even in the Pacific) needs no help from Hollywood. It is a magical island in its own right, even more colourful than the film in which a new colour process was tried. (In some prints all the leading players had complexions which changed hue every time they turned round.) Bali's colour is 100 per cent genuine and it comes not just from the rich fertile countryside, the towering mountains and white sand beaches, but from its people, their traditions and flair for ceremony.

If someone ever bottled happiness and tried to sell it, they would be wasting their time on Bali. The two-and-a-half million population have their own highly successful recipe and if you've heard that before, on Bali this is the genuine article. Quite literally every day is a holiday in Bali as each temple on the island has a festival every year (Bali's year is only half as long as ours) and there are around 10,000 temples. There are about three in every village so you don't have to visit many places during your stay to be sure of happening upon a colourful parade. Even death is a cause for celebration as the Balinese believe it is a release to the next, better stage in life. Some of the best and liveliest shows are cremations.

Balinese are almost all Hindus but theirs is no ordinary branch of the religion. They are Agama-Hindu, which is a more relaxed and joyful version than the one that holds sway in India. Overwhelmingly the Balinese are a people enjoying life and at peace with themselves, a rare experience to encounter in travelling the world these days.

But peace is relative, of course, and there is certainly little peace — as in 'peace and quiet' — to be found in Kuta, one of the three main resort areas. It has a good beach and plenty of the glorious sunsets that you quickly find are

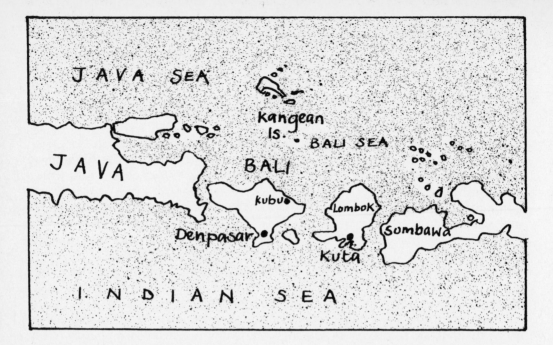

Bali's trademark, but it also has an excess of traffic, too many shops and too many people. If disco/pub nightlife is your thing, it is the only place to be, but it is more like a suburb of Sydney than a Balinese village. Still, like all of Bali, it has charm, even if it is less conspicuous than elsewhere on the island.

Kuta is close to the main airport on the west coast in the south of the island. On the east coast, the other side of Bali capital Denpasar, Sanur is much more attractive, despite a tremendous growth in popularity which has made it the top destination for British and European visitors. The white sand beach is as good as Kuta's, but the sea is much better for swimming as it is protected by a coral reef. The only eyesore is the Hotel Bali Beach, which is from the Costa Concrete school of architecture. It did serve a useful purpose, though, as it so horrified the Balinese that they immediately introduced a rule that no building could be higher than a palm tree. As a result all the other hotels are low-rise. Many have been designed in traditional Balinese styles using local materials and fabrics. The Bali Hyatt at Sanur, the Nusa Dua Beach and the newish Bali Sol are good examples.

Nusa Dua is the newest of the resorts. On a peninsula south of Denpasar, Kuta and Sanur, it is being developed more slowly than the other resorts which means, on the one hand, that the beach and surrounding area remain quite unspoilt, but on the other, that there is little in the way of local entertainment. It is a relaxing away-from-it-all spot but, if you stay there all the time, you will miss much of the magic of Bali.

At the southern tip of the peninsula on which Nusa Dua is found, there is the extraordinary sight of the temple (or *Pura*) Luhur Ulu Watu, clinging — but only just — to the cliff edge. A colony of brave or shortsighted monkeys are its only inhabitants now and they are no doubt entertained by the antics of those chasing Big Surf at the nearby Suluban Beach. Bali has some of the world's best surfing, and there are splendid beaches too, but the range does not, in all honesty, match up to what you will find on most Caribbean islands or even in some of its neighbouring Asian Countries. It is a long way to go just to lie on a beach anyway so you should drag yourself away and do what the Balinese — no lovers of what they see as the demon-infested seas — do and turn your thoughts and steps inland.

It is a pity that so many people see Bali simply as an ideal stopover on the long trek Down Under. It is certainly a great place to wind down and relax in between gruelling flights but a couple of days is no time to do it justice. In fact two weeks is too short but if that's your limit, there are some highlights that should not be missed.

Head first of all for Ubud. Not far from traffic-clogged Denpasar it is a haven of peace, surrounded by terraced rice paddy fields. It is the centre of Balinese art and home to the Palace of Fine Arts which shows off some of the best works in beautiful garden settings. Ubud also has its own Monkey Forest which is less commercialised than the better-known Sangeh Forest although the monkeys are just as tame.

Serangan (Turtle) island can also be a bit too much with the tourists outnumbering the turtles in their pens but it is still worth a visit.

The Sea Temple of Tanah Lot, off the west coast, is equally popular. While there may be a crush on the mainland. Tanah Lot stands in glorious isolation as Mother Nature serves up a series of stunning sunsets as backdrops.

Two mountains take next pride of place. The Holy Gunung Agung towers more than 10,000 feet over the island. It made its presence well and truly felt in 1963 when, in the middle of a series of traditional sacrificial ceremonies, it erupted, killing more than 1000 people and destroying villages in its lava-flow. The Pura Besakih temple, high on its slopes, was spared and so now carries even more significance for the Balinese.

To the north-west is Mount Batur. Also volcanic, its black lava streams are best seen from Penelokan but there is a fascinating trip — by horse and canoe if you like — across Lake Batur in its outer crater to the inner peak. On the opposite side of the crater stands the island's highest temple, and cloud-shrouded Tegeh Koripan at nearly 6000 feet.

One aspect of Balinese culture that should not be missed is the dance shows. These are being staged all the time, for tourists and locals alike. Although the dances are uniquely stylised, the staging and plots are like an old fashioned panto with 'goodies' and 'baddies' clearly identifiable and greeted by audience applause and hisses. The Monkey dance (*Cecak*) is probably the most familiar and popular for visitors but look out for the more graceful *Legong*, danced by a couple of young girls. Most of the dances are accompanied by Gamelan music from a Bali-style band or orchestra. It is their version of a Caribbean steel band. All the instruments are percussion but the sound is quite different if just as insistent.

All the main hotels offer tours all over the island but there is plenty of opportunity for the independent-minded to make their own way. Depending on budget and inclination, there are air-conditioned limos for hire with English-speaking guides, self-drive cars or motorcycles or — for the really energetic — push-bikes. Routes should be planned carefully, however; Bali measures 50 miles by 90 and there are plenty of hills. Sailing canoes (*prahus*) are for hire too, with or without a guide/pilot.

There is plenty to buy on Bali and, in places like Kuta, rather too many people trying to sell to you. The real finds, and the pleasure, in shopping are in places like Mas, the woodcarving centre, and Celuk where the intricate silver filigree work is a delight. Balinese art, which was once confined to temples, is the kind of work you'll either love or hate. (And the same goes for anyone you are thinking of buying it for!)

Eating can be rewarding. Indonesian food, Bali-style, is tasty and often imaginative. *Nasi Goreng* is a staple of most menus. A bit like *paella*: it can cover a multitude of fins although it is supposed to be made only of shrimps and meat with rice. Roast pig (*Babi Guling*) is another favourite but only the hardhearted can stomach turtle steak if they have visited Serangan.

Tasty *satay* — skewered meat in a peanut sauce — is as popular in Bali as elsewhere in South East Asia and a bonus is the huge range of fruit. Visit the night market in bustling Denpasar and you will see huge bananas, mango and papaya and the less recognisable *rambutan*, an acquired taste if ever there was one.

In the main resorts and hotels, a lot of the food is 'international' or westernised Indonesian but, if you get out and about, there are plenty of authentic Bali places from the basic cafés (*warungs*) to restaurants up in the hills where the views over lush forests or rice terraces are even better than the food.

OFF-SEASON BRITAIN

Last winter a friend of mine told me that he'd made up his mind to go and get his eyesight tested but then decided to postpone the appointment until the spring. 'I can't possibly face the thought of looking at Britain in sharp focus until the gloomy grey days of winter have passed,' he confessed. How very shortsighted of him, I thought.

Even though the heart of an English winter can have its depressing moments, there's never any need to hibernate. Most of the country's finest natural assets are in their deserted prime, free of the crowds that merely come to pay warm-weather homage. The countryside in winter is a world of solitude, muted pastel colours, close horizons, general sogginess and regiments of undressed trees. Hit upon one of those crispy, blue-sky days of January, each one launched by mist with the ground covered in a dusting of frost, and even the most chauvinistic of townies will go weak at the knees. Not too weak though, since by far the most rewarding way of absorbing such pastoral pleasures is to walk.

Despite our limited acreage and squashed population it is still remarkably easy to get away from even the most sprawling of urban surroundings. Britain is particularly well-endowed with waymarked footpaths of varying lengths and most of them don't require bionic reserves of stamina. The ten National Parks that cover some nine per cent of England and Wales take in much of the country's most spectacular scenery, a blend of mountain and moorland, downland and heathland, cliffs and seashore, and all offering plenty of great escape potential.

The Great Outdoors even in the middle of winter doesn't imply roughing it, providing you wear sensible warm and waterproof clothing. Besides, the Great Indoors should never be that far away, ready, willing and very able to provide a cosy back-up to your daily treks. The most sensible way to start sampling Britain off-season is to make daily forays from a well-chosen home base. Being a city dweller, my idea of a break from the regular routines and familiar surroundings is to get lost in some rural retreat but be based at a good hotel. Because I know it may well be cold, and wet, the ideal bolt-hole has to offer a

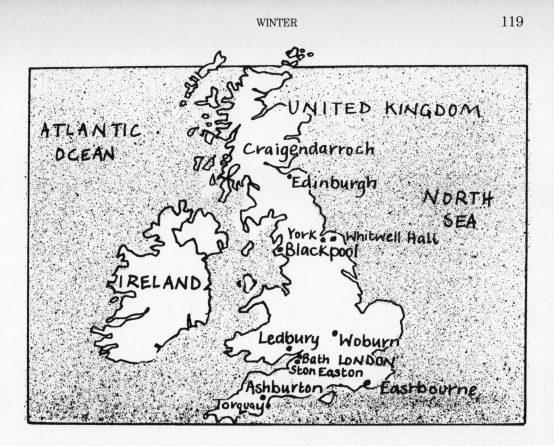

blend of elegance and informality, friendly but unobtrusive staff, well-furnished but cosy bedrooms, have a least a couple of vigorous log fires where I can toast my toes and serve food that is a good deal fancier than I'd bother to produce at home. And this wonderworld shouldn't cost the earth.

'Of all the things the British have invented,' wrote Henry James, 'the most perfect, the most characteristic ... is the well-appointed, well-administered, well-filled country house.' Nowadays you don't have to have a marchioness as your mother-in-law before indulging in such luxuries. Once a jealously guarded perk of the landowning rich, many country houses now heave open their doors (portcullises, drawbridges ...) to paying guests. A weekend break in such historic, architecturally distinctive country houses, is a unique way of savouring a way of life where a gentle pace, highly individual attention and a caring brand of elegance are far from lost in an age of mass-marketed holidays and faceless hotels. They offer, in short, a perfect antidote to winters of discontent.

Country house hotels are different. Don't, for example, be surprised to find that there is no obvious reception or check-in counter, its place having been taken by a fine Chippendale desk topped by a leather elbowed blotter and a silly quill pen. Ring a tiny silver bell and a lackey in knee breeches may spring into action — though the chances are that you were already spotted crunching your wheels up the gravelled driveway.

The best of rural retreats are widely scattered. In Herefordshire, one of England's most underestimated counties, you'll find Hope End, a hotel set in 40 wooded, silent acres near Ledbury. Once the childhood home of Elizabeth Barrett Browning, today's owners, the Hegartys, have built a magnificent reputation for English 'real' or wholefood cookery. Apart from discerning diners, you can tell who enjoys Hope End from a look at the cars outside. As

John Hegarty points out, 'You'll find a high proportion of National Trust and RSPB stickers, walking boots and detailed guides and maps on the back shelf plus a copy of whatever they have been meaning to read for the past few months but could never find the time. Until now.'

The heart of Devon's countryside, somewhere on the fringes of Dartmoor so that one can plot swift forays on to the moor and back again before the bleakness of the scene gets too overwhelming, makes another ideal winter retreat. If you thrive on tranquility, a peace disturbed only by the odd owl hoot and the revs of a distant chain saw, the Holne Chase hotel near Ashburton is as far removed from the world of mega-decibels as you could hope to find. Once a hunting lodge, now with just a dozen simple rooms, books for browsing and open fires, it overlooks the valley of the river Dart and lies just within the National Park boundary.

Some hotels have a knack of taking winter in their stride, literally in the case of Flitwick Manor in Bedfordshire. They have a pine chest full of green wellies ready and waiting for guests, the only passport you need to explore the 50 acres of parkland and the bordering Woburn estate. Ston Easton, perhaps the finest country house hotel in the country, even has a resident overweight spaniel, Lucy, who will lead you through the hotel's 300 wintery acres before leading you back for R & R in the grandest of styles. Other hotels have adapted to the unacceptable face of winter in practical ways. Whitwell Hall, which sits on an escarpment of the Howardian Hills overlooking the Vale of York has recently built a 12-metre heated indoor pool, sauna and orangery equipped with a gazebo and twittering canaries, while Craigendarroch on Deeside, just down the road from the Royals, has a 'trimnasium' complex of mini-gym, pool, squash courts, jacuzzi, snooker and sauna.

Don't forget the seaside when drawing up your winter escape routes. Out of season resorts can be both bracing and romantic — a couple of brisk walks along the beach, deserted but for men and their dogs, will soon blow the cobwebs away. More than half the total number of hotels in the country are to be found at the coast but, surprisingly, they attract only 20 per cent of the short break business. Of course the winter weather is going to be a bit of a gamble, but if the prospect of getting rained on puts you off, you'll find them equipped with plenty of waterproof distractions.

Several of the golden oldie resorts have been spending small fortunes in the hopes of shaking off those images of holidaymakers swaddled in thermal undies and cling-filmed in pacamacs at the end of a wet pier — and that's just in the summer! They have been investing enormous amounts of money in state-of-the-art leisure centres packed with facilities and entertainments designed to keep everyone smiling no matter what the weathermen may threaten.

Brash and brassy Blackpool, for example, claimed to have pioneered 'Britain in the Rain' when it built its Tower back in the 1890s. More recent undercover operations have included the three-and-a-half-acre £15 million Sandcastle Centre, Europe's first indoor resort with three pools, water slides, garden terraces, all-day and evening entertainments, restaurants, cafés and a children's 'play paradise'. They all sit among palm trees imported from Barcelona, bask in a constant 83°F and are housed under the largest roof in Britain. Arguably, given the current trends in travel, resorts have had little choice but to spend — those that don't invest in their future may find themselves without one.

Two hotels well worth a final mention in these winter dispatches are the Grand at Eastbourne and the Imperial at Torquay, both perfectly poised for relishing the off-season seaside at its most unhurried, uncrowded best.

TOURING

There is an awful lot of snobbery about travel. The word 'travel' has a cachet mere 'holiday' does not, summed up by the subtle distinction: I am a traveller / You are a tourist / He is a holidaymaker / They are trippers.

If there is any distinction, it has to do with movement. Holiday is static; travel is going places. If, in Robert Louis Stevenson's words, 'To travel hopefully is a better thing than to arrive,' then holidays are all to do with arriving.

When the business of getting there and back became cheap and simple, along came the holiday. Travel became simply a means to an end, which was probably a beach in the Mediterranean, and people in their thousands were only too happy to be deposited in the sunshine for either seven or 14 nights — to use the industry's somewhat paradoxical terminology. Even in Britain the general mentality was to go somewhere and stay put.

Now, I am delighted to say, journeys are back. Whether you go independently or on a tour operator's package, the travel business is geared to keeping holiday-makers on the move. With round-the-world air tickets, more ferry services to mainland Europe than ever, greater flexibility in car rental, hundreds of budget-priced flights and computerised hotel reservation systems, touring has never been easier or more popular. Mass travel can now be mass adventure.

Some countries are natural touring areas, America for one. The area I have picked is Florida, surely the most comprehensive holiday land on earth.
India is addictive: the more you see, the more you will want to see, and package holidays, have been designed with this condition in mind. The same goes for the game parks of East Africa.

Scotland is another explorer's country — which perhaps explains why so many were born there. France is too. Even the bit that lies immediately across the Channel has that unmistakably Contental flavour.

Travel hopefully, therefore; travel merely to arrive and you could miss it all.

FLORIDA

America is run on roads. So are most American holidays. Sitting comfortably in your glass-tinted, air-conditioned limo, you glide in a stately, muffled procession along sunshine strips at the statutory 55 mph limit or less. Outside, Florida flickers past in slow motion. 'Get Shrimpnotized ... when you're hungry for fun.' 'Tall on Taste.' 'The World's Longest Oyster Bar.' 'Fitness Plus — State of the Art Facilities and Equipment.'

Roadside reading, US-style, adds another dimension to motoring. The shorthand language is always graphic, sometimes baffling, uniquely American. So are the roadside eateries. Jack's Skyways Diner sits, roughly, where Tampa Bay meets the Gulf of Mexico, just before you hit the Sunshine Skyway Bridge, which speeds you south to Sarasota and Fort Myers. Jack serves breakfast all day — some say the best in Florida.

It's the cramped haunt of local fishermen, truck drivers, highway patrolmen, sharp-suited salesmen and tourists. At the next table, a large American sat under the revolving fans, ordering up his breakfast. Two eggs, sunny sides up. Crispy bacon, hash brown potatoes. Buttered toast. English muffins. Waffles with pecan maple syrup topped with ice cream. And coffee till the pot runs dry. 'OK so I'm on a diet. Otherwise I could run right through that menu.' He sighed. The waitress nodded sympathetically.

This is the still recognisable America you see in old movies, little changed by the latest fads and fashions. On Florida's east coast is a salt-licked wooden pier. Fishermen fish from its plank walk and surfers surf on the mini rollers below. The sands are endless. You can drink beer or sip Bloody Marys from plastic cups in the hot sun, listening idly to the chatter. 'I managed a New York store, now I'm working my way down to the Virgin Islands or Dominica ... or anywhere hot,' the waitress confessed. 'Guess I'm a beach bum at heart.' This could have been anywhere, too, in listless, sun-doped America but was in fact Cocoa Beach on Florida's Atlantic coast.

Then again, jump into your car and head out south west straight into the setting sun along the Florida Keys. Down the Overseas Highway, a 100-mile ruler-straight ribbon of road linking islands by 42 bridges that span swift, unpredictable currents. Through Key Largo, where Bogart outwitted the baddies, Duck Key, Pigeon Key, Big Torch Key, Cudjoe Key, Saddle Bunch Key and Blue Coppitt Key into the cloudless Gulf of Mexico and the last key of all, Key West.

The pace of life along the Keys must be the slowest in Florida. Key West is the liveliest but the atmosphere remains relaxingly languid. It's a great place for fishing, snorkelling and simply soaking up the sun. In the old quarter, some buildings, graceful white wooden houses with fretted balconies and louvred shutters, peel and splinter in a losing battle with the hot sun and salt-laden air. 'Fall-Apartsville,' one person opined, though she was referring as much to the diverse and quirky set of people as to the architecture.

A rented self-drive car not only gives you the freedom of the freeways but it's absolutely essential for visiting the scattered attractions — and don't be put off if the hire company offers you one of those long jobs — it's amazing how quickly you get used to them. Car hire is relatively cheap, petrol around half our price and driving along the straight, well-signposted roads is easy, though signs in built-up areas around Miami and Orlando can be initially confusing. Make sure you've got adequate third party liability cover and personal accident insurance — points to check before you leave home. Once there, roadside

motels, often with family rooms sporting two double beds, are outstanding value and you can often book in at any time of day or night. Even if you are staying put in one resort a car is necessary, as distances are often huge. Otherwise, you will become trapped in your hotel.

Florida, with its variety of attractions and clean, safe, sandy beaches, is unusually well geared to families. You can now fly from Britain to three airports — Miami, Orlando and Tampa. After the long trans-Atlantic flight, pick up your car and book into a local hotel before setting out, refreshed, the next morning. When planning where to go, bear in mind that distances are great and the low speed limit makes for longer journeys than you first expect.

One place, where imagination is king, tops most people's holiday shopping list. Orlando must surely be the world's family entertainment capital. Sculptured out of woods and lakes, the 43-square mile Walt Disney World complex is far larger than most resorts. Its Magic Kingdom mixes childhood fantasies, good-humoured amusements and the ultimate in thrilling white knuckle rides. As you queue up for the Space Mountain roller-coaster, signs repeatedly warn of the danger to anyone with bad backs or weak hearts. I chickened out first time, but took the plunge at the next opportunity — exhilarating!

In contrast, Disney's EPCOT has a more serious side. It stands for Experimental Prototype Community of Tomorrow; 'Engineered entertainment,' the creaters call it, a look at life in the future. Some 20 major rides and attractions use all the inventive Disney wizardry. And that invention shows no sign of abating. Five new major projects are scheduled to open during 1988 and 1989, among them the Disney MGM studio and Pleasure Island with its six acres of night-time entertainment.

You'll need at least two days, probably three, to *do* Disney World properly, and you must be prepared for long queues. Other 'musts' in Orlando include

Sea World, with its eerie Shark Encounter and outstanding water-ski shows, and the stomach-churning slides, shoots and splashes of Wet 'n' Wild.

The nearest seaside centre to Orlando is Cocoa Beach, just one hour's drive away. It's a quietish, typically family resort on a 12-mile beach that shelves, clean and uncluttered, into the Atlantic. No souvenir stalls or hot-dog stands are allowed on the beach and even real dogs are banned. You might share the sands with pelicans, the occasional racoon — they are quite harmless, you'll be pleased to know — and in summer turtles arrive to lay their eggs.

Of the several beachside hotels, I recommend the British-owned Oceanside with big bedrooms overlooking the sands — another good family spot. It's air-conditioned, an essential in Florida, particularly if you go in the hot, humid days of summer. The best times of year, when both humidity and prices are lower, are spring and autumn.

Cocoa Beach is also near another great attraction, the Kennedy Space Centre and Cape Canaveral, where NASA's Apollo moon missions and space shuttles were launched. Still fully operational, despite the Shuttle disaster, it is open to the public. A regular earthbound shuttle service of coaches takes you on a fascinating two-hour tour. Before you are bussed around the familiar landmarks, see the film shot by shuttle astronauts — shown on an IMAX screen bigger than most houses, it is as gripping as any science fiction fantasy.

On the opposite seaboard, around two hours' drive from Orlando, is the Pinellas Suncoast. From St Petersburg (or St Pete, as it's affectionately known) up through Treasure Island, Madeira, Redington and Indian Rocks to Clearwater lie 28 miles of soft sand and warm seas. All the way, the scenery is similar: a familiar strip of hotels, motels, restaurants, hamburger and pancake places, glossy shopping malls. In hot and sunny March, the sea glinted invitingly behind swaying palms and each evening the huge, ochre sun sank so slowly from the sky you could almost hear it hissing into the Gulf of Mexico.

Good value restaurants abound: steaks with baked potatoes, generously topped with sour cream and chives, at the Brown Derby; seafood with jazz at the Hurricane; a conjurer dressed like a tramp performing miracle sleights of hand at tables in Silas Dents; a note outside the seafood Crab Market warning 'closed for Christmas and hurricanes'.

Miami is the big time. And there's far more to it than vice. If you have preconceptions about Miami, a lot of it will come as a surprise. It is enormous, spread across beach, mainland and islands — you'll need that car. Hotels stand shoulder-to-shoulder along ten-mile Miami Beach; the fashionable end is where the resort began, the cluster of restored 1930s Art Deco hotels. In total contrast, the Cuban quarter, with its ethnic restaurants and traditions, is now on the tourist circuit. So too, of course, is the Everglades National Park, much of it a labyrinth of mangrove swamps and sawgrass marsh, the home of spectacular wildlife, including the famous alligators. The Everglades can be explored by high-speed air boat, swamp buggy and on foot.

Miami is too far from Orlando for a day trip (the Viscount Hotel in Disney World, incidentally, has rooms large enough to sleep a family of four). So, too, is a favourite spot of mine, the tranquil and uncommercialised island resorts of Sanibel and Captiva on the south-west coast. Pelicans flew alongside as we drove along the three-and-a-half-mile causeway from Fort Myers to Sanibel and when you swim in the Gulf you may be accompanied by dolphin. Sanibel is a sanctuary, summed up by two of the island's laws: don't feed the alligators and don't take away a turtle. The beaches, wild and unspoiled, are among the best in the world for collecting shells — some 300 different types, at the last count.

Plushy waterside holiday homes can be rented. The apartments of Casa y Bel come equipped with washing machines, spin dryers and self-cleaning ovens and the swimming pool is magnificent. Across on Captiva, we ate at Mucky Duck's, a simple wooden restaurant with an engagingly eccentric host. He wore a stuffed parrot hat, sported a shocking pink revolving bow tie and playfully squirted mustard and ketchup at you — from joke bottles that emit no more than coloured cord. It's a wonderful place to go with children. Florida echoes America's bemusing mix of moods, moments and lifestyles.

NORTHERN FRANCE

The cross-Channel ferry from Newhaven sails straight to the heart of Dieppe — instant France. As it noses into the inner harbour the salty air seems garnished with garlic. Cheerful little restaurants ring the port and from the deck you can see check table cloths and bowls of steaming *moules*; you can almost hear, beyond the thud of the ship's engine, the splintering crust of crisp French bread as it is dipped into the sauce.

If you haven't eaten on board — and the meals on these French boats are the best on the Channel — this is where you must start. Menus should always act as an aperitif and here they certainly do. In Newhaven, it was fish and chips. In Dieppe, it is *assiette des fruits de mer*, a plate piled high with oysters, *langoustines* and other marine mysteries, accompanied by enough spikes, scoops and probes to perform a major operation.

Eating is taken seriously; among traditional-style restaurants in the Arcades de la Poissonerie is La Moderne. It has an ambitious list of dishes and service comes with a professional polish missing from some of the more touristy establishments. But by far the best place to try the local speciality, *Marmite Dieppoise*, a fishy stew embellished with cream, is the little restaurant of the same name tucked away in rue St Jean.

Unhappily, Dieppe, the most interesting of the Channel ports, is just too far for a day trip — the crossing takes over four hours. But, for touring northern France, it is a good point of arrival and an even better point of departure. Time your return for a Saturday when you can stock up at the street market in the Grand Rue. Stalls groan under their sumptuous loads of newly-baked pies and flans; mounds of game and paté, fruit and vegetables; piles of cheeses and barrels of butter from the surrounding farms; rickety barrows of fresh fish — sole and scallops, glossy mussels and pink shrimps.

It's about time we rediscovered the French Channel coast. Easy to reach, it could hardly be more different from our south coast. Beaches are bigger and resorts smaller; some have a piquant M. Hulot period charm, others are genuine fishing ports. Somehow, they have resisted the dreary ribbon development that mars too much of Kent and Sussex by the sea. With regular crossings to seven French ports in northern France, we are spoiled for choice. The ferry companies' five-day excursion fares allow just enough time for an appetising taster. The permutations of where to go are endless — you could, for instance, tour from Dieppe or turn right at Calais and return home from Cherbourg, dipping into Picardy and Normandy as you go.

Both scenically and historically, Normandy is the best bet. Between Dieppe and Le Havre, resorts are squeezed into rocky clefts and wooded, suntrap coves — Veules-les-Roses, Yport, Les Petites-Dalles and Les Grandes-Dalles. The impressionist Monet once painted Varangéville, and the twelfth-century

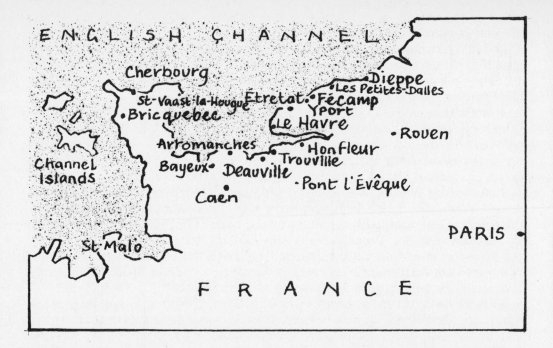

cliff-top church there has a coloured window by Braque, the Cubist painter who lies buried in the churchyard. Painters have always been attracted by the clarity of the light and the sea and skyscapes — elegant Etretat, edged with high cliffs, was another favourite spot.

In Fécamp, a bizarre skyline of spires, figures and turrets catches the eye. This gothic and baroque fantasy, like a prop from a Hammer horror film, is the Benedictine distillery and it's not as old as it looks. In the sixteenth century, a Benedictine monk perfected an elixir made from 27 herbs but when the monastery was destroyed during the French revolution, the recipe was lost. A local merchant, M. Alexandre Le Grand found most of it, capitalised on it commercially and produced today's version of Benedictine, building the distillery itself in the late nineteenth century. A French king once commented: 'Upon my faith, I never tasted better.' And after a tour of the distillery, with its giant copper stills and cellars full of barrels, you are offered the opportunity to agree.

Across the Seine, Honfleur is a gem. On a sunny day, the ambience is almost Mediterranean, toned down by the tall grey slate-faced houses that overlook the inner port. The narrow streets are cobbled, cramped and full of charm. You can sit for hours by the harbour, sipping a drink, watching the hustle and bustle and the painters, who can't resist such a picture. They are in good company. Boudin, the forerunner of Impressionism, was born here and a local museum has some of his pictures, along with superb Dufys and Monets.

There's a nice touch of irony about the wooden church of Ste Catherine. Its roof, is in the form of an upturned boat and was built by ship's carpenters to celebrate the departure of the English after the 100 years' war.

From Honfleur to Cherbourg runs a coast of war and peace. Deauville is full of wistful period whimsy and architectural eccentricities; one beach hut is actually a scaled-down chateau. In summer, Deauville remains *très snob*, when society descends on Les Planches, the plank walk by the beach, to see and be seen. Next-door-neighbour, Trouville, is marginally more workaday with a faded air of grander times, when it shared with Deauville the society success of the champagne years between the wars.

And it's the scars of war, now permanent memorials, that mark the coast well into the Cherbourg peninsula. The D-Day invasion beaches resound with evocative overtones: Sword, Juno, Gold, Omaha, Utah. Bunkers, batteries and blockhouses; the fractured remains of the Mulberry harbour at Arromanches; a tank squatting aggressively in an innocent-looking village; the stark white simplicity of military cemeteries and their moving inscriptions. The graveyards tell more of the horrors of war than the many museums, which can come perilously close to the glorification of battle, fascinating though some of them are. A signposted circuit ensures you won't miss the main sights.

'Defeated by William, we liberated the land of our conquerors.' So reads a double-edged inscription in Latin on the huge, arched memorial opposite the British and Commonwealth cemetery on the edge of Bayeux. In the town itself, the famous Bayeux Tapestry tells the tale of that other invasion. 'Naïve primitive film strip with Latin subtitles,' begins the English commentary on the 70-metre-long masterpiece chronicling the events leading up to the Norman invasion of Britain and the 1066 Battle of Hastings itself.

With a newish Channel ferry service to Caen, this area is suddenly more accessible. Caen itself, largely re-built following near-annihilation towards the end of the last war, is dominated by the massive ramparts of William the Conqueror's castle and the lofty splendour of the Abbaye aux Hommes, where he lies buried. Between here and medieval Rouen, centuries of history are etched across the countryside.

Forget wars and you can relish the sandy beaches and the jaunty fishing ports right the way up to Cherbourg. The east coast of this long peninsula is less well known harbouring little fishing towns like St-Vaast-la-Hougue, its harmony of mellow buildings built in pale, Cotswold-type stone. Those in the know pay return visits to the Hotel de France, creeper-clad, comfortable and outstanding value; local oysters have appeared on the cheapest menu and some ingredients come straight from the owner's family farm.

A mantle of peace hangs over the serene Normandy countryside. Turn off ruler-straight roads heading south and you find yourself lost in a gently undulating landscape of hedgeless fields, large forests, quiet villages, ivy-tangled castles and shuttered manor houses, some grey stone, others half timbered and topped with tea-cosy thatch.

Calvados, cider and cream are the reassuring ingredients of the area around Bayeux, Caen and timbered Pont l'Evêque, where the cheese comes from. The *route du cidre* takes you through apple orchards; road signs marked *cidre bouché* direct you down country lanes to farms where you can taste and buy home made cider and calvados.

You might slip over to France for one reason alone: to sleep and eat in those small, family-owned hotels that for value have no equal in Britain. Always personally run, often by colourful personalities; the owner chef in his tall white hat in control of the kitchen, madame dragooning customers to the right tables. Places like L'Auberge de la Hauquerie on the Lombard's stud farm near Pont l'Evêque, where an abiding memory is of taking breakfast in front of a cheerfully crackling log fire one spring morning, watching through tall windows elegant racehorses exercising in the paddocks. Or the Hardy family's Hotel du Vieux Château, actually inside a medieval castle, right in the old town centre of Bricquebec, within striking distance of Cherbourg. Try the *Poussin Victoria*, served in a rosy-hued lobster sauce and named after the Queen, who stayed here when opening the Cherbourg–Caen railway.

In spring the banks and deep hedgerows are carpeted with primroses, the colour and density of which I haven't seen since childhood. And I am sure the impressionist painters would still recognize the workaday seaports with forests of masts and men in chunky blue sweaters, clumping around in big boots and knocking back glasses of fiery, post-breakfast calvados in bars with steamed up windows. So far, the Common Market hasn't achieved what the Channel has prevented since 1066 — a merging of Anglo–French life styles. Nor will it ever.

THE ROAD TO COMPOSTELA

This is a holiday with a difference, a long car journey across the remoter areas of two beautiful European countries. It is certainly an experience, and may even be an adventure, a journey unlike any other.

The Road to Compostela is one of the oldest journeys known to the Western World and, incidentally, the subject of the world's first ever guidebook. This was written by a French monk, Ameri Picaud, in about 1149, although this journey, or pilgrimage, to the shrine of St James of Santiago (the patron saint of Spain) had been going on for at least two centuries before Picaud set out on his trip.

There are, in fact, four Roads to Compostela, beginning in Paris, Vezelay, Le Puy or Arles, running from these four French starting points to cross the Pyrénées into Spain and combining to form a single road, which the Spaniards call the *Camino Frances*, the French Road, in the little town of Puente La Reina in Navarre. I recommend the road from Le Puy. This is the most difficult but also the most interesting route and wise travellers will allow two days for crossing the Channel and central France, before they reach Le Puy, in the central Auvergne, and the start of their travels west to Compostela.

This journey is really a pilgrimage, but even the agnostics might care to begin it with a visit to the great cathedral in Le Puy, or the long walk of 268 steps up that slender spike of rock — a *puy* — to the little chapel of St Michel de l'Aiguilhe, which overlooks the red-tiled roofs of this attractive town. Le Puy is full of good hotels and restaurants and the road out down the Rue de Compostelle, leads across the valleys of the Loire, Allier and Truyère, over the grain of the country. This is, therefore, a very up-and-down road but quite an easy one to follow, through Saugues and the empty Gevaudan country to the first night-stop at the two-star Hôtel Prouhèze at Aumont. This belongs to the Prouhèze family, who see to it that the food and service are always impeccable, and can boast a Michelin rosette in consequence.

Next day begins with a beautiful run west, across the open moorland of the Aubrac plateau, through the little village of Aubrac, which was built by a Flemish nobleman in 1120 to shelter pilgrims on the road across this bleak, if beautiful, moor. A coffee stop in Aubrac might be a good idea, before taking a short walk along part of the old road, which is now the famous GR (*Grande Randonnée*) footpath No. 65, *Le Chemin de St Jacques*. Then back into the car again and steeply downhill to St Chély d'Aubrac and the beautiful valley of the Lot, or as they call it hereabouts, the Olt.

The road runs along the valley, right beside the sparkling river, and through three towns that no traveller in France will want to miss — St Côme, Espalion and Estaing. Each one is a gem, particularly in the summer season, but Estaing

tops them all. The feast day of St James is 25 July, so travellers — or pilgrims
— start to pass through the Lot valley in mid-June, and can be identified by
the scallop shells they all carry — the *coquilles de St Jacques*.

Estaing is topped by a splendid castle. It belonged to the Estaing family, who
were Admirals to the Bourbon Kings, and you can eat a very good and very
French lunch in the Aux Armes d'Estaing hotel, before pressing on over the
steep hills of the green Aveyron country to the little hill-town of Conques.

Whatever you do, don't miss Conques. Conques is beautiful, a dream in
golden stone, with a fine hotel, the Ste Foy, and a huge Romanesque cathedral
which contains the shrine of Ste Foy, who was martyred here by the orders of
Emperor Diocletian. But the great reason for stopping here is the famous
medieval treasury, the last of its kind in France, full of jewelled reliquaries from
the time of Charlemagne. Conques itself, though, is the real jewel, a quaint,
peaceful town with cobbled streets set above a rippling river; terribly romantic
and definitely a place to linger in a while.

The road rises steeply from Conques, a second-gear climb from the river, and
then swoops up and down over the mountains, first to the town of Figeac and
then on to the river Tarn and the town of Cahors. Cahors has a famous rich, red
wine, the 'black wine of Quercy', and an equally famous fortified bridge, the
Pont Valentré, which was built in the twelfth century with the aid of the Devil
... well, that's what they say. The road actually crosses the Pont Valentré, and
rolls on to the town of Moissac, where the Hôtel Chapon-Fin is ideal for lunch
or dinner or an overnight stop. It is very close to yet another cathedral. There
are so many fine cathedrals on this Pilgrim Road to Santiago that you can afford
to be selective, but the one at Moissac is well worth including in your itinerary.

South-east of Moissac the road crosses the Gers, the Armagnac country, passing through Lectoure, Condom, Eauze and — another essential stop, but one that hardly anyone knows about — the tiny, walled village of Larressingle. After a delightful run through more vineyards, it drops into the valley of the Gave de Pau. The snow-tipped Pyrénées are now in sight but it is worth taking another full day to reach them, if only to explore some of the fine places lying en route, like Orthez, Sauveterre de Béarn, Oberon and St Palais, before arriving at St-Jean-Pied-de-Port, and the country of the Basques.

After a night at the Hotel des Pyrénées in St Jean, you cross into Spain at Val Carlos and begin the long, steep climb through the famous pass of Roncesvalles and then down to the city of Pamplona. When the pilgrims are passing through this city in the early days of July, the Basques of Pamplona are holding their seven-day-long St Firman festival. Each day begins with the *Encierro*, the Running of the Bulls. Only those who are very agile or very fleet of foot should join the Basques in this dangerous diversion.

The *Camino Frances* runs through the centre of Pamplona, and due west to Puenta La Reina, where all four Pilgrim Roads meet. From there it continues to Estella and Logroño, which is the capital for the wine country of the Rioja. All this is across Navarre, a country green with vines, golden with grain, blazing in the summer sunshine, with the pilgrim-dotted road running like a black ribbon over the landscape to the dusty little town of Santo Domingo de la Calzada. Wise travellers will stop for a night in the medieval *parador*, and visit the cathedral, which features among the legends of the road, and was built by Santo Domingo (St Dominic) in the eleventh century.

From Santo Domingo the road climbs over the Montes de Oca, the Goose Mountains, out of Navarre into Castile, and down to Burgos, the city of El Cid. Here is another one of the cathedrals you must see before pressing on, following the *real* road which keeps to some very minor, very Spanish roads, through Hontanas and Hornillos del Camino, past Castrojerez, which has a magnificent castle high on the hill, and on to Leon.

In Leon, travellers must stay in, or at least visit, the Hotel San Marcos, part-church, part-museum, part-monastery, all magnificent. It was built as a pilgrim hostel in about 1170 by the Military Knights of Santiago, and it still makes a special effort to welcome pilgrims on the road. Leon also contains another marvellous cathedral, pure Gothic and built from 1205, with no less than 182 stained glass windows, so many that the very structure is said to be weakened by them. Inside the cathedral on a sunny day, the spectacle of all that glowing glass is quite unforgettable.

Between Burgos and Leon, the countryside is fairly flat, for the road crosses the northern edge of the *meseta*, that great plain that occupies much of Spain between the Sierra de Guadarrama, north of Madrid, and the coastal mountains of Cantabria. West of Leon though, the countryside begins to ripple again as the road passes through Astorga, where the curiously-built Bishop's Palace now contains the *Museo del Camino*, the Museum of the Road. Beyond Astorga it rises to climb over the Montes de Leon. Motorists follow the newly-opened main highway to Pontferrada and so into the green wine country of the Bierzo to the town of Villafranca, and up to the pass at Pedrafita. From Pedrafita a minor road leads up to the little hostel at El Cebrero which has been welcoming pilgrims for over nine hundred years. There are only eight rooms, so you will have to book ahead or arrive early or sleep in one of the curious thatched barns, or *pallozas*, which are peculiar to El Cebrero. In summer they are always full of pilgrims, sleeping comfortably on great piles of straw.

From El Cebrero the road rises a little to the pass of Puyo, and then falls away into the green, misty mountains of Galicia, first to Tricastela, then to Somos, and for the last night-stop before reaching Compostela, to the little town of Puertomarin. Puertomarin has several hotels, including a modern *parador* set high above the river. Puertomarin once stood in the valley but then the river was dammed. Before the waters rose, the buildings were carefully dismantled and moved, piece by piece, uphill to their present position. The numbers marking the stones of the Church of St Nicolas can still be seen.

There is still a lot to see on the last day, as the road presses on towards the sunset, past Villar de Donas, then through Palas do Rei, and finally past the Lavacolla airport to the hill of Monte del Gozo. From there you can see 'the good town of Compostela,' as my worthy predecessor Ameri Picaud puts it in his *Guide de Santiago*, 'the most exalted, and most fortunate, of all the Cities of Spain.'

Santiago de Compostela is a magnificent city. The first stop should be the cathedral itself, where those who have come all the way down one of the roads must touch the Pilgrim Pillar in the entrance as a sign they have ended their journey and kept their vow. Countless hands down the centuries have worn fingerprints in the stone. On any feast day, visitors to the cathedral will be able to see the flight of the famous *botafumiero*, the Great Censer of St James, which is hauled up on ropes to the roof and then allowed to swing in great arcs, roaring and smoking, high above the fearful heads of the congregation. The Hotel de Los Reyes Catolicas nearby, like the Hotel San Marcos in Leon, was built for pilgrims by the Knights of Santiago. Those who have completed the pilgrimage and obtained evidence in the form of stamps in their notebooks from churches passed on the way, can still get a certificate — a *compostelle* — from the Cathedral chapter. If this is shown to the Hotel de Los Reyes Catolicos, the pilgrim gets a free meal. Incidentally, it is better to hand in a photocopy as the hotel will retain it, and you will want to keep the real *compostelle* as a unique souvenir.

Santiago is full of hotels which range from the luxury Reyes Catolicas, to the small Hotel Suso in the Rua del Vilar. Most of the true pilgrims seem to gather at Suso's, especially on or about the Day of St James, 25 July, which is the ideal time to arrive in Compostela, because the whole town is *en fête*.

It is possible to go to Compostela by sea from Portsmouth via Santander, or even by air. But if you have two or three weeks to spare, follow one of the Pilgrim Roads all the way across France and Spain. At all the other pilgrim centres in Europe — and there are a surprising number of them left — the object of the journey is the shrine itself. How you get there hardly matters, but that is not the case with Compostela. Travellers have been making their way down the *Camino Frances* since 951 AD, when the route was pioneered by the Bishop of Le Puy. After a thousand years, therefore, it is not too surprising if the big attraction on the Road to Compostela has become the road itself.

THE COWAL PENINSULA

I love Scotland. That should not be too surprising, for Scotland is a land which invites affection and, after all, I do have Scottish roots. I like the kilt and the purple heather on the hill and I am by no means averse to kippers or the occasional helping of haggis.

The Scottish Highlands is a vast and empty region where it is still very easy to escape the crowds and just wander away into the hills on those narrow roads

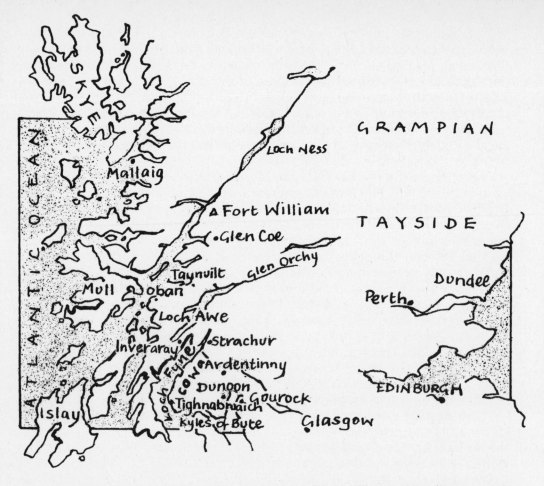

that are said to owe their origins to General Wade. Those old military roads
probe into the Grampians, along the Great Glen and make up much of the
famous Road to the Isles. But for this tour I suggest another way to Skye, up the
Cowal Peninsula, from the resort town of Dunoon, to Mallaig at the end of the
West Highland Railway. It is a journey with both scenery and romance, where,
as a bonus, the hotels are excellent, the food fresh and the prices — at time of
writing — marvellously low.

The only snag — quite literally a little one — is the West Highland midge, a
real *beastie*. Wise travellers will make this trip in the spring or autumn.

Start at the Gleddoch House Hotel at Langbank on the Firth of Clyde. This
fine hotel was a mansion built in the last century by a Clydebank shipbuilder.
It's still an imposing place, with such modern additions as an 18-hole golf
course and central heating. The hotel is now owned by the working manage-
ment, so everyone is on their toes and eager to please, and mellowness sets in
among the guests over a vast Highland breakfast. The bedrooms are spacious
and comfortable, offering great views across the Clyde to the snow-capped
peak of Ben Lomond and the bar serves a wide selection of single malts. At
Gleddoch House the menus offer good fresh Highland food: casserole of hare
and pigeon from the Gleddoch Estates, collops of venison and veal, kipper
pasties from Loch Fyne — all of it delicious. Throw in log fires and fresh
flowers, add the fact that this hotel is only ten minutes from Glasgow airport,

and it is hard to think of a better place to begin a visit to the Western Highlands.

Our road north, up the Cowal Peninsula, begins just across the Clyde, 'the watter', from Langbank. The river can be crossed from Gourock to Dunoon on a Caledonian-MacBrayne ferry. These little Cal-Mac ferries ply everywhere about the Highland waters from shore to shore or island to island, and I can't think of a better way to start a Highland journey than with a brief, bouncy trip across the Clyde to Dunoon. Dunoon, the capital of the Cowal Peninsula, is a resort town and very quiet out of season, but the tourist office is always open and very eager to equip visitors with brochures and leaflets on the charms of Argyll — which are considerable.

One of the attractions hereabouts is the weather, which tends to be mild even in the winter. The prevalence of rain in Scotland is a point on which the Scottish Tourist Board is often somewhat reticent, but those fat clouds which sweep in from the Atlantic on the westerly winds tend to ignore the Cowal and dump their rain or snow on the Grampians further east.

From Dunoon the route lies north, on narrow Highland roads with little traffic, plenty of passing places and no real hazards except the occasional slumbering sheep. Spring or autumn are the seasons for a Highland tour. Drive up Holy Loch, where the dark hulls of nuclear submarines lie out in the water beyond the protester-fringed fences of the US Naval Base, to see the Younger Botanical Gardens, a riot of rhododendrons in spring, and stop for coffee at Ormidale House. This was once the seat of the Campbells of Ormidale and is now an adventure centre where Colonel McLuckie puts his guests through their paces on his assault course, or takes them tramping in the hills, fishing in the streams or sailing on the loch.

The best route north from Ormidale lies through Ardentinny village, on the shores of Loch Long, and slow motoring should ensure that visitors arrive at the Ardentinny Hotel just in time for lunch, which can be taken out in the garden while enjoying clear views across the loch.

The road across the Argyll Forest Park runs past a memorial erected by that most Scots of entertainers, Sir Harry Lauder, in memory of his son who died in the Great War. Sir Harry lived nearby and is well remembered by the local people. Then on past Strachur and south on the A886, climbing steadily to the spectacular viewpoint overlooking the Kyles of Bute above Tighnabruaich and the hills and islands around the Sound of Bute. Far below the Sound stretches away, out towards the blue Western Ocean, across the great island-dotted waste of water, empty of life except for one small yacht cutting a slow track across one of the more distant bays ... breathtaking.

Tighnabruaich is one of those places that time has somehow overlooked, a dreamy, forgotten little port. Here there is another excellent hotel, the Kames, which offers windsurfing, sailing and fishing, plus full board accommodation and much Highland hospitality for a moderate sum. Careful planning will have you there just in time for high-tea, with scones and sticky cakes, before picking up a minor road and heading north again to the shores of Loch Fyne and a night-stop at the delightful Kilfinan Hotel.

Next day, after a very late start and another walk to the loch, you can lunch at Sir Fitzroy Maclean's Creggans Inn at Strachur. The seafood is superb. Then wander, first to Inveraray to see the great castle of the Dukes of Argyll, then up to the top of Loch Awe for a look at the romantic ruins of Kilchurn Castle, before moving on to the next night stop at the Taychreggan Hotel at Kilchrenan by Taynuilt, right on the shores of the loch. From Kilfinan to

Taychreggan is no great distance, but the Western Highlands is not the place for rushing about. At Taychreggan a five-course dinner (with haggis) is quite likely to end with the guests singing in the bar — accompanied on our visit by a County Court judge playing the mouth organ! Unplanned, unexpected evenings make Highland wandering so enjoyable.

Wander on, across the Highlands to the Isle of Skye, driving across Glen Orchy and across the bleakly beautiful wastes of Rannoch Moor and down Glencoe to Fort William. If you can find a volunteer to take the car to the Skye Ferry at Mallaig, you can take a steam train for the last lap of the journey. A trip on the West Highland Line is one of the great train rides, and a beautiful way to see this wonderful country between Glasgow and the Isle of Skye.

From Mallaig a Cal-Mac Ferry takes you across to Armadale on the Isle of Skye. There you can stay in considerable comfort at the Clan Donald Centre and perhaps have dinner at the Kinloch Lodge Hotel, owned and run by Lord and Lady Macdonald. Lord Macdonald is the present chief of the Macdonalds of Sleat, while Clare Macdonald is a cookery writer of note.

This tour up the Cowal Peninsula from Dunoon to Skye will stand the test of time and memory. You could just go a little further on the West Highland Line, up to Oban perhaps, or by train across Rannoch but, whatever route you take, this is a trip to remember.

AFRICAN SAFARI

Africa is special. Every part of it is special. But few areas have quite the magic for we British as East Africa. Here are the names that have grown with us since childhood — Serengeti, Kilimanjaro, Ngorongoro, Manyara, the Masai Mara. These are the stuff of which Daktari dreams are made.

This is the land of khaki and the Great White Hunter, the land of Hemingway and Adamson. A land born free. The land of the safari.

A safari sounds strenuous, even dangerous. In reality it is neither. The image of trekking through impenetrable bush and, at least once a morning, having to raise one's trusty Martini Henry rifle, cool and steady, and bring down a charging rogue is, thankfully, now somewhat wide of the mark. Today, the accent is on cameras and conservation and the only Martini you'll come across will be on the verandah of your lodge before dinner.

Instead of the tents and campfires of yesteryear, comfortable lodges provide air-conditioned havens in the remotest, most breathtaking locations. And if all this sounds a bit antiseptic, don't worry. Africa itself will provide all the excitement you can handle. Most of a safari holiday is spent in game reserves and national parks which bear about as much resemblance to our British safari parks as the Outback does to a window box. This is Africa as it was before Man trod all over it, cut out his farms, built his cities and laid his railroads. This is the bush.

Once East Africa boasted three great safari countries but since Uganda has become such an excellent place not to be, we're left with Kenya and Tanzania. Together they offer perhaps a dozen of the most beautiful, most exciting game areas in the world. But they are, however, very different. Politics has seen them take different ideological and economic roads and so today not only does each offer its own unique parks and reserves but a very different holiday experience.

Kenya is the self-styled king of the safari and the quality of the lodges, hotels, guides and safari vehicles is very high. Most visitors to Kenya arrive in Nairobi.

It is a perfect soft-landing for the first-timer in Africa. Although it sits virtually on the equator, its altitude gives a climate of perpetual European summer. The mass of jacarandas, oleanders, hibiscus and bougainvillaeas that adorn its avenues and private gardens have won Nairobi its name as Africa's 'City of Flowers'. But the bush is the thing and after an overnight in the city you'll be on road. British tour operators offer an enormous variety of safari itineraries covering all the famous parks and reserves. There isn't enough space here to do all the game areas justice but some must be singled out.

Amboseli, for instance, in the south, is where all those postcard views of Africa — with Mount Kilimanjaro in the background and a browsing elephant/ giraffe/rhino in the foreground — come from. Game you're likely to see includes elephant, lion, rhino, giraffe, cheetah, hippos and the ubiquitous wildebeest. The Masai Mara on the Tanzania border is the topmost end of the Serengeti and is at its best in August and September when the massive zebra and wildebeest herds move up from the plains on their annual migration. Tsavo, divided into east and west, is most famous for its 'red elephants' so-called because of the red soil they throw over themselves and the mud which, given the slightest opportunity, they will spend hours wallowing in. It is estimated that Tsavo's elephant population is now around 20,000. Meru is the park where Joy Adamson finally managed to return the lioness Elsa to the wild. In fact, many other animals have also now been brought in and resettled as part of government conservation programmes — among them a herd of white rhino from Natal. And, finally, there is Aberdare, perhaps the biggest game reserve in the world and boasting the world's two most famous game lodges — Treetops and the Ark. The former was where the Queen was staying when her father, George VI, died.

Lakes Naivasha, Nakuru and, in the north, Turkana are a paradise for

birdwatchers with millions of flamingo and other water birds. South of the
border in Tanzania, the game is even better and the scenery if anything even
more stunning. However, the standard of the lodges is unpredictable, sometimes a little more than a little unpredictable. Visitors are advised to pack their
own loo paper. That said, the tour operators receive virtually no complaints
from their Tanzanian safari-takers, and when you look at what this extraordinary country has to offer, it really isn't surprising.

If there is one name which more than any other evokes everything that is
safari, it's Serengeti. Wedged between a trough of the Eastern Rift Valley and
Lake Victoria, Serengeti is a wild, primitive landscape. From December to May
the enormous herds concentrate in the southern grasslands but by early June
they're on the move northward. The numbers are staggering — one and a half
million wildebeest, a million gazelle, 75,000 impala, 74,000 buffalo, and so it
goes on. In Serengeti it's not uncommon to see 30 or more lions in a single day.

The Ngorongoro Crater is a vast ecological amphitheatre and a drive down
into it with its sheer forest walls rising around you is unforgettable. Most
visitors stay in one of the two lodges perched on the crater rim. The views from
both are stunning. However, the view from Lake Manyara Hotel high on the Rift
Valley wall in the Manyara National Park, is altogether unbelievable. As you
walk into your room and across to the window, there, a thousand feet below is a
silver lake stretching out into the shimmering distance, its edges tinged with
the delicate pink of a million flamingos. The forest around the lake is famous for
its tree-climbing lions — and, unfortunately, for the failure of most of its
visitors ever to see one.

All the major long-haul operators feature both Kenya and Tanzania plus
combinations of the two and although the minibus and game lodge formula is
the most common, tented safaris, walking safaris and even camel and balloon
safaris are there for the asking. All the main operators also offer the option of a
week's safari and a week's beach holiday on the golden Mombassa coast — the
perfect end to an unforgettable holiday.

INDIA

The sun tipped below the edge of the hills pouring darkening gold across the
valley and into the lake. The fisherman nodded and began to row slowly toward
the sparkling palace that seemed to float like an iceberg in the centre of the
lake.

But the palace, far from being inhabited by the princess it so obviously
deserved, is a hotel — the Lake Palace Hotel at Udaipur. Built originally not for
a princess but a much-loved queen, it is now one of the most romantic places to
lay your head anywhere in the world.

In fact, Udaipur itself is probably one of the world's most romantic cities.
Known through the centuries as the 'City of Dreams', it is dominated by the
Maharajah's main palace that rambles along a ridge overlooking the lake.
Towering battlements protect sumptuous apartments, secluded courtyards
and roof gardens with views hardly believable.

But then, so much about India is unbelievable. Its size and variety is
daunting. It is a country of a million contradictions. Great wealth and great
poverty. Great spiritualism and extraordinary materialism. Frightening
passions and extraordinary kindness. All of which adds up to one of the most
exciting holidays any of us is likely to experience. I say 'experience' because

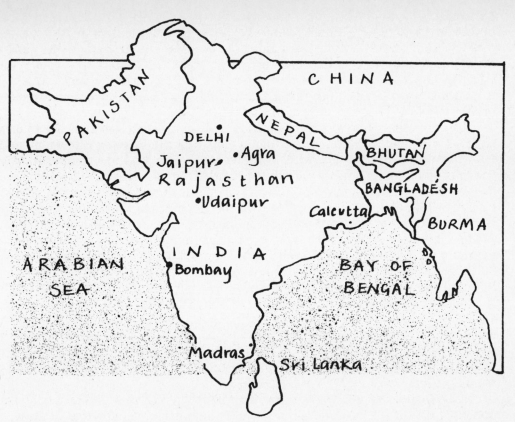

that's exactly what an Indian holiday is. The images and colour of India will remain with you long after the memories of a thousand beaches have faded.

One of India's greatest contradictions is, of course, its relationship with Britain and the British. There is a strange affinity between India and the British — an affinity understood instinctively by many of the pre-war generation but one that current generations are only now beginning to rediscover. The instant popularity of virtually any film or television series about India shows just how much this unique sub-continent continues to fascinate us. 'Gandhi', 'Jewel in the Crown', 'The Far Pavilions' — it seems we are just as deeply under its spell as Kipling's audience was a hundred years ago.

But stories and books are all very well — just how does one go about discovering India? Well, these days it's all very simple. All the best long-haul tour operators feature it in their brochures and the choice of tours is excellent. It's just a matter of choosing one that suits you best. If you have never been before, the tour that has become known as the 'Golden Triangle' is the one to start with. The triangle is formed by Agra, Delhi and Jaipur. Udaipur is only a short flight to the south-east of Jaipur and so it's often part of a 'Golden Triangle' trip.

Agra is the town of the Taj Mahal — and, yes, it *is* every bit as beautiful as it is meant to be. Its hypnotic symmetry, its glowing white marble, its mosaics of hundreds of thousands of precious and semi-precious stones take away the breath of the most blasé of travellers.

But for me, it's the story of the Taj Mahal that really makes it so beautiful. Unlike so many man-made wonders, the Taj Mahal isn't just another meglomaniac's ego trip. The Taj Mahal is a monument to love. In 1612, Arjuman Banu, herself the neice of a queen, married the great Indian Emperor Shajahan and took on the name by which she was to become known to history — Mumtaz Mahal, Exalted of the Palace. Over the next 18 years she bore her Emperor 14 children and their love became legend. But in 1630, when Shajahan was away at war, she died. On his return the Emperor was stricken and within a few months his hair turned grey and he exchanged his royal robes for clothes of simple white muslin. Shajahan vowed to build her a memorial more beautiful than anything the world had ever seen. Over 17 years an army of more than 20,000 craftsmen from as far afield as Persia and Turkey, France and Italy worked at his creation. Finally, the sad Emperor had his wish. Later, when he himself died, his son had a new tomb built next to Mumtaz Mahal's and the two lovers were reunited to lie together through the centuries.

However, stunning though the Taj Mahal is, it's not the only place of interest in Agra. The city was once the centre of the great Mogul Empire and Agra Fort was the source of all power. Within the Fort's massive walls are a fabulous palace and the beautiful mosque of Moti Masjid, also built by Shajahan.

Only 124 miles from Agra along the royal road built by the Mogul emperors is the capital of modern India, Delhi. Vast and sprawling, Delhi has been an imperial capital on and off for more than a thousand years. The last empire to hold sway here was, of course, ours and today Delhi is divided into Old Delhi and New Delhi, the ceremonious Government buildings in the latter built by the British and designed by Sir Edwin Lutyens and Sir Herbert Baker. Exploring Delhi is a giant task, so a word of advice: don't try to do too much or you'll merely find yourself overwhelmed. If it's your first visit just keep to the main places of interest — there are enough of them to keep you on your feet from dawn to dusk.

New Delhi, with its spacious boulevards, green cool parks and impressive, though sometimes curious architecture, is a strangely comfortable marriage of east and west. From the shady acres of New Delhi, it's a sudden step into the cacophony and chaos of Old Delhi, a maze of twisting lanes and crowded bazaars, magnificent mosques and milling mankind.

The Red Fort is the ultimate symbol of Mogul power and elegance. Its outer walls are of red sandstone but inside the defences, all is once again the purest marble. Close your eyes and you can almost see the swaying imperial elephants in their cloth-of-gold livery, almost hear the chimes of the silver bridles of the young princes' ponies. And then out once again into the teeming streets. All life is here. Turn a corner and you meet a bridegroom's procession on its way to the bride's home, the bridegroom himself a maharaja for a day astride a borrowed horse, his turban flashing with cut-glass jewels. Round another and you're pinned to the wall by a passing cow, sacred in India and allowed to roam free in the streets. Another and it will be a dancing bear or group of Jains carefully sweeping insects out of their path lest they harm the least form of life.

In these narrow streets, you will also meet poverty. New Delhi or Bombay will probably be your first encounter with a large Indian city and it's as well to be prepared for the grime as well as the glory. Despite enormous progress over the last ten years, the beggars and lepers are still there. It is impossible to remain unaffected.

After the human swirl of Delhi, escaping into the peace of Rajasthan is an escape into a dream. Rajasthan is the India of legend and chivalry, of princes and knights, of music and culture. 'The Country of Kings', it is the brightest jewel in India's crown. Rajasthan wears its historic past like a glittering coat of many colours — in some cases quite literally. Everywhere colourful and picturesque costumes reflect the people's pride and gaiety. Some men wear a pink or yellow beaked turban, the *safa*, while the women are often covered in traditional jewellery literally from head to foot.

Capital of Rajasthan is Jaipur, the 'pink city'. Built almost entirely of local rose-pink stone, Jaipur at sunset seems hardly real. Compared with Delhi and Agra, Jaipur is a relatively modern city founded by Maharajah Jai Singh in 1727 when he decided to move his capital down into the plains from its original mountain fortress of Amber, for six centuries the capital of Rajasthan whose women wear the most exotic saris. All that remains of the ancient stronghold today is the beautiful, sleeping Amber Palace.

Like Udaipur, Jaipur also boasts a former Maharajah's palace-turned-hotel. Although not quite as breathtaking as the Lake Palace, Jaipur's Rambagh Palace Hotel is nonetheless set in beautiful gardens and is still a wonderful place to stay. Both are run by the Taj Hotels group and were among the first Indian palaces to take on a new lease of life as hotels. Today, though, there is a score or more of lovely palaces to choose from. Like all first-class hotels in India their service — and of course, cuisine — is marvellous.

Mark Twain once described India as 'the one land that all men desired to see and, having seen once, by even a glimpse, would not give that glimpse for the shows of all of the rest of the world combined.' Twain, as usual, wasn't far off the mark.

BEST KEPT SECRETS

Travel writers are accused of telling too many secrets. We are the ones who are supposed to give away all those unspoiled little haunts that no one else knows about. One mention in print and the next minute the hordes are turning up in their hundreds and the place is never the same again.

Well, that is the theory. It used to be most vehemently propounded in the late Fifties and early Sixties when the package holiday was moving in on any beach in the western Mediterranean where there was room to swing a tower crane. But then, as now, when the cement mixers are advancing on the pristine shores of Turkey, the argument assumed that developers were incapable of recognising for themselves empty sands, azure seas, uninterrupted sunshine and a good thing when they saw it.

Yet there are still some secrets in travel, not so much about places you have never heard of, as about places you have never thought of. That was the case with Orkney for me. I knew about it — I had ancestors who lived on Orkney — but it was not until I went there that I fell under its spell. East Anglia, which is no farther from London than the Cotswolds but nowhere near as well known, is another of my retreats.

Then there are two cities, Berlin and Istanbul, each with their own mystique but nonetheless well served by the holiday industry.

Holiday prospectors do still discover some new crannies of the world although I am not sure that they have yet found Samoa. I am happy to be able to introduce it to them and to you, while closer to home, the Aeolian Islands are one patch of the Mediterranean that the developers have so far passed by.

But if the biggest surprises are those that are closest to home, you will be amazed by what London has to offer away from the Abbey, the Palace and the Tower. All these have remained secrets which not too many have shared. On second thoughts you had better not say I told you.

BERLIN

Ask a Berlin taxi driver to take you to the zoo and he'll know you don't necessarily want to see the monkeys. The zoo is right at the centre of things, right where the main tinsel-and-glitter street called Kurfurstendamm ('Ku 'damm' for short, the 'boulevard between flair and fantasy' for long) intersects with its equally brash tributaries. But this innermost tantrum of consumerism is, of course, just a tiny part of the Berlin story.

Greater Berlin was created in 1920 by a pair of compasses with very long legs. It is huge. West Berlin alone is four times bigger than Paris although it has less than a third of its population; nearly half of its grand circle is, in fact, swallowed up by woodland and water, parks and recreation areas — some 80 farms lie within the western, smaller half of the city.

Berlin is not, you would rightly surmise, a city easily explored on foot. Everywhere you want to visit seems to stand on a distant horizon with a vast tract of greenery or a long belt of tarmac in between. Most of Berlin was wiped away by wartime bombs — the highest point in the entire city consists, in fact, of rubble heaped from the ruins. Even the trees of the Tiergarten, Berlin's organic heart, are newish, planted to replace the ancient oaks torn down and used for fuel during the years of post-war austerity.

The one sure-fire thing you could never feel about Berlin is indifference. The overriding fact of city life is its location, slap in the lap of Iron Curtain geography and closer to Warsaw than Munich. 'It is a place of action and suspense, not a fossil in time,' maintained my zoo-bound taxi driver. 'This is not the capital but it is where you always feel a part of the current news and international affairs.'

The number one tourist attraction is the Wall. The Cold War nowadays is a far less frigid affair but Berlin is still the only place in Western Europe under military occupation. Even when cosseted by the capitalist comforts of hotels like the Inter-Continental, watching yesterday's US ball game or the latest screening of 'Dynasty' on the American Forces TV channel, a lonely, insular feeling can creep up on you, sharply tinged by the knowledge that, if anything *did* happen, here will be the first to go.

The Wall, covered in graffiti on one side, pure white on the other, is a disturbing, almost medieval spectacle, the emotional response to which can only be handled by cliché. The best initial encounter with this head-on clash between East and West ideology is from one of the peeking platforms beside the Brandenburg Gate, the original pre-war, pre-zoo city centre. On the far side lies a swathe of wasteland populated only by armed guards (the *Volkspolizei* or 'Vopos') and, peculiarly, scurrying rabbits. From their perspective we must appear like rows of peeping Kilroys. I would loathe to be one of 'them' but equally felt resentful about being one of 'us' when several voyeurs on my side of the fence began to perform rude gestures towards the Vopos. You can't, surely, condemn a system for its autocracy at the same time as taunting its victims?

Defecting for the day — back at midnight, or else — is a lengthy, red-taped but fairly straightforward procedure. Although perforated in a few places the most popular hole in the Wall for foreigners is Checkpoint Charlie, à la *Smiley's people*. Be prepared to wait for anything up to a couple of hours in the open air (extremely cold air, at that, in the middle of winter) humiliatingly locked in one of a series of pig pens, before they stamp your passport, accept your 'entrance fee' of five marks, allow you to change a mandatory 25 marks and let you in.

Unter den Linden, over the border, is the most gracious cul de sac in the world. Once the site of all the grand hotels and cafés, it starts (or finishes?) at the Brandenburg Gate and runs for nearly a mile past glamorous Prussian buildings including the Staatsoper, the ivy-covered State Library where Lenin worked, the Humboldt University, and the Neu Wache, with its eternal flame to the 'victims of facism, and militarism' guarded by soldiers wearing wok-like tin hats and marching in goose-step, a sharp reminder of the roots of Berlin's currently split personality.

Alexanderplatz marks the eastern end of the 'under the lime trees' avenue. It is a spacious, Soviet realist dream of the city of tomorrow, complete with happy families and dominated by a giant of a television tower, the second highest structure in Europe. It is the main centre of consumerism, such as it is, at its least lively on a Saturday afternoon when virtually every store is closed. Despite the marked shortage of luxury goods you may be surprised to learn that East Germany now has a higher *per capita* income than Ireland and more people have their own TV set than in France.

Visit East Berlin just before Christmas, and as the day fades to dusk the entire square becomes illuminated by wave upon wave of 40-watt bulbs, a plain, unostentatious but magical prelude to the holiday. There is a joyously-spirited fair, with brass band and hurdy-gurdy music, warming cups of *Glühwein*, hot doughnuts, sausages and *zucker watter*, the local brand of candy floss. There are 'goes' to be had in the *Spuk in Schloss* (haunted house) and jars of pickled gherkins to be won on the hoopla stalls. There are bears from the Urals, tigers from Malaysia and wolfhounds from wherever.

West Berlin, given its highly contrived role as the glittering showcase of capitalist values, inevitably enjoys a monopoly on the more decadent, hedonistic ones. Potpourri is a favourite word used in guidebooks to describe the after-hours menu, ranging from Isherwood-style cabarets to those featuring transvestism as the main theme, from satire to strip-tease, from heavy rock to even heavier. It is hardly surprising that West Berlin's 24-hour, anything-goes lifestyle (just in case tomorrow doesn't) is as fascinating to other West Germans as to foreigners.

But both Berlins compete in the more serious cultural stakes. In the late nineteenth century, unified Berlin was the greatest museum city in the world; now there are still two of the greatest to be seen, one in the East and one in the West. In the former, the highest density of art and artefacts is to be found on Museum Island, bordered on three sides by the river Spree and on the north side by Marx-Engels Platz. The Bodel, National, Altes and Pergamon museums form part of the complex, the latter containing the single most famous exhibit, the Pergamon Altar, an enormous white Hellenistic temple which was brought virtually intact to Berlin. The equivalent museum complex in the West is the Dahlem which contains, amongst its many treasures, a staggering collection of Rembrandts. Even the former Reichstag is now in part a museum of German history.

With so much to do, not to mention the legwork involved in doing it (though the snappy yellow *U-Bahn* will help), most visitors will rejoice in the ample style of eating in which Berliners are apt to indulge. Instead of standing in front of the Wall, perhaps President Kennedy could well have been eating a large sausage when he declared '*Ich bin ein Berliner*'. The cosy, wood-lined Hansel and Gretel neighbourhood taverns called *Kneipe*, plus the numerous restaurants and tea rooms make welcome 'ins' from the cold in between a hectic schedule of winter weekend sightseeing fixtures. So huge are the plateloads of steaming spuds, *sauerkraut* and shanks of port that you'll never want to look a pig in the face again. So huge are the cakes (and most of the customers) in Café Möhring on Ku'damm that they ought to figure on the agenda of the SALT talks.

All things considered, Berlin for most British visitors is likely to be a moody weekend filled with bizarre sights and chronic indigestion. Well, they say it takes all sorts — especially in Berlin.

ORKNEY

Kittiwake or guillemot? Razorbill or fulmar? I stood on Marwick Head, field glasses poised, learning my ABC of ornithology. The cliff-face was shrouded in clouds of seabirds. My keen-sighted guide spotted a wheeling and dipping arctic skua. Better still, we picked out two portly puffins on a rocky ledge, for all the world like an elderly couple on a dignified day out by the sea.

Since that windswept morning in Orkney, I have been a paid-up member of the birdwatching brigade. I carry a pair of slim but powerful binoculars in my handbag. In spare moments between filming, I am to be seen sweeping far horizons, focusing on hedgerows, peering into trees, often with muttered exclamations to anyone who cares to listen. It is a wonderfully satisfying hobby for a traveller.

Orkney — in the singular, as islanders are quick to point out — is a surprising place. For a start, the jet age has yet to reach this ragged jigsaw of islands spreading some 50 miles off Scotland's north-east coast. Sunday's newspapers arrive on Monday. Shops are sometimes shut when you think they might be open. A bar or two may be open when you think they should be shut. The best way to arrive is by boat. Take the sturdy ferry from mainland Scrabster to Orkney's salty seaport, Stromness, passing that sheer, 450-foot rock stack, the Old Man of Hoy, and soaring, gull-haunted cliffs. You feel the remoteness, catch an all-pervading sense of times past.

Even by air, the pace is slow. Propellers whirring, your plane tilts over grey seas and green fields towards the rural airstrip rimmed by water. There's no sense of urgency. The pilot may detour over Scapa Flow, that vast natural anchorage and maritime graveyard, now so deceptively peaceful, and point out a dim shape vaguely outlined beneath the sea like an old war wound. Which is just what it is: an oil slick marks the spot where the battleship, Royal Oak, lies on the bottom, sunk in the early days of the last war by a stray German submarine with the loss of more than 800 men.

At first, Orkney's locker of promise seems as limited as a politician's pledge. Much of it is flattish, fertile and treeless. Only Hoy, of the 70 odd islands, mirrors the rugged grandeur of the distant Highlands. But you quickly come under its spell. 'A land where the sky never ends,' wrote a poet about this open landscape fashioned by wind and water. It is also a land of sun and cloud, of rock-sliced seashores, of pewter-coloured lochs, of distant headlands. Clean and uncluttered, you quickly come to appreciate its timeless beauty and its limitless peace.

And there is a foreign flavour about the place. In the capital, Kirkwall, you stand closer to Oslo than London. Island names ring romantically: Shapinsay, Rousay, Sanday, Stronsay. Papa Westray's claim to fame is the world's shortest scheduled flight — all two minutes of it from big brother, Westray. The islanders are self-sufficient, doughty and hospitable. Somewhat confusingly the

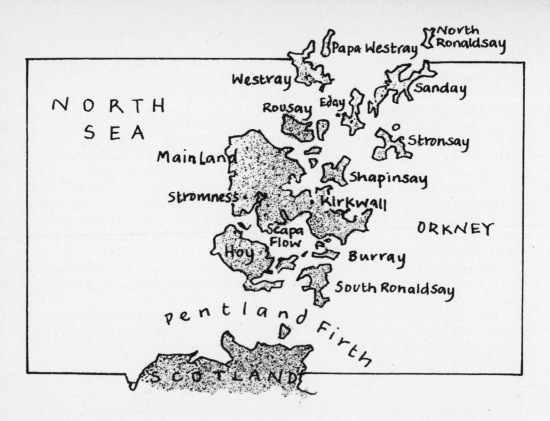

biggest island is called Mainland, but then the independently-minded Orcadians refer to the bulk of Britain simply as an off-shore island. My father's grandparents were born and lived in Stromness and Kirkwall and there are still Chalmers living on Stronsay. No wonder I felt at home on Orkney.

Standing alone on a distant seashore, you feel you are on the outer edge of the world. Yet Orkney has always been very much *on* the beaten track. All over the islands are mounds of prehistory, signposts to the past. On Mainland, among fields of buttercups, stands the formidable Ring of Brogar, 27 standing stones dating back to 2500 BC.

Older still, at 5000 years, is Skara Brae, one of the best-preserved prehistoric villages in Europe. Far from the popular conception of cave dwellers, stone-age man lived with a modicum of comfort. You can see the little houses connected by passageways with their stone box beds (which would have been softened with heather and animal skins) and the cupboards above them; a dresser for food and pottery and a water box for keeping the fish fresh. And they knew how to pick the best spot: Skara Brae overlooks a vast sweep of sandy bay.

Another wonder of that age is the stone burial chamber of Maes Howe. It, too, is a marvel of prehistoric engineering. You crouch along a narrow passage into the tomb itself, a lofty room with walls of stone, blocks of three tons or more cut so precisely that you can't slip a knife between them. When the Vikings invaded Orkney thousands of years later, they may have plundered the tomb of treasure ... or found that someone else had beaten them to it. Mysterious Norse runic inscriptions can be seen cut into the grey stone. At the winter solstice, the shortest day of the year, the sun shines fleetingly in through the long corridor, illuminating the chamber itself.

The Vikings, the medieval rulers of Orkney, have also left their mark. In Kirkwall, they built the impressive St Magnus cathedral which dominates the pocket-size capital and the busy little working harbour. Stromness's narrow main street of jumbled houses and its quayside has an engaging old-fashioned feel about it: a few fishing boats, wicker lobster pots, the arrival of the ferry from Scrabster with its flock of attendant gulls and cormorants. Well-waterproofed visitors make straight for the tourist office, where the notice board is smothered in cards offering cheap bed and breakfast.

Ferries from here and other ports maintain low-cost, shuttlecock services between the main islands: to Hoy, the most spectacular and ideal for walkers, where you can see the great skua soar across rugged mountains and moors starred with wild flowers; to lobster-shaped, highly-cultivated, low-lying Sanday with miles of glistening beach, disturbed only by the surf and the birds which nest in the dunes; to Eday, in contrast looming large and darkly from the sea; to almost circular Rousay, with its trout lochs — such rare birds as the hen harrier and peregrine falcon hunt here. On Papa Westray's North Hill is Britain's largest colony of arctic terns; the high-decibel bird cries are ear-shattering and, if you're lucky, you may watch breathtaking aerobatic chases as arctic skuas pirate food from terns in mid-air.

On Mainland, there are moorland reserves at Hobbister and Birsay, with hides for viewing meadow pipits, skylarks, birds of prey and the ubiquitious curved-bill curlew with its haunting 'curlee' call. If you are at all interested in the islands' rich wildlife, two slim but most helpful booklets are published by the Royal Society for the Protection of Birds.

In summer, the evenings are long and light until well past midnight. To view the kind of sunset that would have done credit to Hollywood, I took out a boat with Angus MacDonald, who runs a small hotel overlooking Loch Harray. It's difficult to deflect Angus from discoursing about fishing but even he was moved momentarily to silence by the sunset. He was more moved, though, by the sudden twitching of his line; up came a large fresh water trout. Harray is renowned for the fighting qualities of its wild brown trout and each night successful anglers proudly show off their catch on the hall table in Angus's hotel.

The Merkister is personally run by Angus and his wife Elma. You are treated with friendly informality, rather than as a room number, and the bar turns into a real 'local' each evening. Only a few of the 18 bedrooms have private bathrooms; it's a matter of 'first come, first served' for that evening shower. After which I can recommend a fresh trout supper served in the dining room overlooking the loch.

You don't have to be a birdwatcher or an angler or an archaeologist to enjoy Orkney. You can combine a bit of all three and add a pinch of modern history, too, that adds another evocative dimension to these unique islands. Drive down through Mainland to Burray and on to South Ronaldsay. The road crosses massive concrete causeways, known as the Churchill Barrier, built after the sinking of the *Royal Oak* in 1939. The half-sunk, rusting 'block' ships, which formed part of the defences, are a gaunt memorial to war in a part of the world thick with the mantle of peace.

The barriers seal off the vulnerable, eastern approaches to Scapa Flow. This vast, island-locked, natural harbour was the scene of earlier drama. On 21 June 1919, Rear-Admiral von Reuter of the Kaiser's Imperial Navy ordered the scuttling of the captured High Seas fleet. All 74 vessels sank — and a party of schoolchildren, cruising in the bay, innocently clapped as the fleet went down.

There are pictures of some ships and the log of the submarine captain who sunk the *Royal Oak*, in the little naval museum in Stromness.

But the most poignant monument to war is the tiny chapel that stands, almost unnoticed, on Lamb Holm. Italian prisoners in Camp 60, working on the Churchill Barrier, transformed two Nissen huts into an elaborate Italianate chapel using scrap, driftwood, barbed wire and concrete. Just outside the chapel, the prisoners left a memorial in concrete of St George slaying the dragon, symbolic of their triumph over defeat and loneliness during their years of captivity. Another unexpected chapter in the story of Orkney's long and absorbing history.

AEOLIAN ISLANDS

The seven Aeolian islands are unmarked on most maps. They sit like stranded whales in the Tyrennian Sea just to the north of Sicily, forming one of the most unusual archipelagos in the world. Supposedly named after the Greek God of Wind, Aeolus, who lived on Vulcano, the surrounding seas are among the most violent in the Mediterranean — something Odysseus, according to Homer, found out to his cost when he was sent packing home to Ithica with a present from the King of the Islands — a bag of wind.

The Aeolians are far from windy in summer, though there is a welcoming cool breeze. Relatively unspoilt and largely undiscovered (except in August when wealthy Italians drape themselves over every available rock, and moor their yachts in otherwise secluded bays), the islands are a traveller's dream. They are small enough to explore thoroughly in a week or two yet big enough to offer some decent hotels and restaurants.

They are all volcanic, though Vulcano and Stromboli are the only two actively so. The danger to visitors, however, is probably a lot less than crossing the road in Rome.

The beauty of holidaying in the Aeolians is that all the islands are different and near enough to each other to make exploring easy. There are few good beaches (Panarea has the best) but plenty of other unique holiday components from curative 'mud' on Vulcano that you can wallow in, to a nightly display of 'real' fireworks on erupting Stromboli.

Lipari is the capital, the biggest (13 square miles), the liveliest and the most fertile (they grow capers and tomatoes). The old town, dominated by a hilltop castle, lies within medieval walls, fronted by a rainbow of boats and awnings in its colourful port. There are a couple of beaches, a bustling main street, good hotels and *pensione* and numerous bars and restaurants. Most visitors base themselves on Lipari, with perhaps a night on Stromboli, hopping over to the other islands on the regular boats and hydrofoils.

Vulcano, its nearest neighbour, is less conventionally attractive. You can climb to the crater of its volcano and down again to bathe in the sulphurous mud that bubbles and gurgles in pools behind the black sand beaches. There are some decent hotels nearby which are very popular, in spite of the strong smell.

Stromboli's beaches are even blacker, the slopes of the volcano scorched by the nightly lap of fire (it erupts every 15 minutes or so). Panarea is the prettiest and the tiniest island (1.3 square miles) and the most popular with Italians. The walk along the clifftops to the best beach (yellow sand) is idyllic.

Salina is dominated by twin peaks, two survivors out of six now extinct

T Y R R H E N I A N   S E A

volcanoes. The slopes produce Malvasia, the islands' best wine. Alicudi and Filicudi are the most remote; the surrounding seas thick with sponges, turtles, seahorses and flying fish. Diving is excellent and in early summer swordfish with their long black snouts swarm past the islands in droves.

At one time the islanders were quite wealthy. Some say the money came from slavery. Certainly they traded in the jet black obsidian you can still see today on Lipari (the only other place you'll find it is on the moon). Invaded by both the Greeks and the Romans, remains of successive civilizations (dating back to the fifth and sixth centuries AD) are preserved in the museum in the acropolis on Lipari which houses one of the best collections of neolithic remains in the world. Up by the museum the Greek amphitheatre comes to life in summer when visiting theatre companies perform against a backdrop of the sea and distant Stromboli.

The islanders may seem a bit withdrawn compared to other southern Italians. Years of poverty and occupation have seen to that. But once you get to know them they'll go out of their way to be friendly and helpful. In summer distant relatives arrive from far-flung corners of the world to help out in family restaurants and *pensione,* to drive the trikes that shuttle visitors from their hotels to the port and man the boutiques. Apart from tourism, which occupies a brief four months of summer, they live on the income from their vines, and a flourishing pumice industry. It covers the north west of Lipari in a fine white powder that now and again gently avalanches down the cliffs and into the sea like a cloud of talcum powder.

The urge to explore is irresistable and catching a boat is as easy as catching a bus. The huge ships from Naples and Sicily regularly deposit visitors and provisions, dwarfing the yachts, fishing boats and throbbing hydrofoils. There is much hysteria at the foot of the gangplank, even complete strangers find themselves embracing as they bump into each other for the third time in two days. It is easy to make friends. There are cheers above the clanking of the anchor and the wail of the siren. Then once again the chairs in the quayside cafés fill up and, depending on the time of day, the waiters take orders for a campari or *cappuccino*.

Vulcano is ten minutes away from Lipari. At first sight it isn't particularly inspiring. Most visitors come to climb to the rim of the crater or to wallow in the stinking mud. There are several hotels but not a lot else. The hot springs that bubble up into the sea like a non-stop jacuzzi are volcanic gases forcing their way up to the surface. The best idea is to wallow in the mud like a hippo and then sit around in the sun until you bake like a cake. Dirty brown bodies with white staring eyes can be seen hopping over the steaming rocks to wash it off in the sea. The 'treatment' is free, though locals will tell you not to stay in too long.

While Vulcano steams away silently and residents panic if they hear it, Stromboli rumbles every 15 minutes or so and they'd worry if it didn't. Whitewashed hotels and villas covered in bougainvillaea stand out starkly against the jet black, lava-pitted rocks and dusky sands, with Stromboli looming majestically behind. It was here that Ingrid Bergman fell in love with Rossellini while filming 'Stromboli' and the island hasn't changed much since then. Few people can resist the lure of the volcano and expeditions are mounted daily. You can be serious about it, put on your walking shoes and rucksack and hike it to the top where you unroll your sleeping bag and camp out on the summit for the night. They say that the rocks up there are so hot in places that you can heat a can of beans on them. The temperature drops at night, however, so go prepared if you intend to camp out.

There are less energetic ways of watching the nightly show. Boats leave at regular intervals for the best vantage point at the foot of the *sciara del fuoco* (fiery path). From there you sit in silence under a silvery sky until a rumble heralds the next display. Then to 'oohs' and 'aahs', brilliant red and yellow fireworks shoot out into the night sky and trickle slowly down the mountain. It is addictive viewing. Everyone *knows* that the next eruption will be better than the last.

Alternatively you can have a slow amble up to the 'observatory' which in true Italian style turns out to be a pizzeria. It is open until the early hours. Diners pause between mouthfuls at each distant rumble and watch tiny pinpoints of light as the torch-lit processions of climbers wend their way up and down the mountain until the dawn camouflages the show and the sun draws everyone to the beach.

Panarea's beach is *the* one to head to for relaxing; a delightful walk along clifftops that are ablaze with wild flowers in springtime, past the rubble of a prehistoric village and deserted bays lapped by crystal clear seas. On the way there are a couple of beachside *trattoria* serving platters of seafood.

Fish on the islands is excellent. One of the best restaurants in southern Italy is Filippino's on Lipari. It is regularly awarded a rosette by Michelin. It has been there for years, run by several generations of the same family. You sit under awnings and choose from trayfuls of gleaming fish or home-made pasta, each a creation served with pride as though it were its first night out of the kitchen. Try *riso nero* (rice in squid's ink), a *boccancini* (roll of) *pesce spada*, swordfish with pine nuts, their own *zuppa di pesce alla pescatora* (fish soup), and the wine from neighbouring Salina.

There are some excellent hotels on all the islands, perched on the cliffs or in pleasant gardens a little way inland. Stromboli's best hotel is La Sciara, set in a pretty garden, though the small, whitewashed La Sirenetta-Park across the road from the beach is no less comfortable. Lipari has several large hotels and many *pensione* as well as a youth hostel high up in the grounds of the Norman castle. Apart from August, when visitors without a reservation simply get put back on the boats, the choice is yours. As your boat or hydrofoil noses into the harbour you'll be met by young locals anxious to offer you a room in their home. Before you know it you'll be trying to keep up with a small blue wheelbarrow containing your bags as it bumps its way over the cobbles. If you do arrive without a booking the local tourist office will help; Lipari's is opposite Zuu Bob's pizzeria. Private rooms cost from around £6 a head in low season to £12 a head in August. The tourist board will ring round for you and check availability.

The islands may be relatively unknown but they are not as remote as all that. You can fly to Catania on Sicily and then take a coach or train north to Milazzo where boats or hydrofoils take less than an hour to get to Lipari. Alternatively there are boats in summer from Cefalu, Messina, Naples and Reggio di Calabria. The Aeolians are for travellers not tourists. Long may they stay that way.

EAST ANGLIA

East Anglia is a cul-de-sac. That is what keeps it secret. You do not go to East Anglia in order to go somewhere else. There are no through roads, unless you count the A45 which hustles the container lorries into Europe through the port of Felixstowe. Set off into East Anglia in almost any direction and you will end up in East Anglia.

Mercifully it has some of the worst trunk roads left in Britain. Even the motorway system, which stalks the area up to the M11 from the south, loses heart and makes a last minute swerve to the left to come to nothing somewhere west of Cambridge. That leaves the A11 and no one in their senses would choose to drive on its primitive single carriageways without some pretty compelling reason.

So the combination of geography and the Department of Transport's Highway Division works a process of natural selection, weeding out the casual visitors. Few people happen on East Anglia. You have to make the effort to go there. It has its rewards if you do.

To the purist, East Anglia is Norfolk and Suffolk with the northern fringes of Essex and the eastern edge of Cambridgeshire admitted if you must. Draw a circle with the centre in Thetford and a circumference that follows the bulge of the north Norfolk coast, and you are talking about an area with a radius of no more than 45 miles. Within that circle, though, not only is there scenery unique to the British Isles, but a landscape and coastline that changes theatrically within the space of a few miles — from the cosy thatched villages of Suffolk to the bleak Norfolk fens; from the muddy Essex estuaries to the saltmarshes and sand dunes of the north Norfolk seaside; from the wild heath of Breckland to the Broads.

And what amazes me to this day is that this little-known reserve of extraordinary countryside is within 60 miles of London; not much more than 100 from Birmingham. Yet still there is a remoteness about East Anglia. You feel it on the coast on solitary walks along the windy sands of Norfolk, or inland among the villages of Suffolk, so close to one another on the map, but connected by a crazed pattern of lanes bent between dishevelled hedges and enormous fields.

Of course there are parts which are far from secret. Great Yarmouth is the

east coast's answer to Blackpool. Built on a thin spit of land that dangles from the mainland, it has the sea on one side and the River Yare on the other. As a consequence the town has two fronts. The oldest faces the river. This was the original port of Yarmouth and along the quayside overlooking the Yare is a remarkable line of merchants' houses, Tudor, Georgian and Victorian. Behind them are The Rows, a grid of alleys which is all that remains of the original medieval settlement. The other front faces the North Sea across the beach. It has all the trappings of a big resort — two piers, starry summer shows, a pleasure beach and, with one eye on the British summer, an indoor leisure centre.

The other part of the area that is hardly secret is the Broads, though they too are not entirely well known. They fall into two distinct halves which are joined by the Yare at Yarmouth. There are the northern Broads, comprising the rivers Bure, Ant and Thurne, and the southern Broads on the Yare and Waveney. The rivers in the north are smaller and prettier but with more than 250 miles of waterways, as well as around 30 Broads, or lakes, themselves, it takes more than a two-week holiday to explore them all.

Even without a boat, the flat meadows of Broadland, reedy and green, are still an extraordinary place to visit. Often the rivers are lower than the fields and yacht sails appear to slash the scenery like blades pushed up from beneath the farmland. And all in the same view there could well be a windmill — there are particularly fine ones at Horsey Staithe and the Berney Arms — and a monumentally-sized church tower.

In a sense the two are connected because they both represent East Anglia's links with the Low Countries. It was Dutch engineers who oversaw the big land reclamation schemes in both Broadland and the Fens in the seventeenth and eighteenth centuries; it was Flemish weavers who crossed the North Sea to work with East Anglian wool in the Middle Ages. That was a time when Norfolk and Suffolk were among the wealthiest regions of Europe. The East Anglians 'struck sheep' in much the same way as their descendants struck oil 500 years later. The weavers arrived in a 'wool rush'. Their traces survive. Several old houses have Dutch-style gables and the crinkly pantiles, still used for roofing today, were originally introduced as ballast in the wool ships when they tied up empty from the Continent at the east coast ports.

But it is the churches, pocket-sized cathedrals out of all proportion to their villages, that are the most spectacular relics of that age. Blythburgh, Long Melford and Framlingham are all particularly splendid, but the prize is Lavenham. Here, besides the church and its mighty tower, are complete streets of 500-year-old half timbered houses, sagging and warped, twisted and tottering, architecture's walking wounded. Twenty years ago they took away the telegraph poles and hid the cables underground. If you want to find the fifteenth century more or less intact, here it is.

Lavenham is a showpiece, yet scattered in the gentle swell of the Suffolk countryside is a company of pretty villages — Cavendish, Clare, Walsham-le-Willows, Woolpit, Kersey. Some are plain streets of flint houses; others, blushing clusters of snug pink cottages — Suffolk pink — topped with dollops of thatch and with walls of 'wattle and daub', the local plaster slap. This is country to get lost in, an intimate landscape of neat plough and big fields, trim woods and efficient farms. Too low for great vistas, the biggest thing in Suffolk is the sky. The horizon only ever comes up to your ankles.

East Bergholt is another special village and the birthplace of John Constable. Flatford Mill, where his father was the miller, and Willy Lot's Cottage, subject of one of his most famous paintings which now hangs in an Ipswich museum, are a mile away. The scene is almost unchanged except for the coach parties.

There are other obvious pleasures: Cambridge and punting on the Cam along the Backs behind some of the university's oldest colleges; Norwich market and walking down the cobbles of Elm Hill between over-hanging Tudor houses the colour of plums and primroses; lofty Norwich Cathedral clad in stone that was shipped from Caen in Normandy 800 years ago; Sandringham, where the grounds are open in summer if none of the Royal family is around.

But the real secret of East Anglia lies in the wealth of smaller pleasures, the ones you can only ever really discover for yourself. There is July's heavy scented harvest in the lavender fields near King's Lynn; the sailing village of Blakeney and boat trips to the nature reserve in the sand dunes and marram grass of Blakeney Point; Burnham Thorpe where Nelson was born and the pub with no bar which has not changed since he celebrated his first command in a room upstairs; the Stone Age flint mines at Grimes Graves near Brandon; Bury St Edmunds, where twentieth-century traffic has to funnel through the original Norman street plan and, bearded with ivy, the Angel Hotel where Dickens stayed. It faces the gatehouse to what was, before Henry VIII got at it, one of the greatest abbeys in the land.

There is crunching along the shingle at Aldeburgh; driving through the pine forest to Orford to eat oysters in the Buttery; browsing in the antique shops in Woodbridge; hoping to spot an avocet in the bird sanctuary at Minsmere; buying wine in Southwold; drinking it at Pin Mill beside the Orwell estuary where the Thames barges are left sitting on the mud flats when the tide goes out; listening to the sing-song local dialect that few will dare to imitate. It alone is cryptic enough to be the code in which all these secrets are kept.

WESTERN SAMOA

Far from Edinburgh's 'windy parallelograms', the consumptive Robert Louis Stevenson chose the South Pacific islands for his last escape. 'I go there only to grow old and die, but when you come, you will see it is a fair place for the purpose,' he wrote to a friend. Stevenson chose well. Western Samoa, in spite of a cannibalistic history, is a tranquil spot of sun, beauty, flowers, welcome and a gentleness at odds with the appearance of the huge and powerful islanders.

RLS had himself pictured with his servants (noting 'cannibal' beside the pantry boy), and gave local-style banquets on his verandah, his guests sitting in two long lines with food piled on banana leaves between them. He is still revered as *Tusitala*, the teller of tales. Vailima, his house on Upolu island, above the capital Apia, is now the government official residence, the rooms mostly empty except for beds on which the Queen has slept. Wide verandahs cool the rooms, but a nostalgia for 'Auld Reekie' is betrayed by the fireplaces on both floors.

Through the well tended tropical gardens a trail leads steeply up Mount Vaea to the writer's tomb, a glorious spot from which to watch the sunset flashing green into the ocean. Tomb visiting may not seem the happiest of sightseeing, but Samoans like to keep the most beloved of a family buried as close to the houses as possible while the rest go to the communal cemetery. The high, stepped concrete tombs have fresh flowers placed on them daily; the tropical scarlet blooms often threaded on thin coconut palm sticks to create bouquets. Women often do their sewing, vegetable preparation and chores seated comfortably on top of a tomb.

The 'cannibals' are now devoted Christians. Sundays awake to an extra deep silence and the scent of wood fires drifting through the misted trees. The day's supply of food has been cooked at dawn for the Sabbath and the streets of Apia are shuttered and empty. The people are on their way to the dozens of churches, the men in dark suits, the women in long white dresses, gloves and hats. They are joined by tourists who go along to hear the magnificent hymn singing.

It was only recently that Western Samoans, the largest pure Polynesian group in the world, allowed a single flight in on Sunday. The 15-mile ride from Upolu's airport, the terminal of which resembles a hot scruffy market, to Apia, is one of the most beautiful in the world, even if it is seen from the bone-shaker open-sided buses. Certainly it gives an instant insight into Samoan traditional life which, in spite of a thorough raking over by anthropologists, remains its own in style.

The people live in villages in *fale* houses. These are simple, thatched-roofed constructions over a concrete or wooden platform with open sides. Roll-up grass blinds can be lowered for privacy or during storms but on the whole Samoans lead a home life open to public gaze. The platform contains family possessions: sewing machine, chests, bedrolls. To a Samoan, the riches of life are a good-looking wife, healthy children, house, canoe, pigs and coconut and banana trees.

The visitor feels like a voyeur peeking into the *fale* while men doze and

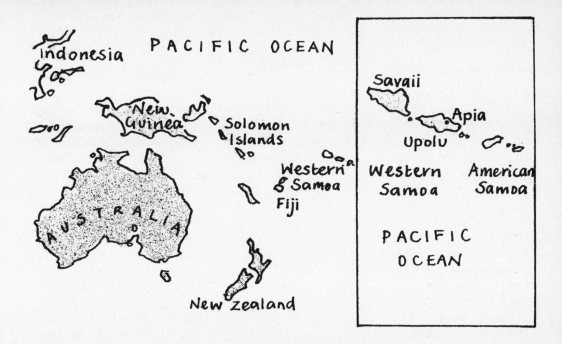

children play and there is a strict code of Samoan etiquette which the tourist
office leaflet spells out for visitors. A *fale* should always be entered from the
back and left by the front to show nothing has been stolen. Inside, one should
sit cross-legged on the mat, not stand, and it is rude to stretch the legs unless
they are covered by a mat. If chiefs are meeting (and the tribal hierarchy
persists) one should not drive or ride past, but walk, umbrella lowered if it's
raining. Flowers should not be worn in a church; quiet should be observed in a
village during evening prayers and no brief clothing should be worn. Nor should
any tips be given. The last is a delight of South Pacific travel.

In Western Samoa tours consist of a visit to ex-teacher Bob Rankin's batik
shop where an amazing range of tropical fruit wines and (potent) liqueurs are
made in a solar-powered still. The white wines are delicious chilled for evening
poolside sipping or for a beach picnic. Other island coolers are the waterfall
pools in the interior National Park or at Pula on Falefa bay.

The south coast beaches are magnificent. Lotofaga and Salamumu are 'best
beach' award winners, backed by shady casuarina trees and palms, and empty
of people, apart from the occasional fisherman. They gently shelve to clear,
warm waters. Apart from finding yet more beach beauties, there are few 'musts'
to list. Apia is a seafront, one-street-stroll, with its market, new Tusitala
thatched hotel, small guest houses, bars with disco music, restaurants and old-
fashioned, dusty stores. On Saturday mornings early, the few vehicles are
halted while the police band rehearses with great oompah along the main
street, twirling batons, clashing cymbals, thundering drums, the naturally
massive figures of the men extended by British-style helmets. They are quite
incongruous when worn with native *lava lava* wrap-round skirts ... worn by
men.

The place to stay is Aggie Grey's on the fringe of Apia. A modest frontage
hides an expansive back garden development. Aggie Grey began 40 years ago

with ten grass huts. Now she is in her late eighties and a Queen Mother lookalike. Her son runs the business but Aggie will occasionally still perform the seductive *siva* dance, akin to the Hawaiian *hula*, at weekend *fia fia* feasts held at the hotel. Aggie is said to be the original for James Michener's Bloody Mary in his South Pacific story. Michener has a *fale* named after him (this one a rather superior thatched and air-conditioned bungalow) at Aggie's in the lush gardens. Others are named after the Hollywood stars who have stayed there, like Bill Holden and Gary Cooper. There are more rooms in two-storey blocks around the edges of the garden. They are simply furnished but spotless and each has an ironing board and a fridge with fresh milk for tea or coffee making. The gardens are dense with tropical trees and plants around the swimming pool. It also is a place for cat lovers: there are dozens and each will mark out a visitor as 'theirs', purr loudly, curl up on the verandah chairs and hope for a saucer of that milk. Few begrudge it.

No hotel serves more generous portions at every meal than Aggie Grey's. Breakfasts are the full house of eggs, bacon, fruits, cereals and bread. Lunch is a continuous carry-in buffet of curries, Chinese dishes, salads, meats and fruits. And just when you think you are finishing, the neat linen-suited waiters bring yet another dish or beg you to try a few more candied sweet potatoes. Afternoon tea — sandwiches and home-made cakes — arrives next, served on a terrace shaded by scented pink frangipani trees, while dinner will try and outdo the lunchtime procession of dishes. Taking a picnic is no escape. A huge packet of sandwiches, cold chicken and fruits is sent with you to the beach.

At the *fia fia*, the weekly traditional-style rave up, the chefs go to town, producing a superb island buffet of fish and seafood salads, curries, roast suckling pig and fruit delights all laid out on long tables and piled high in huge clam shells. You eat in a large barn-like hall, high raftered and thatched, and with a stage at one end. Here drummers encourage the stomping beat and the stage quivers with the gyrations of the hefty dancers who, for the last dance, swing themselves from the rafters to a cannon volley of drumbeats.

Real Samoan seclusion, sleeping in the sight of stars beyond open *fale* walls, can be found on Savaii, Upolu's sister island. It's a ten minute flight away, though the aircraft do not run to strict timetables. There is also an erratic ferry. This is the 'big island', 660 square miles spread round the 6094-foot volcano, Mount Mauga Silisili. Past eruptions have created strange overhanging cliffs of lava at the coast. Savaii seems hardly to belong to the twentieth century; land tenure is still in the hands of the Matai, heads of extended families.

Here there is another potential Aggie Grey to host and show off the Samoan life style. Mrs Vassili Moelagi Jackson — her full title — is a chief's daughter. Plump, smiling and with *tipani* (the local name for frangipani) blossoms in her dark hair she will greet you at the grass airstrip. Her late husband, an eccentric Englishman called Barry Jackson, set up the Safua hotel here in 1978.

Driving with Moelagi in her rickety truck up the Australian road, which was built recently to open up the area, you pass iron-roofed churches, lava-edged pools, and games of *kirikiti*, village cricket that marries the English version with American baseball and in which every inhabitant joins in.

'Hotel' is perhaps too grand a word for the Safua's few *fales*. The largest acts as reception, restaurant, lounge, bar and library. Guests sit in low-slung chairs or curl up on rush-matted floors. The meals are excellent, served by giggling *pareo*-clad girls at a long narrow table headed by Moelagi. Seafood, especially fresh lobster, curries, crisp vegetables, home made breads and plenty of tropical fruits are typical fare included in the inexpensive daily rate.

Barry Jackson was a South Seas character, a hard-drinking ladies' man Moelagi says. His funeral was the biggest gathering of 1984 and now his stepped tomb, scattered with flowers, is in the place of honour just outside the main *fale*, and happily close to the bar as he would have wished. Hotel bills are often made up by girls perched on the tomb.

Beyond the main *fale*, the garden stretches away, shaded by flowering trees and palms. Little black pigs root among hibiscus bushes. A handful of *fale* rooms — the ideal instant hotel room to build — are set among the flowers. They are identical to the traditional native Samoan dwelling with open, pillared sides and thatched roofs, roll-up blinds and beds with mosquito nets. The only difference is that they have an attached shower room.

Days are spent on the deserted beaches. Many people come to paint the tropical plants and rocky coves. Then it's back for dinner by paraffin lamp and Moelagi telling traditional Samoan stories, the ones they didn't relate to the anthropologist Margaret Mead on her visits here. A lamp is carried to the candlelit *fale*, and it takes only seconds to unwind a *pareo* for bed. Most guests live by the sun clock. One explained: 'We don't roll down the blinds, we just merge into the night'.

ISTANBUL

Turkey has burst upon the holiday scene in a big way only quite recently. It has rapidly become one of those destinations which everyone wants to visit at least once, and where those who have been end up going again and again. Turkey, in short, is addictive.

The bulk of British visitors head south for a summer holiday along the Aegean or Mediterranean coasts, staying in small hotels or villas at Marmaris or Bodrum, or taking coach trips to Ephesus, Side, Aspendos or Troy. They may cruise down the coast from Kas to Antalya, or simply stay in one spot to enjoy those three great Turkish delights, good food, cheap wine, friendly people. Those who fancy something a little more out-of-the-ordinary, however, should take a trip to one of the world's great cities — Istanbul.

Istanbul, the ancient Constantinople, is a child of the Bosphorus. Sitting at a table in the open air restaurant below the Topkapi Museum, you can see that instantly. Just below, on this southern side of the Golden Horn, lies the old city of antiquity, the one that was the capital of the Eastern Roman Empire, first called Byzantium and later, Constantinople. Across the Horn, above the bustling ferry port, lies modern Istanbul, a much cleaner city than it used to be, with a jagged skyline where the pencil-slim minarets of the mosques find themselves in competition with office blocks and high-rise hotels above the narrow, traffic-jammed streets. Far away, arching over the water, lies the great Ataturk bridge which links Europe with Asia. Between the two continents lies the mighty stream of the Bosphorus, flowing between the Black Sea and the Sea of Marmara, once the Hellespont, the 'Greek Bridge', surely one of the most attractive and most famous waterways in the world. In the past few tourists visited the fascinating city on its shores.

Twenty years ago only independent travellers or hippies bound for India made the long journey across Europe to spend a few days resting in this then ramshackle city. A great deal has changed since then and mostly for the better. The streets are now much cleaner, the people obviously more prosperous; beggars are few and the street vendors much less persistent, which, since I

don't find squalor particularly romantic, all helps. That apart, most of Istanbul remains as it always was, a charming, noisy, fascinating city, full of interest.

Until the fourth century AD, this city was Byzantium and the Eastern capital of the Roman Empire. Then it became a Greek city, Constantinople, named after Constantine, the first Christian Emperor. His empire endured more or less intact for the next thousand years. Though it was briefly overthrown by the Fourth Crusade, it was only finally extinguished in 1453 by the Ottoman Turks. The empire of the Ottomans didn't last as long as that of Byzantium. Old Turkey, which came to be called the 'sick man of Europe', finally died in the First World War to be replaced by the modern Turkish State, created, almost single-handed, by Kemal Ataturk. His image still looks down on you from every square, office and schoolhouse in the country. Ataturk was a wise man, and a rare politician, who kept all that was best of the old country and only changed those things that needed changing.

Ataturk decreed that Turkey should be a modern European state. And so it is, even though the region of Thrace on the Western side of the Bosphorus is tiny when compared with Anatolia, on the Asian shore. Anatolia runs deep into Asia, eventually butting up against the borders of Syria and Iraq, making Turkey a land bridge between the two worlds of Europe and Arabia.

Most visitors to Istanbul will begin with a tour of the ancient sights, the relics and palaces of the Ottoman Sultans. The Blue Mosque pokes delicate minarets into the sky above the old city; the Hagia Sophia Church is now a museum but well worth a visit, and the 5000 shops of the Covered Bazaar are full of Eastern promise and rare goods — silks, leather, carpets, brass, silver, gold. To my personal relief, haggling in the Bazaar seems to be a thing of the past.

All city tours end at the Topkapi Palace, best known to Western visitors for its starring role in the famous Peter Ustinov–Melina Mercuri film 'Topkapi'. The various museums inside the Topkapi are crammed with armour, costume, porcelain, and marvellous jewels including the Imperial emeralds, and, of course, that famous dagger. Visitors can wander at will around the Topkapi, into the Old Harem quarters, past the courtyard of the Black Eunuch, and around the tinkling fountain where the palace executioner, who was also the Imperial gardener, used to wash his sword after every execution. The tour leads out to the edge of the cliff at Seraglio Point from which unwanted concubines were dumped by the sackful into the Bosphorus. You can lunch in the open air restaurant up here. A good meal will cost around £4 and a bottle of excellent Turkish wine only £3. Far below Russian tankers come forging down from the Black Sea, city ferries hurry to and from the Asian side, or go chugging away east to the Anatolia ports and the many islands in the Sea of Marmara. It is easy to see that Turkey is a nautical nation, besides which those ferries of the Bosphorus and the Sea of Marmara are a wonderful way to get about.

Evening is a glorious time in Istanbul, when the setting sun deepens the smoky-blue shadows over the rooftops. In this complex, mysterious city, this is the time to notice the contrasts. The *muezzin* calls the faithful to prayer from every minaret, while at the same time neon signs spring to life around the city skyline and the nightlife begins along the shore. Istanbul nightlife is a mixture of the very modern, with nightclubs and discos, and the traditional — and inevitable — belly-dancers and performing bears. Good restaurants in the centre of the city include the Cuneyya and the Camdan, very popular with the locals. Any taxi-driver will take you to them. The night can finish with an after-dinner drink on the rooftop terrace of the Sheraton Hotel, overlooking the moonlit waters of the Bosphorus.

Turkish cooking rather resembles that of Greece, although the ingredients are usually much fresher and better presented. Notable dishes include stuffed aubergines, kebabs, lamb, liver, salads and excellent fish and shellfish — the lobsters in particular are marvellous and wonderfully cheap. Wine is cheap, good and readily available — a bottle for £1 is typical in any small restaurant, and the price remains moderate even in the more exclusive establishments.

For something a little different, and a very well worthwhile excursion, it is possible to take an evening cruise on a schooner. The *1001 Nights* sails every evening from the quay by the Dolmabache Palace, a marvellous trip up the Bosphorus under the Ataturk Bridge out through the old, crumbling walls that once encircled Byzantium, and up to the yachting port of Tarabya, where a gipsy may well bring his dancing bear aboard to entertain.

Istanbul's ferries run everywhere, so do not fail to take to the waters again to cruise across the Bosphorus to the resort islands of the Sea of Marmara, especially to the Prince's Islands and to Buyakada. There you can go ashore for lunch and take a tour around the island in horse-drawn Victorias. These islands of the Marmara are green and very beautiful, but the people on the ferries are the real attraction. Who else but the Turks could sing, dance and pass bottles of *raki* around the boat — at half-past eight in the morning? A ferry trip from Istanbul is an experience not to be missed, and it gives the visitor a chance to meet the Turks whose hospitality is one of the real delights of this beautiful country.

Istanbul could easily offer enough attractions to last a whole holiday, but it is also a good excursion centre. One idea is to travel south and east round the Sea of Marmara. You pass through the most beautiful countryside, full of olive trees, first to Iznik, the ancient Nicea, and then up into the mountains to the resort town of Bursa. It was the summer capital of the Ottoman Sultan and is now a popular ski resort.

It is also possible to take a small overnight bag and island-hop about the Sea of Marmara, staying a night or two on one or other of the islands at very little cost — £4 for a hotel room is typical. North of Istanbul, at the northern end of the Bosphorus, lies the resort of Kilyos on the Black Sea. If you cross to the Asian shore you can travel along the north coast of Turkey to the great city of Trabzon, the famous Trabizond. It is yet another place where the tourists still don't go — yet.

In Istanbul it is still possible to wander about the old town, peering into little workshops, accepting a glass of tea — *çay* — from the traders, shopping for *kilim* (carpets), hammered brass or leather, or just settling gently into a way of life that in all its essentials has not changed a lot since Suliman the Magnificent ruled half the world from the Sublime Porte.

Istanbul is really much more than another big, cosmopolitan city. It is a surprise, a total mixture of East and West, of ancient and modern, of the familiar and the bizarre. Using the Bosphorus ferries, which are cheap and frequent, you can slip over into Asia, and travel to the port of Yalova for a visit to the Uladag mountains. Sail the other way up the Bosphorus and you arrive at Kilyos on the Black Sea, the perfect little resort for working up a winter tan. The weather is good, the people pleasant — and it's not even expensive. Who could ask for more?

If you are stuck for a new destination this winter, why not try Turkey? It might not stay a secret for much longer ....

LONDON'S DOCKLAND

Although 'Eastenders' currently rates as TV's smash-hit soap opera, it is a fair bet that most of its fans remain unaware of the real life drama that is now being staged in London's real East End. Visitors to the capital who venture just a few minutes from Tower Bridge will come across the outer fringes of a London that is undergoing massive redevelopment on a scale only ever seen on two previous occasions — after the Great Fire and during the Fifties when Londoners set to work repairing the ravages of war.

The area destined to become the new London is the old dockland, a vast network of enclosed expanses of water where, during Britain's turn-of-the-century economic heyday, exotic cargoes were unloaded from the colonies and manufactured goods exported to the rest of the world. With the gradual loss of empire and the undermining of our commercial supremacy, coupled with the growth of containerised traffic that led to the end of traditional methods of handling cargoes, the docklands, which had become increasingly inaccessible to the larger vessels, gradually dwindled in importance. Decline led to decay and the vast landscape became a giant urban wasteland.

In 1981 the London Dockland Development Corporation (LDDC) was set up and given the formidable ten-year task of regenerating the area, exploiting its rich historical past by preserving scores of listed buildings and generally breathing new life into the corpse. A budget of some £250 million was allocated from public funds, subsequently matched by four times that amount from private sources, for what has become the most important and exciting inner-city renaissance in Europe.

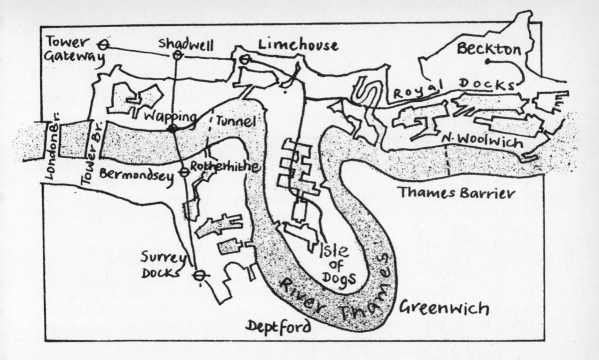

Today, where once bulging ships were unloaded and their cargoes stored, existing buildings are being converted and foundations laid for wine bars, up-market stores, conference and exhibition centres, apartments, craft workshops, galleries, museums, boat marinas, artists' studios, floating restaurants, an airport and several hotels. Top names in architecture have been recruited to both renovate old warehouses and design new residential and commercial buildings in the same dockland vernacular. Sir Terence Conran, for example, fresh from revitalising our high streets, is already at work on Butler's Wharf, an outstanding remnant of original nineteenth-century Thameside warehousing, transforming it into shops, homes, restaurants, offices, the site of the V&A Boilerhouse exhibition and a Conran Foundation Design Museum.

Typical of the renovation is a vast old Grade 1 listed tobacco dock, now destined to become an Eastenders' Covent Garden — and twice as big — providing shops, restaurants, leisure facilities and workshops. Another classic transformation is the long-neglected pumping station on Shadwell Basin in Wapping, a beautiful red-brick, ivy-clad building, which will become the recording and rehearsal home to the Academy of St Martin's in the Field, the world's most recorded orchestra.

When Dockland was dock land, high security walls meant that locals were never able to see, let alone enjoy, their backyard acres of water. Today, with the building of scores of river, canal and dockside walks, an entire waterscape is opening up before their eyes. With its eight miles of River Thames and 460 acres of retained water, people are already muttering comparisons with Amsterdam and Venice.

The best way to begin exploring Dockland London is to take a ride on the new Lite Railway. You can travel from the Tower of London some 20 feet above street level, crossing many of the original Victorian viaducts, all the way to the Isle of Dogs. From the train's riverside terminus, those with time on their hands can enjoy the striking perspective of the Greenwich skyline before taking the foot tunnel under the Thames to visit the Cutty Sark and the Maritime Museum, perhaps returning to town by the new high-speed river bus which runs as far upstream as Chelsea.

The most exciting aspect of docklands from the visitor's point of view is not what is new but what is old. Historic watering holes like the Prospect of Whitby, Town of Ramsgate, Three Suns, Angel, Grapes, Mayflower and the aptly-named The House They Left Behind, are all part of the dockland fabric. Several back on to the Thames — on a fine summer evening you'll find it hard to find a more absorbing sight than, say, the tiny balcony at the back of the Grapes, looking across the drift of the tide to the Surrey docks.

There are more than a hundred listed buildings in the area including half a dozen Hawksmoor churches which are all being spruced up, their courtyards cleared of years of matted vegetation. Restoration work has even uncovered long-lost history — when they began digging foundations in the vicinity of Rotherhythe docks they came across Edward III's moated manor house. A large chunk of Britain's maritime history was spawned by London's docks — most eighteenth-century Royal Navy vessels, for a start, were made here as was the Great Eastern, the largest ship built in the last century. Some are now berthed back in the docks as tourist attractions, including the *John W. Mackay*, probably the oldest steam-driven cable-laying ship in the world.

Dockland is also Charles Dickens country. Lizzie Hexham lived in Limehouse, as did Miss Abbey Potterson, the proprietress of the Six Jolly Fellowship Porters — alias the Grapes — in *Our Mutual Friend.* Jacob's Island, Bermondsey, was where Bill Sykes was hung in *Oliver Twist* while Southwark's George Inn of both *Pickwick Papers* and *Little Dorrit* fame is now owned by the National Trust. At the time of writing, Dockland's attractions are mostly embryonic rather than operational, a hundred building sites and a thousand blueprints sharing places with historic landmarks. But the leisure potential of the area has already been firmly demonstrated. St Katharine's Dock has already been converted into a complex where the bars, old boats in the Historic Ships Collection, the Dickens' Inn and other ancient buildings, shops and medieval feasts are all in full swing. And anyone who has visited either Boston or Baltimore in the United States will have seen a supreme example of how a combination of historic surroundings and a waterfront setting is a superb formula for tourism.

In many ways the success of this Water City of the twenty-first century, as it has already been billed, is guaranteed. But the essential characteristic of Docklands is a living environment, not an artificial stage-set specially designed, packaged and presented for tourist consumption. The population is expected to double with a mix of celebrities, journalists working for *The Times* and other Fleet Street immigrants, yuppies, artists, city slickers and genuine Eastenders drawn back from the Essex estates to which they emigrated. But, as a tourism project alone, its scale is unparalleled with anything Europe has to offer.